Enid Blyton

Enid Blyton

a biography by

BARBARA STONEY

HODDER AND STOUGHTON
LONDON SYDNEY AUCKLAND TORONTO

To my husband and family

Foreword

SOME YEARS AGO, IN THE COURSE OF AN EVENING'S CONVERSATION, MY Mother expressed the hope that I would write her biography if it ever came to be written in the future. I would have liked to have carried out this wish of hers and, indeed, gave much thought to doing so in the months immediately after her death. At that time we had recently moved to Yorkshire and my family of four children were all still young. It was difficult enough to get down to London once a month with my husband, to see friends, never mind to find the time to carry out lengthy interviews all over the South of England with people connected with my Mother's life. I decided that a biography would have to wait for a few years until I had more time on my hands and was freer to travel away from home. In the following year, one of my Mother's closest friends became very ill and died a few months later. Some of those acquainted with my Mother's youth were now very elderly, some a little younger than she had been when she died; I realised that the documentation of her early years could no longer be delayed.

Very soon after my Mother's death, a number of people wrote to me asking for permission to write her biography. Most were genuinely interested, but they seemed to me to be unsuitable for the task, either because they were young and unmarried, or because they were male, and I thought that to fully understand my Mother's life, a mature woman with experience of marriage and children was essential.

About this time, Barbara Stoney wrote to me. She had been working on the life of a master thatcher, who had roofed my Mother's home 'Old Thatch'. He had taken her to see the house at Bourne End and, living there still, were the people who had bought it from my parents in 1938. Mrs. Stoney was particularly interested in talking to them because it had been suggested to her by a publisher that she might contribute to a biographical series for children and she had considered Enid Blyton as a possible subject. The series was temporarily shelved but she had become so intensely interested in my Mother's life she had continued to search out material, reading everything that had been written about her and talking to everyone she could find who had known or worked for Enid Blyton.

I agreed to meet Mrs. Stoney and discuss the subject of the biography with her. To my surprise, she had more information on those days at Old Thatch than I had, even though I had lived there as a child. She seemed to have an instinctive understanding of the sort of person my Mother was and to be particularly interested in the way her environment had formed her character and affected her life. Very quickly I agreed that she should write my Mother's biography and that I would let her have all the papers and diaries that existed. Unfortunately, much of importance had been destroyed before my Mother's death, and of the many diaries she had kept throughout her life, only the early ones were left. This meant that she left behind her very little personal evidence as to her thoughts and feelings from the 1940s onwards.

We agreed that the book would be the story of the life of Enid Blyton: it would not be a book of literary criticism nor would it be a deep and learned psychological study of why she wrote as she did. We were concerned that the book should reveal as far as possible the human being with all her faults and virtues who was known to so many as Enid Blyton. It was not an easy task. Vital witnesses to her early years were either untraceable or dead. My Father, her first husband, died just after Mrs. Stoney had discovered where he was then living. As must often happen in biographies, one person's memories completely contradicted another's and trying to ascertain the true facts must have been extremely difficult. I know from my conversations with the author that there have been many such incidents during the three years in which she has been working on this book.

I was very pleased that Paul Hodder-Williams of Hodder and Stoughton, with whom my Mother had worked closely for many years, is the publisher of this book. He knew her well over a number of years but he confessed that he has been surprised to discover details of my Mother's early life that he didn't know about at all. I was too, despite the fact that I was very close to my Mother, and talked with her freely from early childhood. But she is an important writer for children all over the world. And it is best that the very private drive and the very personal talent that made her so should be known and understood. It is best too that this should be done by someone as honest and as detached as Barbara Stoney.

Gillian Baverstock

Acknowledgments

IT WOULD HAVE BEEN AN IMPOSSIBLE TASK TO CHART THE LIFE STORY of Enid Blyton without the generous assistance I have received from many quarters, in particular from Mrs. Donald Baverstock, who gave me not only access to her mother's papers, but great help and encouragement throughout. I am also indebted to Enid Blyton's younger daughter, Mrs. Imogen Smallwood, and to Mr. Hanly Blyton, who gave much time and thought in helping my research into his sister's early years and — with his cousin, Mrs. Sylvia Conway — provided me with many valuable photographs from family albums.

Among those who also lent photographs and letters or supplied personal recollections of Enid Blyton's early life, I would like especially to thank: Miss Mabel Attenborough, Miss Margery Dawson, Dr. Mirabel Harrison (née Davis), Mrs. Kathleen Murray (née Harrison), Mrs. Mary Potter (née Attenborough) and Mrs. Phyllis Samuel (née Chase); Mrs. Ida Haward (née Hunt), Misses Kathleen and Nan Fryer, Miss J. Gilchrist, and Mrs. Ann Style, Secretary of Ipswich High School for Girls; Mrs. Joyce Dunn (née Brandram), Mr. A. Robert Dickinson, the Reverend M. Martin Harvey, Mr. Derek Hudson, Mr. T. R. Twallin, and Mr. E. I. Childs, Headmaster of Bickley Park School; the Thompson family — Messrs. David, Brian, Peter and John — Mrs. Frances Peterson, Miss E. D. Moore and others associated with 'Southernhay' during the 1920s.

I am grateful, too, for all the other help I have received during my research into the writer's later years, particularly from her executor, Mr. Eric Rogers, and his daughter, the late Miss Patricia

Rogers; solicitors, J. D. Langton and Passmore; literary agents, Mr. George Greenfield and Miss Rosica Colin; medical advisers, Dr. Raymond Daley and Dr. R. M. Solomon; and representatives of her many publishing houses — especially the directors and staff of Evans Brothers Limited, the Hon. Mrs. Audrey Evans, Miss Audrey White, Mr. Ronald Deadman, and the editorial department of *Teachers' World*, who gave me access to much interesting archive material covering her long association with this company.

Among Enid Blyton's friends, business associates, household staff and others whose help has been invaluable to me are: Mrs. Mary Bale, Mr. Victor Broadribb, the late Mrs. Margaret Calvert (née Norris), Mrs. Joyce Chapman, Miss Doris Cox, Miss Dorothy Collins, Mrs. S. Colledge, Mrs. Joan Dashwood, Mrs. C. Emmett, Mrs. Hilda Guest (née Russell-Cruise), Miss D. Herbert, Mr. and Mrs. R. Hughes, Dr. J. P. Jackson, Mr. Stephen Jennings, Mrs. Lorna Jones, Miss Olive Jones, Professor Peter McKellar, Miss Jessie Mangan, Mrs. Betty Marsh, Mr. K. Martin, Miss Olive Openshaw, Mrs. Ida Pollock, Miss Rosemary Pollock, Mr. E. A. Roker, Mr. Malcolm Saville, Miss Eileen Soper, Miss Grace Stuart, Miss Margaret Summerton, Mrs. Marjory Twitchen, Mr. and Mrs. Uphill, Miss Diana Ward, Mr. Ewart Wharmby, Mr. David White, Mr. Michael Woods and Mrs. M. G. Woollerton. My thanks also to the B.B.C., the Chairman and Committee of the Essex Branch S.L.A., and to the officials of the Friends of the Centre for Spastic Children, Sunshine Fund for Blind Babies and Young People, and the People's Dispensary for Sick Animals.

Illustrations

ACKNOWLEDGMENTS
[1] Department of Postal Administration, Jersey.
[2] Associated Newspapers Group Ltd.

CHAPTER

I

IT IS SAD TO WATCH THE DEMOLITION OF A HOUSE, THE TEARING away at walls which once enclosed the joys, sorrows and triumphs of its former occupants. When this has also been a home known to millions and around which many dreams were spun, such a scene takes on an added poignancy.

So it was on a warm, sunny day in the late summer of 1973, when the last of Green Hedges at Beaconsfield came tumbling down. Here, for thirty eventful years, lived Enid Blyton — the most prolific, successful, yet controversial children's writer of all time. It was to this house that hundreds of her readers from all over the world continued to address their letters long after she died in 1968, and from which many thousands once received her distinctive, hand-written replies. Under its roof most of the characters from her books were created and many of the dramas of her own private life enacted — a life which began some thirty miles away, in 1897, at East Dulwich in South London.

Enid Blyton's early forebears are believed to have come over to England at the time of the Norman conquest and to have settled in Lincolnshire, where the name appears under various spellings in many of the early chronicles for that county. There is a village called Blyton in the Lincolnshire Wolds and a chantry was founded in Lincoln Cathedral in 1327, apparently bequeathed by a de Bliton who was mayor of the city four years earlier. For several centuries the family were concerned with farming or the wool and cloth trade — but George Blyton, Enid's great-grand-father, was a cordwainer.

George Blyton was thought by his relations to be something of an eccentric. He spent much of his spare time tramping through his home county of Lincolnshire preaching to all who cared to listen and it was said that his main ambition was to go to the Fiji Isles to 'convert the heathen'. Instead, he stayed at home in Swinderby making fine boots and shoes and raising a large family. With such aspirations, however, it is not surprising that he gave his elder son, Thomas, the second name of Carey, after one of the founders of the Baptist Missionary Society. Thomas Carey, Enid's grandfather, eventually left Swinderby to become a linen draper in Sheffield, but there is no record to show how he came to meet and marry his Irish-born wife, Mary Ann Hanly, in Camberwell in 1864.

Family rumour has it that Mary Ann was descended from the Dukes of Hamilton and was born at the house of her grandfather — a Doctor Hamilton of County Tyrone — but little is known of her background prior to her marriage. By all accounts she was a surprisingly well-educated woman and made a great impression on all who met her, including the young Enid on the few occasions she visited her grandmother at Swinderby.

Enid's father, Thomas Carey junior, was born in 1870 and was the fourth of Mary Ann's seven children. One of his sisters became a professional musician, another an elocutionist, and a creative, artistic thread seemed to run throughout the family. Thomas himself had many talents and an engaging personality. There was nothing particularly striking about his appearance, being rather short in stature, sallow of complexion and with a nose just a fraction too large, but his eyes — dark brown and arresting — gave a hint at the restlessness within. At the time of his marriage in 1896 to Theresa Mary Harrison, a pretty, raven-haired girl from his home town of Sheffield, he was a salesman with a cutlery firm, but his interests outside his work were many and varied. Even in those days his thirst for knowledge led him into studying astronomy, teaching himself French, German and shorthand and learning to play both the piano and banjo. He painted in water colours, was no mean photographer, sang with a fine baritone voice, wrote poetry — and read voraciously. Books were his great love and he acquired new ones whenever he could. During his courting days he would each week allot one sixpence towards a box of chocolates for his future wife and another to buy one of a series of 'sixpenny classics' then being published by Cassells. In this way he was able to accumulate almost the complete set, and these books, along with many hundreds of others on a wide variety of subjects, were to delight the young Enid in later years.

Soon after his marriage Thomas moved from Sheffield to represent his company in London and it was on August 11th, 1897, at 354 Lordship Lane, a small, two-bedroom apartment above a shop in East Dulwich, that his first child, Enid Mary, was born. A few months before the birth, his job with the cutlery manufacturer had come to an end and at the suggestion of an uncle he joined his two older brothers in the family 'mantle warehousing' business of Fisher and Nephews, which was also based in London. This proved a happy change for Thomas and from then on his fortunes improved — as did the houses rented by him for his growing family.

His first move, when Enid was only a few months old, was into the neighbouring suburb of Beckenham in Kent where, at a semi-detached villa in Chaffinch Road, Theresa gave birth to a son, Hanly, in 1899. Three years later, at a slightly larger house in nearby Clockhouse Road, a second boy — Carey — arrived.

There had been little more than a back-yard at Chaffinch Road, so the garden at the new home was a delight for the two older children. Here they could play contentedly for hours, providing they kept off Thomas's well-kept borders. Hanly's memory of that first garden at Clockhouse Road was of a front privet hedge behind iron railings, with irises and lots of snails. But his sister was to remember far more, especially of the small patch allotted to her by her father in which she invested most of her pocket money. Many years later she described this 'garden' as being square in shape, running from the path to the wall. In it she planted virginia stock, candytuft, mignonette, clarkia, poppies and 'many hardy nasturtiums that climbed high over the wall, thick with orange flowers.' Her father understood her excitement when the first green shoots appeared from the carefully bought seeds for he, too, loved his garden and working there together was only one of the many interests they shared.

Thomas delighted in his young daughter, so like himself both in appearance and temperament. She had the same dark hair, alert brown eyes and sensitive, highly-strung nature, intent upon seeking out and enjoying life to the full. Almost from the beginning he felt a special bond had been welded between them, and he was often to tell her of the occasion on which he was convinced he had saved her life. She was barely three months old at the time and dangerously ill with whooping cough. The doctor, when called on that cold November evening, had looked grave and, shaking his head sadly, had told Thomas and Theresa that he doubted if their baby girl would survive until the morning, but Thomas refused to accept the doctor's opinion. He took the sick infant from his wife's arms, and all through that long winter night sat cradling her to him, keeping out the cold and willing her to stay alive. In the early hours when the crisis had passed and he had finally been persuaded to go to bed he had lain awake for some time, exhilarated by the thought that he had undoubtedly saved his daughter's life.

Enid loved hearing this story and would ask him to repeat it to her many times. She enjoyed listening to all her father's tales — whether of his own boyhood in Sheffield, of the leprechauns, fairies and 'little people' once told him by his Irish mother, or those based on history or the classics. Many of these he would relate to her on the long walks they took together through fields and woodland when Thomas, also a keen, self-taught naturalist, would enthusiastically air his knowledge of the countryside to his eager companion.

'He knew more about flowers, birds and wild animals than anyone I had ever met and was always willing to share his knowledge with me,' Enid wrote years later, adding wistfully, 'These were the happiest times, when looking back it seems the days were always warm and sunny and the skies deeply blue.'

Often her father would quote extracts of poetry as they walked and sometimes they would make up little rhymes of their own, laughing over the nonsense of these when they finally returned for tea at the well-kept house in Clockhouse Road. Afterwards Thomas would take out his banjo and sing popular songs or nursery rhymes to amuse his family and then, when the children were in bed, he would seat himself at his much cherished piano and play long into the night. For most of her life, Enid could never listen to certain sonatas by Beethoven or works by Chopin, Liszt, Mozart and Rachmaninoff without recalling the days of her childhood, when she would lie in bed, almost asleep, listening to her father playing hour after hour downstairs.

He gave Enid her first piano lesson when she was six years old and, as with everything else, she was quick to learn. He nevertheless insisted that she practise daily, and this she did religiously. She and Hanly had by then started school — a small nursery class run by two spinster sisters at a house called 'Tresco', on the corner of Clockhouse and Cedar Roads, almost opposite the Blyton home. The Misses Read found Enid a bright and alert pupil, who appeared to enjoy every minute of her schooling. Although she found even the simplest of sums difficult, she wrote, read and sang well and, due no doubt to Thomas's influence, was one of the best pupils at art and nature study.

From the moment she learnt to read, it was rare to see her without a book, in or out of school, and her father's bookcase in the small sitting room was a veritable treasure trove. She read Arthur Mee's encyclopaedias from cover to cover, fascinated by, and memorising, some of the more curious facts she found there. She always enjoyed books by this writer and his influence on her thought as she became older is apparent from the many pencilled observations and underlinings, made in her teens, throughout a copy of his *Letters to Girls*. Her reading tastes in those early years were fairly general. She loved mythology and fantasy, but not of the horrific kind — *Grimms' Fairy Tales* she found particularly cruel and frightening. *The Princess and the Goblin* by George Macdonald was her favourite book for a long while and she relished the humour of *Alice in Wonderland* and the excitement of *The Coral Island*. Although she found it sad, she also enjoyed

17

Black Beauty, and *Little Women* she read many times over, because she felt it was about 'real children' whom she could understand. It was not long before she was reading many of her father's adult books and he was quite annoyed one day to find her engrossed in a volume he felt to be far too advanced for a child of ten, as she then was. Later, however, when he realised that his young daughter's interest in literature was as keen as his own, she was allowed to choose freely from his shelves.

Her visual memory, like her father's, was exceptional. At the age of nine, she could scan a page once, shut her eyes and then repeat the whole of it almost word for word. Years later she was able to describe 'Tresco' and remember clearly 'the room, the garden, the pictures on the wall, the little chairs, the dog there, and the lovely smells that used to creep out from the kitchen into our classroom when we sat doing dictation'.

In 1907 Enid became a pupil at St. Christopher's School for Girls in Beckenham, and around this time the family moved yet again to a larger house a few doors away in Clockhouse Road. It was at this new home that she was to experience some of the unhappiest days of her life.

Tension had been growing between Thomas and his wife, Theresa, for some years. The dark good looks which had first attracted him to her were not now of themselves sufficient for this mercurial man. Apart from the children, they had little in common, for Theresa had never shared her husband's interests — indeed most of them she barely tolerated. The family, house and kitchen had always constituted her entire world. Tall and upright in bearing, she ruled her children with a rigidity not easy for the strong-willed Enid to accept, whereas Hanly, always of a gentler nature, and her 'baby Carey' she found easier to understand. To her mind, Thomas spoilt Enid and she had little time for their music, poetry, painting and 'other nonsense'. She felt that, as her only daughter, the girl should help about the house and spend more time learning to cook and sew, instead of 'sitting around reading books' or going off with her father on some excursion or other. Apart from 'training' the young Enid for what she considered to be the only proper future for a girl — marriage, home

18

and children — Theresa felt that she could well do with her daughter's co-operation. Very houseproud, she coped with all the cooking and most of the chores not dealt with by the young general maid, and as she had no time, nor need, for any other activity, it exasperated her that Enid had no similar inclinations. Thomas aggravated the situation by supporting his daughter's resistance to Theresa's disciplining and this, in turn, only added to the already growing discontent of their life together.

As time went on the wranglings between them became more frequent, for a new aspect had now crept into the relationship. Enid and Hanly, tiptoeing one night out of their bedrooms to listen at the top of the stairs, wide-eyed and frightened, to the heated argument taking place below, heard mention for the first time of another woman's name. Enid could not bring herself to believe what she had heard: that her mother and father could behave to each other in this way was bad enough, but that her beloved father could ever consider bestowing his love on anyone outside the family — let alone another woman — was something she found impossible to accept. When she and Hanly eventually returned to their beds that night, she tried to put the thought from her and to take comfort from the little stories that she had for some time been able to conjure up out of what she called her 'mind's eye'.

These semi-conscious 'thoughts' would come to her most evenings just before she fell asleep. They were made up of many things gleaned from stories she had read or heard and often concerned people she had met or places she had seen, but always they sorted themselves into definite patterns which had beginnings, middles and ends. These fantasies increasingly became her escape from the harsh reality of the violent scenes enacted downstairs, for in the happy, carefree stories she wove, there was no room for the angry voices or the slam of the front door which invariably seemed to terminate the quarrels.

Inevitably there came a time, not long before her thirteenth birthday when, after another of the all too familiar clashes, Thomas left the house and did not return and Theresa was forced to tell the children that their father had gone away. He had also

19

left Uncle Fisher's firm and was branching out on his own, starting a new life altogether.

Although this marked the end of the troubled atmosphere within the household, the shock to the highly-strung girl of what she felt to be her father's rejection of her for someone else, was incalculable. With her chief ally and confidant no longer there under the same roof to encourage her with her music, painting and first exploratory efforts at writing down the stories and verses which came to her so easily, life seemed suddenly empty. Hanly was a good companion when it came to swimming together in the local baths or taking occasional cycle rides, but beyond these more sporting activities they had little in common and Carey, closer to her in temperament, was, she considered, just that much too young really to understand her needs. If she could have shed a few tears it might have helped her to face up to and eventually accept, the situation — but she could not bring herself to tell anyone of her real thoughts and feelings. Perhaps if Theresa had not been so preoccupied with her own troubles, and had possessed some true understanding of her eldest child, Enid's future might have been very different. As it was, she was the one who unwittingly made it easier for her daughter eventually to resort to the only means she knew of counteracting the hurt — ignore its very existence.

'Keeping up appearances' was a very real factor in 1910 suburban Beckenham, or so Theresa thought. She had seen the treatment meted out to a divorced woman living in the same road and upon whom 'nobody, of course, would think of calling' and had no intention of letting this happen to her. Divorce, she decided, was out of the question for the Blytons and no one in Clockhouse Road must be aware of the true situation. The children were instructed to tell everyone that their father was 'away on a visit' and in this subterfuge Enid was a more than willing participant.

The neighbours were given little time to speculate, for Thomas had agreed to Theresa and the family moving once again — this time to a large, detached, three-storey Victorian house with a pleasant garden in tree-lined Elm Road, then considered to be one of the 'better' residential areas of Beckenham. Here the residents appeared to be more concerned with their own affairs than were their counterparts in the slightly more confined semi-detached houses of Clockhouse Road, and Theresa, her children and Annie, the young general maid, prepared to settle down to their new life.

From the beginning, Enid knew the room she wanted. It overlooked the garden on the first floor and was large enough to take her desk, books and other treasures. Spiritually isolated from the rest of her family, as she now felt herself to be, this room was to become the only place where she could be alone to continue the creative activities her father had tried to foster. As time went by, she fixed a knocker on the door, turned the key on the inside and within this snug cocoon lived for a time in the happier world she created for herself, in the poems and stories she now found so easy to write and which she hoped would one day be published.

Thomas meanwhile had established himself in an office in the City of London and had set up what proved to be a successful wholesale clothing business of his own. From here he arranged for money to be sent regularly to support his family and also made it his business to see that his children's education continued in the way he wished, by paying the fees for Enid and Carey at the private schools they were attending, and arranging for Hanly to be sent away to boarding school at the age of thirteen. Theresa was also made to agree that she would ensure Enid kept up her hour of piano practice each day, for Thomas was convinced that his daughter was destined for a musical career as notable as that of his sister May — if not more so.

Away from home, Enid put up a front quite remarkable for a girl of her age. No one, not even her best friend at school — Mary Attenborough — ever guessed that her father lived away from the family. After a while the deception was easier to keep up, for Thomas started visiting from time to time, usually to take Enid on outings to the theatre or to the country. She would look forward to these but, although the scar was beginning to heal, the fact that he was now living with someone else created a small barrier between them which prevented a complete renewal of the rapport they once had. The expensive presents he brought her were no compensation, she felt, for what she had lost.

Some forty years later in *Six Bad Boys* — which was an unusual attempt, for Enid, at social realism — she described a similar family situation in which the three 'Berkeley' children (two girls and a boy) were deserted by their father after numerous, violent quarrels between their parents. The effect his departure had on the children and the subsequent behaviour of the mother — even to the pledging of the family to secrecy over his disappearance — was an echo of this desperately unhappy period of Enid's life, yet such was her reticence about her early years no one guessed at the time that she was writing from personal experience.

The Berkeley children's comments on 'being glad of dear old school — even French and Maths' to take their minds off their troubles, must have been Enid's own feelings about St. Christopher's, for at no time did her work there appear to have deteriorated. She was popular with pupils and staff alike and really appeared to enjoy her school life, throwing herself into all the activities with enthusiasm and many of the characters and happenings she was later to describe in her school stories, were based on the people she met and incidents that took place during those years.

Her fellow pupils remember her as a vivacious, intelligent girl with a sallow complexion, large nose, dark hair and eyes — and a penchant for playing practical jokes, which carried over well into adult life. She would plague the mistresses and her classmates with an assortment of rubber- and tin-pointed pencils, artificial blots and other 'tricks' bought from a local shop and, although her friends found them fun at first, her exuberance invariably carried on the joke just a trifle too long. She is remembered by many for her 'great daring' in being the first girl in the school to have her long plait cut off and to wear her hair at shoulder length, tied back with a bow on a large slide, which earned her the nickname — among the girls who were boarding at the school — of 'the hairless day girl'.

Although she had once played the title role in Tresco's production of *Alice in Wonderland*, she was not, apparently, considered

22

to be a good enough actress to perform in St. Christopher's School plays. This rather vexed Enid, whose love of theatricals stretched back to her early childhood, when Thomas would take her and Hanly to musicals or plays at the nearby Crystal Palace Theatre. Undeterred, however, she set about organising her own concert party and, dressed in mauve with white ruffles and black pom-poms, the subsequent 'Mauve Merriments' troupe of eight senior girls eventually became a popular end of term entertainment for the whole school. Her friend Mary Attenborough usually took the lead in these small shows, which comprised several short sketches, dancing and the singing of popular songs, accompanied by Enid on the piano.

Her agility and enthusiasm for games led to her becoming both tennis champion and captain of the lacrosse team and her ability to put the same effort into everything she undertook undoubtedly accounted for the number of prizes she was awarded for various subjects and for her being made head girl during her final two years.

Out of school Enid was also the instigator of a small magazine *Dab* — named after the surnames of its three contributors: Mirabel Davis, Mary Attenborough and herself. This usually consisted of a few short stories written by Enid, poems by Mirabel and illustrations by Mary. When the three were away on holiday they would correspond by coded postcards in order, as Enid would tell them, 'to mystify the postman'. She even sent one of these from France during the summer of 1913 when Mlle. Louise Bertraine, who taught French at St. Christopher's, took Enid for a memorable holiday to her home in Annecy (see overleaf). It was the sixteen-year-old's first trip out of England and the excitement of the journey, the beauty of the lakes and mountains of the Haute Savoie and the happiness of her stay with the family were remembered always. The First World War broke out the following year and there were no further holidays with Louise, but their friendship continued for many years.

The war did not appear to affect Enid very greatly at the beginning. She had no close relatives involved in the fighting and, understandably perhaps at that age, was far more concerned with

Translation: Dear Mirabel, it is simply glorious in France. The French are awfully greedy here. I can't eat half the things. Write to me soon. I will send you a letter soon. Love from Enid.

the trials and pleasures of her very busy home and school life — a life in which her close friend, Mary Attenborough, played a considerable part. They had first met in kindergarten days and, although Mary was her junior by some three years — and consequently nicknamed 'Kid' by Enid — in the senior classes at St. Christopher's the pair were inseparable. Both were alert, intelligent and invariably at the top of their forms — due, in no small part, to the competition between them. Mary always excelled at art and Enid at music, but otherwise their school work followed pretty much the same pattern. Out of school they would play long games of tennis at the home of Mary's grandfather in Oakwood Avenue, on the outskirts of Beckenham, and on Sundays would go to services at the Elm Road Baptist Church. Enid had been baptised here at the age of thirteen and had for some years, with her brothers, attended the Sunday School of which Mary's father was superintendent. His sister, Mabel, ran the girls' classes and from her first meeting with Enid took a great interest in her niece's school friend.

Mabel was unmarried, some twenty years older than the girls, and lived at home with her parents, so visits from the two lively friends were always greatly enjoyed. This tall, rather gaunt woman with the quiet, gentle manner and kindly eyes, seemed to sense, under Enid's usually bright façade, her great need for affection and sympathetic understanding — though even she was never to guess at the cause. The fact that her father was living away from home was something Enid could never bring herself to reveal — even to Mabel, good friend and confidante though the older woman later became. But in other matters, it was to Mabel that she soon began to turn for advice and sympathy, particularly with regard to her writing.

A year or so after her father left the family, Enid had entered for a children's poetry competition run by Arthur Mee in one of his magazines and was thrilled to get a letter from the writer himself, telling her that he intended to print her verses and would like to see more of her work. This encouraged her to branch out further with her writing and to send a selection of stories, articles and poems to other periodicals. Apart, however, from the unexpected acceptance of a poem by *Nash's Magazine*,* some few years later, everything came back — much to the annoyance of Theresa, who soon realised the significance of the long envelopes that dropped with such regularity through the letter box at Elm Road, and considered the whole process a 'waste of time and money'. This was not so with Mabel Attenborough, who continued to encourage the young writer, for she recognised in those early, very naïve efforts a potential that she felt should be fostered.

Enid later admitted that several hundred of her literary offerings were returned to her during this period, but with her usual persistence — and Mabel's encouragement — she continued to send them out, and to enter for literary competitions whenever the opportunity arose. She also avidly read any books she could find about writers and their techniques and for many years kept a diary in which she recorded her feelings and activities in and out of school but, after her mother discovered and read some of the jottings, Enid destroyed this evidence of what she considered to be her 'very innermost thoughts'. Hanly remembers how his sister's fierce temper had flared over this intrusion into her privacy and how she had locked herself away into her first-floor room, tearfully announcing that in future her diaries would include little more than outlines of her day-to-day activities.

Hanly has good cause to remember that fiery rage, for he was the recipient of it himself on many occasions, the most memorable being the time when, in her opinion, he had shown 'extreme cruelty' with an airgun. He had been given the gun for his fourteenth birthday and, bent on trying it out, had crept into the small downstairs lavatory, locked himself in, thrown bread on to the lawn and waited for the small London sparrows and starlings to appear. When they did, he took aim and fired, but his shot was hopelessly off target. He had no opportunity, however, of trying again for a window directly overhead was flung open and Enid, her voice shaking with rage, yelled out, 'You wretched boy, I'll tear you limb from limb'. Hanly did not wait to hear

* Unfortunately it has proved impossible to trace either of these first poems and one can only assume that in the case of the second, at least, she used a pseudonym.

more, for he knew that by then his sister was on her way down and she was a power to be reckoned with when roused. He was out through the window in an instant and ran round into the kitchen, in time to catch a glimpse of her breaking down the lavatory door with her bare fists.

As time went by, the relationship between Enid and her mother deteriorated. Perhaps subconsciously she blamed Theresa for her father leaving home, for she had always objected, as he had done, to her mother's aggressive and domineering manner. She felt resentful that her brothers' interests seemed inevitably to be considered before her own and had no intention of becoming the domestic, home-orientated daughter Theresa wished — nor did she hesitate to make this apparent. Her deliberate withdrawal from the rest of the family, either to Mabel Attenborough's home or to the cosy room upstairs, was a source of constant irritation to her mother and when this also took her away from her piano practice there were even more heated arguments between the two. Theresa had not forgotten her promise to Thomas that she would ensure their daughter practised for the number of hours required by her teacher and this, at least, she was determined upon — however reluctant Enid might be to put aside her writing and other interests. This vigilance was in no way slackened after her daughter left St. Christopher's in 1915, to prepare for her entry into the Guildhall School of Music the following year.

During Enid's final term at St. Christopher's, the family had moved from Elm Road into a smaller, semi-detached house in nearby Westfield Road, which had only two main bedrooms and a boxroom for Theresa and her three teenaged children. The loss of the room at Elm Road, that had meant so much to her, and the impossibility in the smaller house of escaping for long from the critical eye of her mother, drove Enid into spending more time than ever with Mabel and this inevitably aggravated the situation between mother and daughter. As the months passed, Enid's frustrations grew, for she was now convinced that she was being made to work towards a career for which she was totally unsuited.

27

CHAPTER

II

FROM EARLIEST CHILDHOOD ENID HAD BEEN SCHOOLED IN THE belief that she would eventually become a musician. She had always been told how much she resembled her Aunt May, both in looks and temperament, and knew that her father was convinced she possessed a similar musical talent Year after year she had worked doggedly through examinations and practice sessions — not because she particularly enjoyed what she was doing, but because Thomas expected it of her. As she grew older, however, and writing became increasingly more important to her, she begrudged the long hours she was forced to spend at her piano. Playing and listening to music was enjoyable, up to a point, but the idea of working as a professional musician was a different matter. Creating and writing down the poems and stories that seemed to come to her so easily, gave her far greater satisfaction, for she knew she would never be able to express herself in the same way musically. She tried to explain this to Thomas on the rare occasions they met, but he refused to discuss any alternative to the career he had planned for her. It did not help that she had no substantial writing success with which to back up her argument — nor could she expect support from her mother, whose views on 'Enid's scribbling' were only too apparent. When she left school there seemed little alternative but to follow through her father's plans.

By the summer of 1916, however, after months of enforced piano practice and tuition from her music teacher, she felt she needed to get away, if only for a while, from the tensions and tedium of the life she was leading at home. As usual, when she needed advice, she sought out Mabel Attenborough, who came up with a suggestion to which Enid eagerly agreed: that she should spend a short holiday with her friends, the Hunt family, at their farm in Suffolk.

The farm was run from Seckford Hall, a fifteenth-century mansion near Woodbridge, some seven miles out of Ipswich. Although it has since been completely restored, the rambling old house was then partly in ruins and only the portion rented by George and Emily Hunt for their family still retained something of its former glory. The Hunts were great friends of the Attenboroughs, who had spent many holidays at the Hall. For visiting children, the old Tudor building, with its 'haunted' bedroom, secret passage and surrounding farmland, was a source of constant delight. Many were the 'battles' fought in the decaying, partially roofed, banqueting hall, for its minstrels' gallery remained intact and the seed potatoes stored here provided perfect ammunition for the bombardment of 'enemies' beneath.

Enid had heard all about Seckford Hall from Mary and Mabel Attenborough and was overjoyed at the prospect of a holiday in such a setting — especially as it gave her an opportunity to feed and tend the numerous animals on this large, mixed farm. The Blyton children had never been allowed to keep pets — a deprivation which possibly accounted for Enid's intense love of animals which remained with her all her life. She often recalled her sadness at parting from 'Chippy', a small, bedraggled kitten she had once found on a common near her home and kept secretly until it was eventually discovered and sent away — for Thomas was happy to see wild creatures in their natural surroundings, but had little interest in those of the domestic variety and his wife even less.

At Seckford Hall, with horses to ride and dogs to take on walks through the attractive Suffolk countryside, her worries about her future were temporarily forgotten. She went on long cycle rides, or to nearby beaches, with the Hunt sisters — Marjory and Ida — who, though a few years her senior, proved sympathetic companions. Their two brothers, William and Herbert, were both living away, one in the army and the other married, but the Hunt family were hosts to several young officers billeted at the Hall and there was always much friendly teasing and laughter in that happy household.

Ida was a Froebel-trained kindergarten teacher at Ipswich High School — a large day school for girls, with a trainee-teacher, kindergarten section. She also taught at the Woodbridge Congregational Sunday School. Enid went along with her most Sundays to help and Ida was surprised by the way the class seemed to respond to the inexperienced girl. This prompted her to ask Enid if, with her obvious flair for handling young children, she had ever thought of taking up teaching. Up to then this was something that Enid had not even remotely considered, but later that day she thought over what Ida had said.

She certainly enjoyed those Sunday School afternoons and her first close encounters with small children, for from the beginning she seemed to feel a close affinity with them. She loved helping to paint large pictures for the Sunday School walls, making the models and pieces of handwork which illustrated the lessons and, most of all, telling the children stories. From her own Sunday School days with Mary Attenborough at the Elm Road Baptist Church, she had learnt most of the Bible stories she now passed on to the children and found that, without much preparation, she could relate them with the same ease with which she wrote her own, as yet unpublished, stories at home. No 'rejections' from editors here — her listeners were always eager for more.

Quite suddenly, she knew what she must do — become a teacher. In that way she could carry on with her writing and if she were with children all day long — something that now appealed to her greatly — she would be able to study them closely and then, perhaps, learn how to write about and for them. Everything, she felt, had at last fallen into place.

It was typical of Enid that, having made a decision about something, she lost no time in acting upon it. She confirmed with Ida that it would be possible to begin a National Froebel Union course at Ipswich that September, provided her application was accepted, and then set about tackling the greatest obstacle of all — her father.

She walked to Woodbridge village to put through a telephone call to Thomas at his London office and told him that she proposed to give up her place at the music school in September, and train instead as a kindergarten teacher at Ipswich High School. According to her own account of the incident, an astonished Thomas had replied: 'How like you, Enid, to tell me these things over the *telephone*! Why must you be so headstrong? I must think about it. No, I can't give you an answer now. Why, I didn't even know you *liked* teaching!'

Enid said that she did and pleaded with him to agree to sign her application form, adding, 'You can think about it afterwards.'

Thomas's sense of humour was always to the fore and he began to laugh. Many years afterwards Enid wrote that she could still hear that chuckle, so keyed up was she over the call that was to change the direction of her whole life. She was almost overcome with joy when he finally gave his agreement, but was often to wonder afterwards over his sudden capitulation. Was it that he saw a reflection of himself in the 'headstrong' decision of his daughter — or was it the phrenologist's report, which Enid was to find among some old papers many years later, that eventually swayed him?

The phrenologist had visited the house in Clockhouse Road when Enid was about eight years old. Interested, as always, in furthering his knowledge of every subject, Thomas had invited the balding man with the sensitive fingers to 'feel the bumps' on his young daughter's head. He was no doubt disappointed when the subsequent report made no mention of a musical ability but read instead: 'This child will turn to teaching as she develops. It is, and will be, her great gift.'

Whether by luck or skill, the phrenologist was to prove uncannily right for, from the moment she entered her training school, Enid was, as she later described herself, 'a round peg in a round hole'.

But there were other changes for Enid during her first year at

Ipswich. Just as some six years previously her father had made a new start away from his family, so now did she. Hanly never knew exactly what happened to cause the break. It could be that Enid and her mother exchanged heated letters over the decision to give up her musical career, but it seems far more likely that the final severing of the family ties came about through *non*-communication on both sides. For reasons known only to herself, Enid may not have let Theresa know what she was about — and even have asked Thomas and Mabel to keep her movements secret. Theresa might well have stubbornly refused to write to her daughter until an equally obstinate Enid had written herself. This seems more probable, in view of Theresa's strange explanation of Enid's departure to enquiring relations and friends. She informed them that her daughter had left home, against her wishes, to join the Women's Land Army and that when Enid found — as she had been warned — that the life was too harsh for her, she had been 'too frightened to return home and admit her mistake'.

Such subterfuge may be difficult to understand in these days of emancipated women and reformed divorce laws, but in the narrow, suburban circles in which Theresa moved, not only was a wife living apart from her husband treated with suspicion, but an unmarried daughter leaving home and not communicating with her family was thought to be even more suspect. No 'nice' girl would consider such a step unless she had 'something to hide'. Theresa knew Enid had been on holiday to a farm, and in 1916 more and more women were being accepted into industry and the services to help the war effort, so she must have thought this explanation plausible enough to be accepted by the neighbours.

The fact remains that from then on, Enid's holidays away from college were spent either with the Hunt family at Seckford Hall or with Mabel Attenborough, and she was never to live at home again with her mother and brothers — nor did she have any contact with them during the four years that were to follow.

Enid began her training at Ipswich in September 1916, just a month after her nineteenth birthday. She appeared, by all accounts, to have been a quieter and more withdrawn girl among

Enid Blyton's grandfather—Thomas Carey Blyton

Her grandmother—Mary Ann Blyton

Her father—Thomas Carey Blyton Jnr.

May Crossland, his sister, a professional musician

Enid, aged one year

Enid, aged seven

Enid Blyton's mother, Theresa (1924)

her fellow students and teachers than she had been at St. Christopher's, but her occasional bouts of depression very soon disappeared when she was with the children. With them she was always, according to her fellow students, 'relaxed, vivacious and full of fun'. She was no mean artist and carried a small blue book with her everywhere, in which she sketched her charges at play or drew birds and animals seen on the 'nature walks'. She kept a similar book during her last year at school and these two volumes of pencilled drawings provide an interesting insight into how Enid viewed her world at that time: the tousle-headed kindergarten boy, drinking his glass of milk; three small birds, with ruffled feathers, bending a narrow branch with their weight; a round-faced baby asleep in its pram and the rotund back view of a woman sitting on a beach, are all clearly drawn with an eye for detail.

There were three main lecturers in the kindergarten department. In charge was Miss Sophie Flear, who also taught most of the main subjects to the trainees. This small, neat woman was a dedicated teacher with a deep understanding of her pupils — whether at kindergarten or student level — and with her air of quiet authority, did not hesitate to put into practice new methods of teaching if she felt that by so doing she was furthering the scope and standard of her well-run kindergarten. In 1913 she had been chosen by the Council of the Girls' Public Day School Trust to accompany two other teachers to Italy to study and report on the Montessori teaching methods, with a view to their partial adoption in the Trust's kindergartens. Although the training at Ipswich was basically Froebel, Miss Flear drew upon her experiences in Italy to broaden the horizons of her students still further. Her lessons were always enjoyed by the students and Enid was not alone in finding those in psychology particularly interesting. She liked and respected Miss Flear — but she had an even greater affection for her assistant, Miss Kathleen Gibbons.

Miss Gibbons was a large, 'motherly' woman, who taught zoology and botany with great patience and understanding. Her 'nature walks', which she took regularly with the kindergarten children and students, reminded Enid of those rambles with her father when he, too, would point out so much of the teeming life of pond or hedgerow, and the comprehensive notes she took from Miss Gibbons were to be of great help to her years later when she compiled her first book on nature study.

Miss Kathleen Fryer was the youngest of the three lecturers and had not long been out of college. She was a skilful teacher and Enid found her handwork classes something of a relaxation since they gave her an opportunity to think up new ideas for short stories or poems, as she worked away at the cane or raffia articles she was required to make for her course.

Despite her studies, Enid managed to set aside some time for her own writing, and during her training wrote three poems which were accepted by *Nash's Magazine*. The first, in March 1917, was written not long after she began her course and moved into Ida's lodgings at Christchurch Street, five minutes walk away from the school. Here the two women had a bedroom each and shared a small sitting room in which they wrote and studied.

Ida knew that Enid had made the break from home, but not the circumstances leading up to it. On this, as on any other unpleasant subject which had touched her deeply, Enid was as secretive and uncommunicative as she had always been. That the younger woman was lonely and, at times, very unhappy, was apparent. In contrast to the Enid who at home would voluntarily lock herself away from the rest of the family, here at Christchurch Street she was forever seeking Ida out — even after her friend had gone to bed, tired and more ready for sleep than for long hours of talk into the early hours. Perhaps, though she would doubtless never have admitted it at the time, Enid missed hearing from her mother and brothers and secretly wished Theresa would write. It is rather significant that in later years she would frequently say to her daughters, when they thought she was worrying unduly about them, 'You would much rather I did worry about you than not care what happened — which is what I always felt was the case with my own mother.'

Something of her unhappiness is reflected in this first published poem from Ipswich, which she entitled *Have You—?*:

Have you heard the night-time silence, just when all the world's
 asleep,
And you're curled up by your window, all alone?
Have you held your breath in wonder, at the sky so dark and
 deep?
Have you wanted just *one* star for all your own?

Have you seen a streak of glory flash across the summer sky,
When a star is tired of staying still so long?
Have you heard the night-wind whisper, as it softly passes by?
Have you caught the lilting murmur of its song?

Have you listened to the stories that the honeysuckle knows,
As it sends its fairy fragrance thro' the night?
Have you kissed the tiny babies of the clinging rambler-rose?
Have you loved the passion-flowers with all your might?

Have you suddenly felt lonely, have you wondered why you
 should,
When you watched for shooting stars to flash their light?
Have you wanted some one near you, some one dear, who
 understood?
Have you *never* stretched your arms out — to the night?

Enid was overjoyed to find that in the June edition of *Nash's
Magazine*, her rather sentimental little poem evoked a reply,
written by Maud K. F. Dyrenfurth and entitled *I Have.** This
spurred her on to further poetic efforts for the magazine and two
months later *My Summer Prayer* was published, a happier piece
written during a long cycle ride she took with Ida to Felixstowe.
After a busy week at school the pair were spending their usual
weekend at Seckford Hall, and on the Saturday morning decided
to take a picnic and cycle the eleven miles or so to the seaside
resort. It had been a perfect summer day and on the way back
they stopped by some white railings to admire the sunset. Enid
took out the pencil and pad she invariably carried with her and
started scribbling. 'Sorry, Cap'n', was her explanation to an
impatient Ida, 'I've got a poem coming on.' The resultant *Summer
Prayer*, a eulogy of what she saw in the countryside around her

* See Appendix 1.

that evening, was published in the August edition of the magazine.

Enid's habit of coining nicknames for herself and her close acquaintances and then acting out small fantasies with them was something that exasperated the practical, down-to-earth Ida, now engaged to be married to a young soldier she had known since childhood. But Enid continued to call her friend 'Cap'n' and herself 'cabin-boy', or 'Richard', and on walks together she would often act out the part, whistling noisily, plunging her hands deeply into her pockets and putting on a boyish swagger to keep up the pretence. Ida felt this behaviour extremely childish and not in keeping with a trainee teacher, who would soon be responsible for young children herself. Only Mabel, it seemed, understood her young friend's need for these occasional escapes from reality and would laugh over her nonsense, continuing to handle Enid, in her late teens and early twenties, like an irrepressible, lovable child.

During her final year at Ipswich, Enid had another poem accepted by *Nash's Magazine*. *Do You—?*, published in September 1918, again had sentimental rhyming verses and a wistful air. This time no one took up her question poetically in a later edition of the magazine. Another poem, written about the same time, but in a different mood, was in praise of her landlady's date pudding, over which she had enthused at dinner one evening — but this was not to be published until many years later in one of her children's magazines.

With a full programme of assistant teaching in the mornings, lectures each afternoon and private study in the evenings, time passed quickly. Enid took Part I of her National Froebel Union Higher Certificate during her first year, gaining first-class passes in geography, botany, handwork (including drawing) and a distinction in zoology. Surprisingly, she only gained a second-class pass in literature, though her other second-class pass — in mathematics — was not so unexpected, for she had never found this subject easy. By December 1918, she had completed her course with first-class passes in the practice of education, child hygiene, history of education and class teaching of children (between the ages of seven and fourteen) and was awarded a distinction for her paper on the principles of education.

She was now twenty-one years of age, a fully-fledged Froebel teacher and free to go her own way without reference to anyone, but she still welcomed the guiding hand of Mabel. Through her she heard of a junior teacher's post at a new boys' preparatory school at Bickley in Kent. She applied and was accepted. After making her farewells to the staff at the High School and the Hunts, she left Ipswich and closed a chapter of her life that she rarely mentioned again. Except for occasional references to a Froebel training, in later life she told no one, not even her daughters, anything of the people she met during that period or of Seckford Hall and the Hunts. Yet the testimonial given her on leaving by the Head Mistress, Miss M. Gale, was glowing:

> Miss Enid Blyton has been a student in the Kindergarten Department of this school for the last two years. She has very good ability, is both musical and artistic and has shown teaching capacity of a high order. Enthusiasm and energy are marked characteristics. She has a real love of children and handles them well. Discipline is good, and she has an unusual power of interesting children. She has some literary gift herself and dramatic sense.
>
> Miss Blyton has a high sense of duty, is reliable and thorough in all she undertakes, and her influence on children is very good.
>
> As one of the best students we have had for some years, I can recommend her warmly for a responsible post.
>
> M. GALE, Head Mistress

After spending Christmas with Mabel and her parents — 'Grandpa' and 'Grandma' Attenborough, as she was to call them from then on — she began teaching at Bickley Park School in January 1919.

In those days there were about twenty boys at the school, which was run from a small house in Page Heath Lane, Bickley. The Headmaster, Richard Brandram, had not long left the army and was a tall, good-looking man in his thirties, of whom Enid was always rather in awe. She was allotted a bed-sitting room but

37

took her meals with the Headmaster, his wife Maud, their two young children — Dick and Joyce — and the only other member of staff, a Miss Hutson. Enid was now close enough to Beckenham for her to visit Mabel most weekends and she enjoyed the happy, relaxed atmosphere within the school.

This was her first opportunity to try out her teaching ideas on receptive young minds and her skill in handling the children was soon apparent. She had charge of half a dozen boys, aged between six and eight years of age, to whom she taught most general subjects, in addition to taking English classes with the senior boys, and her pupils have happy memories of their enthusiastic young teacher who made her lessons into games and told them such fascinating stories. To those whose work merited special recognition she awarded ribbons, similar to army decorations but worn on the arms, and different colours were used for the varying degrees of progress. When her pupils had reached the 'peak of excellence', as she termed it, they were made 'knights'. Her lessons were equally inventive and she had no difficulty in holding the attention of her classes. She took the children on nature walks, played games and swam with them in the local baths.

Most of her spare time was spent in writing, but with the exception of a poem in *The Poetry Review*, she had no further success with publication. This poem — *The Poet* — looked at the child who gave his own view of the world through his natural poetry.*

By the end of the year, Richard Brandram was well pleased at the progress his young pupils had made under her care, but by then Enid had told him that she would be leaving as she had been offered another post. Once again she took with her a written testimonial which highlighted the ability and flair she was never to lose:

Miss E. M. Blyton held a post on my staff from January to December 1919. During that period she had charge of my lowest form and took English subjects with the other forms

* See Appendix 1.

also. She left me at her own desire to manage a small preparatory school elsewhere.

I was exceedingly sorry to lose her valuable assistance. She inspired her pupils with a real interest in whatever work they were engaged and consequently maintained discipline without any effort. Further, she was at great pains to instil into their minds high ideals of behaviour and manners, with eminently satisfactory results. To be able to lead small boys and to understand their ways is a gift given to few, but Miss Blyton has the secret.

R. A. BRANDRAM, M.A.(Cant.),
Headmaster.

CHAPTER

III

MABEL ATTENBOROUGH HAD SPENT HER SUMMER HOLIDAY OF 1919 in Cornwall, helping to look after the four young sons of her second cousin, Horace Thompson, whose wife, Gertrude, had been seriously ill. As David, the eldest boy, was recovering from diphtheria and had missed a considerable amount of schooling, Mabel had been helping the eight-year-old with his studies and it occurred to her that Enid would be an ideal tutor to continue with these lessons once he returned home. Her suggestion was enthusiastically taken up by the Thompsons, and Enid was subsequently engaged to join the family in January 1920, as nursery governess to all four children.

Horace Thompson was an architect and chartered surveyor and he and his wife had lived at Southernhay — a pleasant, yellow-brick Victorian house in Hook Road, Surbiton — since their marriage. Surbiton in the 'twenties was not the Surrey town of large housing estates and busy roads that it has become today, but a quiet, semi-rural suburb, and Hook Road itself was surrounded by fields and country lanes — something that pleased Enid greatly. She was given a small room at the back of the house with a large window overlooking the garden, and it was here that she was to spend a great deal of her spare time over the next few years, writing. As she had once done at Elm Road, she took to locking her door — but this time it was to shut herself away for a while from her affectionate pupils, who never seemed to tire of her company.

She took her first classes with David and his seven-year-old brother, Brian, in the old day nursery at the side of the house and when the summer came, lessons were conducted in the garden or on the verandah. After a while, the boys were joined by their young twin brothers, Peter and John, and Mollie Sayer, the daughter of a neighbour. Enid's success with her young pupils, and the shortage of schools in the area, soon resulted in several other parents who lived nearby asking if their children also could be included in the classes. Much to her employers' amusement, and Enid's delight, a small 'school' soon developed at Southernhay, with twelve boys and girls being taught at one time or another during the four very happy and eventful years she was to spend with the family.

With ages ranging from four to ten years, lessons had to be conducted with care, but it says much for the skill of her teaching that she was able to handle these so successfully that her pupils progressed remarkably well. She taught every subject herself and meticulously wrote full reports on every child at the end of each term. For the younger members the subjects were Reading, Writing, Numbers, Singing, Painting, Handwork, Games (cricket in the summer, football in the winter) and Acting. Additional subjects for those aged seven and upwards were: Arithmetic, History, Geography, French, English, Music (including piano tuition) and Nature Study. Her General Remarks were always written with care and at length, and these old reports show something of the character of her pupils — and her own sense of humour. She described one child's singing voice as 'a buzzing sound somewhere in his boots', and wrote of another '... Most things come easily to him, and so more difficult things seem sometimes insuperable.' She was quick to praise and give encouragement during her lessons but did not hesitate to wield her authority or reprimand firmly those who misbehaved.

All the Thompsons have happy memories of their teacher, whose 'deep, throaty laugh' could often be heard in and out of the schoolroom. It was her sense of fun which is particularly remembered by them today. One incident which kept the family entertained for many months occurred some two years after her arrival at Southernhay. Horace Thompson was holding a business dinner party and just before the guests were due to arrive, the parlourmaid fell ill. Without hesitation, and to the Thompsons' amusement, the young nursery governess volunteered to deputise. Donning the maid's cap and apron, she assumed what she considered to be the correct air of deference and carried off the whole evening superbly, waiting at table and attending to every need, without the subterfuge ever being discovered by the guests.

Although she was always willing to join in the children's games she was, as Brian Thompson recalls, 'an essentially practical teacher' and even leisure hours were instructive. She would write small plays for the children to act, poems for them to recite and songs for them to sing and twice a year these would be incorporated into a concert for parents and friends. With Enid's help, the children made the costumes, drew up the invitations and programmes, took the pennies at the door and made up the accounts, eventually sending the proceeds to Dr. Barnardo's Homes.

Enid's method of teaching, which was built upon her Froebel training, her knowledge of the Montessori system imparted by Miss Flear and her own creative flair, constantly prodded the young minds to expand in all directions. David and John Thompson both claim that their interest in plant life, instilled into them by Enid's enthusiastic 'nature walks' around Southernhay, led to their becoming nursery gardeners in adult life, and for the other members of the class these happy rambles through woods and meadows were as enjoyable as they were instructive. She encouraged the children to catch pond life and read up everything they could about it, to collect butterflies and moths and follow up the full life-cycle of each specimen. Notes would be made on what the caterpillar fed upon, the time of year caterpillar and butterfly were to be found and the part of the country where they were most common. One summer, she gathered the children around her while she made a large, hot air balloon out of paper and, before it lifted skywards, over a methylated spirit pad, she attached a label giving Southernhay's address. She was as excited as the children when the balloon's label was subsequently returned from Belgium, and this led to an interesting geography lesson for maps were produced and the children were shown the balloon's route and told something of the places over which it had passed and where it had finally landed.

Being always alert to possible teaching aids, her attention was drawn one day at a London tube station to several brightly coloured posters displayed on the platform. Thinking how much the subjects chosen would appeal to her class, she lost no time in tracking down the sales office and buying a selection. These she duly took back to Southernhay and from then on, the child who reached the top of the class each week had the privilege of choosing the picture to be hung on the wall for the following five days.

Handwork for the boys and girls usually consisted of cane and basketwork or threading dried and coloured melon seeds into necklaces and bracelets — an occupation often accompanied by the reading or telling of one of her own stories, which for many was the highlight of their day.

Enid was happier than she had been for many years. She enjoyed the teaching and really felt herself to be a member of a loving family. 'Uncle Horace' and 'Aunt Gertrude' were always there to give encouragement — and to the children 'Auntie Enid', as she was known from the beginning, was someone very special. Undoubtedly this background of affection helped the young governess when, during her first summer at Southernhay, she received some news from her uncle that must have come as a great shock — her father had died suddenly of a heart attack at the age of fifty, while out fishing on the Thames at Sunbury.

His brother, Charles, was the first to be informed and he quickly notified the rest of the family and then arranged for the funeral to take place at Beckenham for — despite having lived with another woman for the past ten years — suburban proprieties dictated that as Thomas was still Theresa's legal husband he must be buried as such.

Enid had never lost touch with her father over the years, even though she was estranged from the rest of her family. She never visited him in his new home, but she would often call to see him at his office in the City and they would talk and laugh over things together, almost like the old days, for nothing that had happened in the past could completely obliterate the deep bond of affection that still existed between them. All the more curious, then, that she did not attend his funeral.

Hanly thinks there may have been two reasons for this. Firstly, she was not to know that the 'other woman', whom she had never been able to accept, would not be present. Secondly, and perhaps more probably, after four years away it would have been painful and embarrassing for her to return to her family at such a time and make her explanations. Her pupils at Southernhay have no recollection of any mention being made of the death — either at the time or in later years — by Enid or their parents, so her feelings on hearing the news and reasons for not being present at the funeral can only be a matter for speculation. Maybe the Enid, who was able to shelve so many other 'unpleasant' aspects of her life, decided to 'put away' the almost unbearable truth that she would never again see her father. If she had attended his burial, she would have been forced into an acceptance of this reality.

Thomas left small bequests to Theresa, Enid and her brothers and due to this some slight contact was re-established between them. Carey had decided to join the Royal Air Force for a seven-year engagement, but Hanly remained at home with his mother at Westfield Road and took over the management of his father's business, where he had been working since his war-time service overseas with the army. As there was still great antipathy between mother and daughter, meetings between Hanly and Enid usually took place at his London office and there was never time for long conversations. They rarely spoke of their personal affairs and he was to learn nothing of his sister's movements since she had left home in 1916. He knew that at the time of their father's death she was a nursery governess in Surrey, but she never told him of her training at Ipswich or of the Hunt family and Seckford Hall. It is therefore not surprising that he assumed Enid had been with the Thompson family ever since her 'disastrous' service in the Land Army so often referred to by his mother

Home for Enid was now with Mabel Attenborough and her

parents at Oakwood Avenue and it was here that she spent most of her weekends and holidays — far enough away from the Westfield Road area of Beckenham for her to avoid painful encounters with her mother It was at a garden party at Oakwood Avenue in the late summer of 1920 that she renewed the acquaintance of an old friend from St Christopher's — Phyllis Chase. The two had known each other since their early days at the school, had played in the lacrosse team together and joined in most of the senior activities, but Phyllis had left first and the pair had then lost touch. Phyllis had always been a good artist and was now beginning to sell some of her illustrations, so it seemed inevitable that before the day was out, the two should decide to try and submit work together. Their first joint sale, early in the following year, was a children's fairy story to one of Cassells' weekly magazines and this was the beginning of a partnership that was to last for several years.

Enid was as determined as ever to achieve success as a writer and during her first year with the Thompsons had been aiming mostly for the adult periodical market but, apart from a small poem for a Presbyterian church magazine — *The Messenger* — everything had been rejected. Her meeting with Phyllis Chase and the acceptance of her story by Cassells seemed to be a turning point. Soon afterwards she won a competition in the *Saturday Westminster Review* of February 19th, 1921 with, according to the magazine editor's comment at the time, 'a pointed piece of nonsense' entitled *On the Popular Fallacy that to the Pure All Things are Pure.**

Later in the year came acceptances by *The Londoner* and *The Bystander* of two short humorous pieces and of a romantic story for *Home Weekly* entitled *The Man She Trusted*. More stories were accepted by *The Bystander* and *Passing Show* during 1922 and she and Phyllis took on a variety of other commissions together. They tackled everything from illustrated rhymes for newspaper advertisements to Christmas and Easter cards for children and adults, Enid writing the verse and Phyllis designing the covers. They also worked on numerous illustrated poems and

* See Appendix 2.

45

stories for children — the majority of which were accepted by *Teachers' World*, an educational weekly published by Evans Brothers.

Having discovered, as she suspected, that the writing she enjoyed most was for children, Enid had begun to study her own young charges to gauge their reactions to the poems and stories she used in her lessons. She found that the boys favoured tales of bravery and loyalty, while girls liked fairy stories. Both, however, shared a taste for adventure, animal stories and bits of nonsense that made them laugh. So certain was she that most children would react in the same way that she decided to send a selection of her most popular items to the educational weeklies.

Miss Hilda Russell-Cruise, the assistant editor of *Teachers' World*, had no hesitation in picking out Enid's contributions from a batch of stories and poems passed on to her by the editor, Mr. E. H. Allen. They seemed to stand out immediately for their freshness and originality. The stories were full of humour, well-constructed, contained plenty of dialogue and, like the poems that accompanied them, were infinitely better than those usually received from free-lance writers. All were accepted and the first to be published was a fairy story about a broken magic dish — *Peronel and his Pot of Glue* — which appeared on February 15th, 1922, with illustrations by Phyllis Chase. From then on, both became regular contributors to the magazine and Enid's happy working association with Evans Brothers was to continue for many years.

But it was the small, twenty-four-page book of verse, published by J. Saville and Company in the summer of 1922, illustrated again by Phyllis Chase, that first brought Enid's name before the general public. *Child Whispers* was dedicated to the Thompson boys: 'four little brothers, David, Brian, Peter and John', and had the following preface:

> The children of nowadays are different in many of their likes and dislikes, from the children of ten years ago. This change of attitude is noticeable as much in the world of children's poetry as it is in other things. In my experience of teaching I have

found the children delight in two distinct types of verses. These are the humorous type and the imaginative poetical type — but the humour must be from the child's point of view and not from the 'grown up's' — a very different thing. And the imagination in the second type of poem must be clear and whimsical, otherwise the appeal fails and the child does not respond.

As I found a lack of suitable poems of the types I wanted, I began to write them myself for the children under my supervision, taking, in many cases, the ideas, humorous or whimsical, of the children themselves, as the theme of the poems! Finding them to be successful, I continued until the suggestion was made to me that many children other than those in my own school, might enjoy hearing and learning the poems. Accordingly this collection of verses is put forward in the hope that it will be a source of sincere enjoyment to the little people of the world.

Enid Blyton, N.F.U.

By all accounts, it was also enjoyed by the reviewers:

... light, lilting, happy tales, told with a charming simplicity of thought and language that should give them an irresistible appeal to all young readers ...

was the comment of *The Bookman*. *The Children's Newspaper* wrote:

A book of real rhymes ... written in the language of a child, and with the thoughts that any child might have ...

This reviewer might well have been referring to *Put to Bed* — verses about a small boy sent to his room on a sunny day because he had been drawing pictures over the walls with an orange pencil. He had just started on a giant's head when he was discovered:

> When Nurse came in so cross and red
> It made me feel afraid.

It ended:

> There's nothing here that's nice at all —
> 'Cept for Granny's patchwork quilt.

The Schoolmistress commented: 'Witches, fairies, goblins, flowers, little folk, butterflies and other delights all live between its pages . . .' Enid's readers were to become increasingly familiar with all these subjects in the years that followed, for she was to choose them many times for her stories and verse.

The following year the same publishing house brought out her second book of poems — *Real Fairies* — which was again very well received. The *Morning Post* was moved to comment, rather whimsically:

> In *Real Fairies*, children have received a new educational charter restoring their right divine to believe in fairies.

The *Yorkshire Post* wrote:

> To get a just estimate we left the judgement of Miss Blyton's work to a parliament of children. The children loved her work and asked for more.

Her ability to 'move into a child's world of fancy' (the *Daily Chronicle*) and to understand 'things dear to the heart of childhood' (*The Schoolmistress*), were phrases often used by the reviewers of this fifty-five-page book of poems. Although most of the verses were about fairies, Enid's ability to write from a child's viewpoint is again evident in poems like *The Open Window*:

> I'm here all alone in the schoolroom
> And the others have gone long ago.
> I'm kept in because of my writing,
> I've really been awfully slow.
>
> You see my desk's right by the window
> And I simply can't *help* looking out,

Enid with her brother, Hanly (1910)

. Christopher's School, Beckenham
Top row—Mary Attenborough, Phyllis Chase, and Mirabel Davis third,
fourth and fifth from left respectively. Enid (sitting) third from right—
middle row.

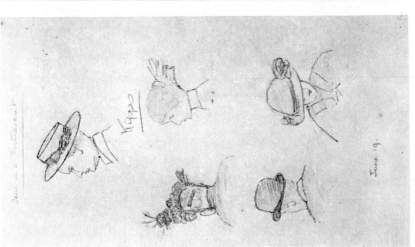

Sketched during Enid's last year at school

And watching the bees in the flowers,
And the butterflies sailing about.

There's buttercup fields in the distance,
And hills that look purple and blue
It's *ever* so hard to remember,
I've got any writing to do.

I never shall finish my writing
With all of these things going on,
I'll have to wait here till the evening
And do it when everything's gone.

By this time, her output of literary work was becoming so
prolific that she began to keep an account book. This shows that
during 1923 alone, her writing earned her well over £300 — the
price of a small, suburban house at that time. In addition to *Real
Fairies*, a small booklet, *Responsive Singing Games*, was published
by J. Saville in March and this was followed by a series of story-
books for Birn Brothers. During that same year no less than a
hundred and twenty other items — stories, verses, book reviews
and short plays — were also brought out under her name.
Eighty-eight of these appeared in *Teachers' World*, fourteen
meriting full pages, and five of her poems were used in a special
Poetry and Song edition which also included contributions by
such noted poets as John Drinkwater, John Masefield, Sir Henry
Newbolt, Walter de la Mare and Rudyard Kipling. Her poem,
January, appeared on the first page of the supplement and her
Teachers' Prayer on the last. On July 4th came the first of a long
series of weekly articles for the magazine — *From my Window** —
a full column or more on a variety of subjects, which told something of her life and thoughts at that time.

Such a programme of work would keep many a writer fully
occupied during the year, but Enid somehow continued throughout to teach, single-handed, her small class at Southernhay — and
from all accounts her pupils progressed satisfactorily. They were
proud of their teacher's ability to write most of the plays, songs
and poems used in their lessons and they, in turn, unwittingly

* See Appendix 3.

49

provided her with plenty of material for her writing. Sometimes she used a situation or happening connected with them for *From my Window — A Dinner in Lilliput* being one example. This was an account of a party for the Thompson children just before Christmas when all the courses of the meal were provided on a miniature scale — even the puddings, jellies and tarts 'the size of a shilling'. This successful 'dinner' was conceived by Enid herself, though she did not mention this fact in her article.

John Thompson was the subject of another *From my Window* in August — *On Being Like Oneself*:

> I have in my care a young, serious, and most profound philosopher. His mind grinds slowly, but it grinds exceedingly small, and he reduces everything and everyone to their lowest common factors. Consequently he occasionally utters observations which, while on the surface appearing superficial, betray a perception and a reasoning which are astonishing . . .

One of his observations that 'people are so "zackly" like themselves', was explained by her:

> . . . He wanted to say that our outward bodies reflected our inner souls and reflected them so astonishingly correctly that even he was able to recognise the fact . . .

The Thompsons remember Enid writing in her diary and she often spoke of having kept one each year from an early age, but there are few remaining today. Those that do, cover only a decade or so of her life and consist of little more than pencilled jottings. The earliest is for 1924 and though incomplete shows something of the general pattern of her life at that time, and of how established a writer she had already become during her four years at Southernhay. According to this diary, there was no easing up on her work even through her Christmas holiday at Oakwood Avenue with Mabel.

Her first entry on January 1st records that she wrote 'all morning' before going out to shop and have tea with Mabel and her sister. The following day she 'Copied out Bimbo and Podge

booklets [for Birn Brothers] until supper . . .' Her entry for
January 3rd was:

> 'To London. Saw Dr. Wilson at Nelson's. It's definitely
> decided I'm to do 36 books for them! [*This was a series of
> readers.*] To Birns. Gave me a cheque for £38 17s. . . .'

She mentioned having tea with Alec Rowley and his sister and
of how the composer played the settings to her lyrics — no doubt
for one of the many songs for children the pair wrote together
for *Teachers' World*, and later brought out in book form. On
January 10th, she recorded going once more to London to see
Birn Brothers:

> '. . . They want me to do a jolly decent book to be brought out
> regardless of expense. To Cassells . . . No difficulty about copy-
> right [*this probably refers to one of her stories that she wanted to use
> elsewhere*] . . . To *Teachers' World*, talked over new ideas for
> poems etc . . .'

There appears to have been no day of her holiday when she did
not spend some time at work in connection with her writing,
and she seems to have retained her boundless energy throughout.
She never failed to get all of her weekly contributions into
Teachers' World on time and even provided Miss Russell-Cruise —
by return post and written to the required length, and seemingly
without effort — extra poems or stories needed at the last minute
for the children's page.

There was little time left for relaxation in this busy life and
even the occasional visits to the theatre or cinema were apparently
used as material for her writings. When she took two of her pupils
to a London theatre at the beginning of January, she noted their
reactions to the play and the visit was later recorded in her weekly
column as *Only Just Us at the Windmill Man*. An afternoon at the
Crystal Palace circus was similarly treated in another *From my
Window* article.

Most of her weekends at home with the Attenboroughs were
spent in writing but she usually made a point of accompanying

Mabel to church on Sunday evenings — although her early allegiance to the Baptists had by this time slackened, and when she was away from home other matters invariably took precedence over church attendance. During holiday time, she knew it also pleased Mabel if she helped her with the creche she ran for East End of London mothers attending Monday afternoon meetings at the Walworth Road Baptist Church, but she refused to join in most of the other social activities around the church at Beckenham and showed no interest in any of the young men she met there.

Most of the men who visited the Thompsons and Attenboroughs were married and older then herself, as were the majority of the publishers she met in the course of her writing, but she appears to have had little inclination, or allowed herself the time, to meet others elsewhere. Her happiness with the children at Southernhay, Mabel's deep affection and, above all, her writing, seemed to provide her with everything she needed — until she met Major Hugh Alexander Pollock.

CHAPTER

IV

HUGH POLLOCK HAD JOINED THE PUBLISHING FIRM OF GEORGE
Newnes as editor of the book department in 1923, after a notable
army career. Born and brought up in Ayr, where his father had
for many years been an antique bookseller and much respected
elder of the Church, Hugh had joined the Royal Scots Fusiliers
on the outbreak of war and fought in most of the major battles,
eventually being awarded the D.S.O. in 1919. A handsome, fair-
haired man with striking blue eyes, he was in his middle thirties
when he came to Newnes, after a short post-war service with the
Indian Army. With his glamorous background, air of quiet
authority and sophisticated manner he charmed the twenty-six-
year-old, emotionally very immature Enid from the start, while
her childlike naïvety and zest for life drew the war-weary ex-
soldier to her from their first meeting.

There is no exact record of this encounter but it is likely that
she began submitting stories to Newnes during Hugh's first year
with the company and probably discussed some of these with him
personally. Whether she knew from the beginning that he was
already married, his wife having left him for someone else during
the war, can only be a matter for conjecture. It is not so much
what she writes about him in her diary of 1924 that intrigues, but
what is left unwritten.

Her first mention of him was on January 10th:

'Pollock wrote and asked if I'd collaborate with him. It was a
lovely letter.'

She evidently agreed to see him to discuss his proposition for on February 1st she called at his office:

> 'Pollock wanted to know if I'd do a child's book of the Zoo. He asked me to meet him at Victoria tomorrow . . . I said I would.'

Her diary for the following day shows that a startlingly rapid progress had been made in their relationship:

> 'Met Hugh at two. Went to the Zoo and looked round. Taxied to Piccadilly Restaurant and had tea and talked till six! He was very nice. We're going to try and be real friends and not fall in love! — not yet at any rate. We are going to meet again tomorrow.'

They met as arranged, walked in the park, had tea and talked — again on a very personal level:

> 'We're going to have a purely platonic friendship for three months' and then see how we stand! Oh dear.'

Obviously this was not to Enid's liking and neither was the letter she received two days later:

> 'He says he is fond of me in a big brotherly sort of way!!!??? I'll small sister him.'

She lost no time in writing a 'long letter' to him —

> '. . . telling him exactly what I think. Guess he won't like it much, but he's going to fall in love if he hasn't already. I want him for mine.'

Such diary entries, all written within the space of a week, would no doubt have surprised the majority of people who only knew Enid at that time as the outwardly naïve young nursery governess, but here was the other Enid who, having determined upon something, was setting about gaining exactly what she wanted.

Her candid letter brought a telephone call from Hugh the next day and they arranged to meet on the following Saturday. After describing how they had lunched at Rules restaurant near Covent Garden, seen a Western film and dined at Victoria, she wrote:

'I know he loves me, but I'm not going to say I love him till he has proved himself.'

By 'prove' does she mean 'shown his love' — or is there a deeper meaning relating to his, as yet, undivorced state? There is no way of knowing, but subsequent entries in the diary, after further meetings in London, show that she proceeded to play him as carefully as any fisherman with a potentially valuable catch:

'... He told me he loved me and asked if I loved him yet. I said I thought I did, *just a little* ...'

On February 16th, following another day in each other's company with 'lots of talking, of course' and a theatre visit she wrote:

'... He's not going to ask properly for my love till Easter. He has got something to tell me first.'

Could this be that he would then be free to marry her? Or simply that he was already married? If Enid guessed, she made no mention of it.

The courtship continued with 'express' letters or telephone calls from Hugh on the days between meetings and by the end of February she was writing:

'Hugh made me say I loved him and he gave me first of all "six incontrovertible reasons" to prove that whatever I might say, I did love him.'

Evidently this declaration of her love did not satisfy him for, after a bombardment of letters and telephone calls, she met him a few days later at the Strand Hotel for dinner where —

'. . . he told me that unless I could give him my real love we must say goodbye after Friday . . . So I told him I did love him, of course. He then gave me his medal miniatures all beribboned and polished up.'

The first token, perhaps, of a possible engagement?

That she had not, up to that time, had much of a social life is clear from the excitement with which she writes of their outings together. Her 'first ever' dance was with Hugh on Leap Year night at Prince's Restaurant in Piccadilly. Felix, Phyllis's husband, had given her a few dancing lessons the previous week and 'Hugh and I danced well. It was such fun.' She wore her newly-bought 'silver tissue dress, grey velvet cloak with shoes and stockings to match' and the evening was a great success: 'I loved it and loved it.' Although she did not get back to Beckenham until early the next morning, she was in London again within a few hours to meet Hugh again. They walked by the river and later had their first argument:

'. . . about which of us was master. Hugh wouldn't give way an inch and I loved him for it. I think I do want him to be master . . .'

Her busy life of teaching and writing continued throughout this time, so it is not surprising that she was soon to record in her diary that she was 'feeling dreadfully tired' and would have to 'put the brake on'. This lassitude, unusual for the energetic Enid, worried Hugh, and on a Saturday in early March, during a 'heavenly all-day walk to Cudham, with a picnic on "Magic Hill" ', he fed her at intervals with spoonfuls of Brand's Essence from a jar, and left her with a tonic to take. Enid described this outing in her *Window* of March 20th:

I think never before do I remember a day like that Saturday. Coming as it did after a spell of cold, grey weather, it was all the more perfect, for everything was in its most rejoicing mood.

She described how she and her 'companion' had set off 'laughing with the joy of spring . . . leaving behind us work, worry and everybody else in the world.' The column finished:

> . . . The hills were soft with blue haze, and the birds were singing of the wonderful, wonderful day. A blackbird took up the tale, and, like a born poet, he wove the sunshine and the spring, the budding trees and the starry celandines into a silvery enchantment of song — a song that came, oh surely not from a bird but from the lightsome, lilting, dancing heart of the sweet Springtime.

The growing sentimentality of *From my Window* had not escaped the notice of the staff at *Teachers' World*. One member of the editorial department commented at this time that the column was becoming 'altogether *too* whimsical'.

The day after the walk, Hugh met her at Beckenham where, according to Enid's diary —'. . . He told me what he had meant to tell me at Easter but it's nothing much, bless him' — and this brief note was the sum total of her reference to a revelation which, to Hugh at any rate, was evidently momentous. No further mention was made of the incident, and meetings continued as before.

During the following weeks they saw each other frequently. They met for dinner or for visits to the newly-opened Wembley Exhibition, the cinema or the theatre — and at times quarrelled vehemently. Hugh was obviously exceedingly jealous, and on one occasion the mention of a casual acquaintance of Enid's was enough to set the pair off on an argument which lasted for days, though he made it up eventually with a small present.

At the beginning of April, Hugh telephoned Enid to tell her that the signet rings they had decided to give each other were ready. Two hours later he rang again to say that Grandpa Attenborough had been making inquiries about him and had found out — 'what we had been keeping secret for a while and sent Uncle Ralph to see him'. Although they met later in London for dinner and to exchange their rings, she made no further reference in her diary to Hugh's urgent telephone call until the following day:

'Met Hugh at 10 and we went to see Uncle Ralph and things are quite straight.'

'Uncle Ralph' Thompson was a solicitor and an Attenborough brother-in-law so, without doubt, this episode related to the family's concern that Hugh was already married or about to be divorced — though Enid made no specific mention of this in her diary. Her entry for April 7th, two days after the visit to 'Uncle Ralph', is rather more explicit:

'Hugh phoned and told me that he'd heard definitely that the case would be heard at Easter and so he'd be free in June. I am so glad.'

At no time did she refer to any actual proposal of marriage by Hugh — though the rings were clearly an indication of their intentions.

It is puzzling that the Enid, who could write at length over other things — and even record such trivia as 'washed my hair' or 'messed about until bed' — could still leave so much unwritten that was obviously so important to her. Perhaps the memory of her mother's intrusion into her secret world all those years before had left its mark. Or was it just that there were some episodes of her life she did not want to remember? An example of this was the brief mention made to the ending of her four happy years with the family at Southernhay. At the beginning of April she wrote, after a weekend at home with the Attenboroughs:

'To Surbiton for last time . . . Went to buy books for children and vase for A.G. [Aunt Gertrude].'

Three days later came the end of the school term:

'We broke up this morning for the last time — the kids were very sweet. A.G. and U.H. [Uncle Horace] gave me a lovely copper jug and the boys gave me a pewter vase.'

These few lines were all she was to write about her leave-taking and the closing of her small 'school', for there had previously been no other hint in her diary that this was impending.

David and Brian were already away at boarding school by this time and neither they nor the twins were told exactly why Enid should have left them before the usual school year was completed. They assumed, later, that her leave-taking was due to her 'impending marriage'. She may have found, with her increased writing commitments, that the teaching was becoming too much for her — and certainly her literary commissions were providing her with a more than adequate living. But whatever the reasons for her departure, it is surprising that she could dismiss so lightly, if her diary entries are any criteria, her parting from the children she had grown to love and the closure of the 'school' she had built up. Little mention is made from then on of her former pupils, though she did write to them from time to time and occasional visits were exchanged — but even these came to an end in the early 'thirties. After that she was never to refer to the Thompson family by name, nor her years as a nursery governess, though she sometimes spoke of the children she once taught in her 'experimental school' — her own description of Southernhay in a 1938 edition of *Who's Who*. Yet an unexpected letter from Brian Thompson in October 1962, evoked some of the memories she had apparently buried in the intervening years, for she replied:

'Your letter recalled the dear old days at Southernhay, where I was so happy with your family and loved you children so much! I think it was the foundation of all my success, for I 'practised' on you, you know . . . Give my love to the other boys — David, Peter and John — if you see them soon — and tell them I have *never* forgotten them! I loved you all — and Mollie Sayer too . . . it was one of the happiest times of my life when I had that little "school".'

Although her teaching days were over, her writing kept her busier than ever before. Even with Hugh as a distraction during those first four months of 1924, she had earned well over £90 from her work for the periodicals alone, and this was in addition to the quarterly payments of royalties on her various books.

The success of her writings for *Teachers' World* and the other educational journals resulted in her now getting a large postbag from schools both in the British Isles and overseas. Teachers thanked her for the stories, plays and songs, which they used for their lessons, and complimented her on *From my Window*, which many of them now read out weekly to their pupils. The children commented frankly. 'I like your "days of the week" poems,' wrote one small girl, early in 1924, 'but "Thursday" is quite wrong. Couldn't you write another for Thursday?' 'I should think,' was the rather prophetic comment of another, 'that if you go on writing nice poems you will be quite famous one day.' A boy wanted to know all about fairies because, '... when I asked the School Inspector what he knew about them, he didn't really seem to know much more than I did.' She answered most of these letters herself, either direct to the child or through the school concerned. The fact that her name was now becoming well known to hundreds of readers of these journals helped towards the sale of her books and this did not go unnoticed in other publishing circles, which again resulted in further commissions.

The Easter of 1924 was spent with Mabel and Hugh at Seaford on the Sussex coast — 'the loveliest Easter that ever was ...' The happiness of the weekend was marred, however, by 'a beastly letter from Grandpa' — again the contents were not divulged, even in her diary, but on her return home:

'Mabel had a talk with him about being so absurdly stupid to me and he has promised to behave better! He has climbed down and I can have a latchkey.'

Evidently Grandpa Attenborough, a religious man of high moral principles, approved neither of Enid's association with Hugh, nor of the late hours she was now keeping. Like many others of his generation and background he frowned upon the newly-found freedom of the young women of that time and even rebuked Enid on one occasion for holding hands with Hugh 'in public'. Twenty-six years of age she might be, but while she was still under his roof, he no doubt felt a certain responsibility towards her.

60

Hugh's divorce case was evidently heard at Easter as planned, for in May the pair started looking for a flat and Enid began gathering a trousseau together. From May 17th to June 4th, she made no entries in her diary, but she recommenced on the 5th with:

'Hugh phoned at 6.15 to say he was coming down to see me and bringing two rings for me to choose from. He came and we looked at them in the summer house. They were lovely but the one I've chosen is adorable! [*a three-tiered diamond and emerald, set in gold*] Hugh was such a dear and I do love him so . . . It will be lovely to be really engaged.'

The following day her pencil appeared to have been almost out of control as she ecstatically wrote:

'I was very excited all day because I was going to meet Hugh and go to a dance with him and have the ring. He fetched me at 7 at Charing Cross and we taxied about in the Park and he gave me my ring. It's a *lovely* one. Then we went to Prince's to dinner and a dance . . . I loved dancing with Hugh . . . It's been a heavenly evening and it's so simply lovely to be engaged to my darling, darling Hugh and have his ring on my finger.'

The following Wednesday, *Teachers' World* announced the engagement. Mr. Allen wrote in his 'News and Views of the Week':

I am sure my readers will be delighted to hear that Miss Enid Blyton is engaged to be married. While I am not at liberty to disclose the name of the happy man, I may say that the marriage will probably take place in August. And Miss Blyton will continue to write for the *Teachers' World* I hope, because, with her, marriage does not mean the end of her career as a writer but merely the beginning of a new phase of it. On behalf of all *Teachers' World* readers I tender good wishes and congratulations. I may add that when the artist drew the cartoon on another page he was ignorant of this piece of news. Otherwise I am sure he would have provided Miss Blyton with assistance in carrying her window.

The cartoon referred to was one showing how some of the regular contributors to the magazine spent their holidays. Enid is depicted carrying a small suitcase in one hand and a large window in the other over the caption 'Miss Enid Blyton took her window with her'.

On June 16th, Hugh decided to lodge at a small private hotel in Oakwood Avenue until the wedding, and from then on the couple saw each other every day. Meanwhile, Enid was writing more than ever. Her first series of Readers, commissioned by Thomas Nelson and Sons earlier in the year, had been accepted without alteration and she had been asked to write a second — and a poetry book. She had prepared a book of fairy stories and poems which had been accepted by Newnes at the beginning of June and finished *The Zoo Book*, commissioned by Hugh for Newnes, on July 3rd. In celebration of the occasion she joined Mabel on a seaside holiday at Felpham in Sussex. Hugh stayed over the weekend and, according to her diary 'spoilt things by being upset because a man is coming to our boarding house next week . . .' Hugh's jealousy understandably annoyed Enid and the quarrel continued the next day, until 'we began to laugh . . . and then Hugh was sweet to me'. But despite their quarrels, they were obviously very much in love.

Enid records having found 'a ripping flat at Chelsea' and of how they both went to look at it on her return from holiday. She made no further entries in her diary for 1924, but her account book shows that she had been busy preparing several columns and regular features in advance, so as to leave the following weeks free for a most important event in her life — though even this went unrecorded in her diary — her wedding on August 28th at Bromley Register Office.

It was a very quiet ceremony, no member of either Enid's or Hugh's family being present. Hanly had had a similarly quiet wedding two months before, but although he, his wife Flossie and his mother were still living in Beckenham, they were not invited — nor was Phyllis Chase, that friend of many years standing. Only Mabel and her parents — 'Grandpa' and 'Grandma' Attenborough — were at the register office and there was no announcement of the marriage in any of the local or national newspapers.

Enid later explained to her friends that this was because 'Hugh didn't want the people at Newnes to know at the beginning that we were married because of the work he has commissioned me to do. They might not have liked it.'

Her honeymoon appears to have been spent in Jersey, for shortly afterwards she wrote two articles for *Teachers' World* — 'La Corbiere' and 'Dawn at Sea' — which described incidents on holiday, though she made no mention of having recently married. Regular readers no doubt spotted, after a while, that there had been some changes in the domestic life of their columnist, for her *Window* of October 8th mentioned 'my husband' and placed her home as now being near the River Thames and Battersea Bridge — though these facts were only referred to obliquely in an article about 'Fire Engines'. The engines had thundered one by one over the bridge until Enid's curiosity had made her persuade her 'reluctant husband' to join her in chasing after them. Despite the fifteen or more engines involved, it proved to be a false alarm and she was about to question one of the drivers about his job and 'whether he was disappointed to see no fire' when a detaining hand pulled her back. 'Alas! Before I could find out what I longed to know, my scandalised husband was hurrying me home.'

There is no diary for 1925 and no further mention of Hugh is made in her columns to help in assessing how the new Mrs. Pollock settled down to her first year of marriage, but that she was happy there is no doubt. She devoted two complete columns at the beginning of the year to 'Happiness'. After writing on January 28th that she thought happy people were the best in the world because they inspired others to be likewise, she received a shoal of correspondence from both children and adults who found 'happiness always tantalisingly round the corner'. Her reply to them on February 18th was:

> I've been looking for it straight ahead all my life and I've always found it. I don't mean content — though that is a very lovely thing — but real, proper, exultant happiness that makes

you want to sing, and gives that lift of the heart which is so well-known in childhood at the thought of some delightful treat!... Happiness is simply an interest in and a keen appreciation of everything in life. A sense of humour doubles the ability to appreciate it.

In a further article on 'Humour', a few weeks later, she wrote that she thought Punch's advice on those about to marry — 'don't' — was 'very silly', which certainly indicates that she found the state satisfactory.

The Pollocks' first home together was a small, furnished top-floor apartment at 32 Beaufort Mansions, Chelsea — a red-brick block of Victorian mansion flats, between the Embankment and the King's Road. Enid described her flat to a friend as being 'in a quiet residential area, which contains a good class of people who keep themselves to themselves'. If she had not been busy with her writing, with Hugh away all day, she would doubtless have felt lonely but, as it was, she had more than enough work to occupy her.

As royalties began to come in on her major books, her income increased yearly. Both the *Enid Blyton Book of Fairies* and *The Zoo Book*, published together in October 1924 by Newnes, sold well — as did another set of six small story books for Birn Brothers, which came out about the same time. She earned over £500 from her writing in that year but by the end of 1925 had increased this to £1,200 for twelve months' work — £500 of that amount being an advance sum for her editorial work on the first volumes of a *Teachers' Treasury*, published eventually by Newnes in 1926.

Her marriage made no difference to her prolific writing output, for in 1925, according to her account book, she wrote thirty-five poems (mostly about fairies and animals) for *The Morning Post*, a song — *The Singer in the Night*, published by Novello, other poems and stories for *Child Education*, *Punch*, *My Magazine*, *Woman's Life* and, of course, her regular features for *Teachers' World*. These now included, from April 15th, a twice-monthly full-page *Nature Notes*, illustrated with fine pen and ink drawings by Enid herself. This was later to be brought out in book form by

Evans Brothers and was selected five years later as one of the four hundred best books for children in a list prepared for the National Book Council. In addition to those shorter items, she produced four more Readers and a seventy-one page book of poems, *Silver and Gold* for Thomas Nelson,* and an *Enid Blyton Book of Bunnies* was published by Newnes. Enid must have enjoyed writing about 'the amusing adventures of Binkle and Flip, the Bad Bunnies' for she had always liked rabbits and brought them into many of her stories and poems. She once described them as:

the quaintest, most adorable animals to be found in all the countryside. Their big eyes and long ears make them look appealing and somehow childlike and I could watch them for hours.

Her weekly column was proving as popular as ever, as evidenced by the increasing amount of mail she was receiving daily. She continued to reply conscientiously to every letter and turn out her usual average of four or five thousand words of writing a day — in longhand, for she had no typewriter at that time.

She went for walks in the early morning, by the river or through one or another of the London parks, but always she longed for the country and the early spring days made her feel restless, cooped up in a city flat, writing. *From my Window* of April 1st, 1925, told of how the sun had made her throw down her pencil, pull on her coat and hat and catch the first train she could out of London. Arriving in the country, she had walked in the lanes and woods, revelling in the bursting buds and the freshness of the spring colours around her. Seated beneath an oak tree, with daisies round her feet, she had listened to a blackbird 'talking to himself in a hazel bush'. She had returned, refreshed, to her work but not entirely happy to be back in the city.

Hugh's boyhood had been spent in the Ayrshire countryside and he, too, longed to live out of town, so it is not surprising that later in the year she wrote that she was 'looking for a house'. In her 'mind's eye' she had a picture of the one she wanted:

* See Appendix I.

5—EB * *

It must be small and friendly-looking with at least one tree in its garden. It must get lots and lots of sun, and look out on to hills and trees, so that I shall see the spring coming and the autumn fading . . .

Soon afterwards she told of how she had found her 'little house'. She had happened to be walking along a quiet, tree-lined road, when she had spotted it 'peeping' at her from behind a large chestnut tree. Fetching the keys from the house next door she had looked inside:

Now I have always said and thought that a new house had no personality. But this little house, new as it was, had a distinct and delightful personality of its own. The primrose-coloured walls and the big fireplaces, the dark oak cupboards and the criss-cross windows with their blue shutters, all seemed to exude cheerfulness and homeliness, kindliness and good humour . . . I loved it. It was just big enough and just little enough. The garden was big, but unmade, so that anyone with a little imagination could plan and plant, and grow what they would. All the main rooms faced the south and great streaks of sunshine bathed the floor and danced on the primrose walls. Soft and blue in the distance stood the Shirley Hills, and fields and woods stretched away at the bottom of the garden, where four sturdy oak trees stood sentinel . . .

It had everything Enid and Hugh had been hoping to find. She finished her article with:

If, in the New Year, you come across a funny little house peeping at you from behind a chestnut tree, look at the name on the gate. If it's called 'Elfin House' you'll know it's mine.

CHAPTER

V

Elfin *Cottage*, as Enid was eventually to call her first 'real home', was one of several newly-built, detached houses in Short-lands Road, Beckenham, less than ten minutes' walk away from Mabel at Oakwood Avenue, and not much farther to Shortlands Station with its frequent train service to London. It was easy enough for Hugh to travel daily into the City and yet, in those days, the area was still fairly rural with fields and woods where now estates of houses stand. Although Elfin Cottage was new, Enid and Hugh both felt it had an air of solidity and maturity with its handmade greyish-yellow bricks, its blue-painted front door and shuttered windows — and the fact that the garden was still unmade, being little more than an enclosed piece of meadow-land, was yet another attraction for them.

Enid could not contain her excitement. She was not by nature domesticated — even the simplest cookery defeated her, and housework was usually delegated to someone else — but for a while she devoted herself wholeheartedly to the affairs of her new home. She scoured the stores to buy furniture and fittings and helped Hugh plan the layout of the garden. She busied herself making cushion covers, lampshades and curtains, frequently visited Beckenham to see how the final work on the house was progressing and planted dozens of bulbs in the garden. Hugh was caught up in her enthusiasm and happiness and looked forward as eagerly as his wife to the move into their new home. This came on February 5th, 1926, and Enid recorded in her diary how she and Hugh had gone on ahead to the house, leaving Daisy, her young general maid, to see their possessions into the van at Chelsea:

> 'All the furniture came during the day and everything went splendidly! . . . It's lovely to be at "Elfin Cottage" at last . . . to wake up and hear the birds, instead of buses and trams!'

She spent the rest of that week organising her new household and did not get back to her writing until Monday the 15th, having taken what was, for her, an unusually long break of sixteen days. From then on, however, the daily stint of work at her desk continued as before and her readers were to learn much of Elfin Cottage, its occupants and garden — particularly the garden — in the months that were to follow, for she wrote about them frequently in her *Teachers' World* column and they appeared, by implication, in many of her poems and stories.

From my Window of March 3rd was entirely devoted to the move and the new home —

> . . . because I can't really think of much else at present and also because I want to say that "Elfin Cottage" is true, and not a place I've invented out of my imagination . . .

She wrote of how she had arranged her furniture 'placing a window seat here, and my desk there and shelves somewhere else . . .' and of how she had lit a fire in the brick fireplace and watched the firelight flicker over the primrose walls and bowls of flowers she had arranged, adding:

> Flowers 'belong' to Elfin Cottage. They look at home there — and that confirms my secret belief that fairies and elves, brownies and gnomes have visited the house and left some of their flower-loving, sunshiny personalities behind. It's such a happy, cheerful, elfish little house, the right place for poetry and fairy stories, dreams and laughter . . .

She insisted on 'christening' the cottage herself, by screwing the name on to the gate, but found it difficult to make the screws go in straight and keep the letters in a line and this resulted in the 'E' finishing up 'a tiny bit crooked'. She explained later that her Peter Pan door knocker was to be used in a certain way — children were expected to knock four times, adults twice, and 'the Little Folk from the woods' seven.

Enthusiastic as she appeared to be about the house itself, the pleasure this gave her was small compared with the happiness she derived from having her first real garden. From her childhood days, when she had so lovingly tended her small plot at Clockhouse Road, she had dreamed of designing and building a complete garden from its very beginning. She and Hugh had started planning its layout long before they moved into Elfin Cottage. With paper, pencils and rulers they had charted out the position of the various paths and had then got to work selecting the best places for flower beds, lawns and hedges. They were agreed that there should be a wild, raised garden in one corner at the back of the house, where such things as heather, foxgloves and bluebells could grow undisturbed and — set in its midst, with an edging of crazy paving — should be a round pond for waterlilies and goldfish. Enid was determined, she wrote to a friend, to have plenty of shrubs and beds of 'old-fashioned flowers like lupins, pansies, hollyhocks and roses' and Hugh wanted a space reserved for fruit and vegetables. The layout of each of Enid's future and larger gardens followed this same pattern but it is doubtful whether she derived the same pleasure over the planning of these as she did from this quarter-acre plot at Elfin Cottage.

Once their plans were complete they lost no time in getting down to work. With Barker, a jobbing gardener, to help, they set about sowing seeds, making lawns, digging and planting and hardly an evening or weekend passed during their first spring and summer at the cottage without one or both of the Pollocks being hard at work outside. Their small garden was soon well stocked for, besides the many plants and shrubs bought by Enid and Hugh, Mabel and other friends provided plenty of seedlings and cuttings, and readers of *From my Window* also sent their contributions from all over the world. Enid was particularly pleased with some marigold and sunflower seeds from Tasmania and told her readers:

> I planted them myself and lo and behold! great sunflowers have sprung up and gay marigolds flaunt in the sun and ask to be picked . . .

On August 4th, she wrote in her column that she had received so many letters asking about the garden at Elfin Cottage, that she had decided to write about it in full when she had received her hundredth request. As this had now come, she would tell her readers something of this place, which five months ago had been a buttercup field and was now 'full of flowers and sunshine, cool greenness and little breezes'. Hollyhocks, mignonettes, poppies, fuschias, foxgloves and roses were all growing there now and although it was not very large she loved everything about it.

Enid's 'Nature' diary, which she started to keep in 1926, was no doubt intended originally to help over the compiling of her twice-monthly *Nature Notes* for *Teachers' World*, but it gives an interesting insight into the progress of the new garden. Just as the eager child at Clockhouse Road had counted each seed that came up and flowered, so did the adult Enid record the first green shoot or bud to appear. She also noted each day's weather and the animal and bird life she saw around her. A typical early entry in this nature diary is that for March 6th, 1926:

> 'A sunny mild day. Hugh began cementing pond. I planted some bluebells Barker gave me, also mint roots. Our chestnut tree is beginning to open some of its sticky buds. There are five violets and a celandine out in wild garden. The owls are hooting every night.'

This close observance of the wild life in her garden provided constant material for her writings. Soon after her arrival at Elfin Cottage she put up a bird-table on which she daily put out food, and outside her bedroom window she hung a coconut and pieces of fat for the bluetits. She noted the progress of some nesting robins in the garage and a pair of chaffinches in the chestnut tree, counting the eggs when they appeared and charting the young fledglings' growth. A great variety of birds bathed in the new pool (the 'twinkling eye' of her garden) and each day in her diary she would enter those she had seen. By the end of her first year she had acquired a tame jackdaw, 'Jackie', and magpie 'Maggie', and Hugh later gave her a dovecote and two pairs of fantail pigeons — 'Bill' and 'Coo', 'Pretty Boy' and 'Ladybird' — all of which soon became well known to her readers. Her *Bird Book* for Newnes, published in the autumn of 1926, contained fifteen chapters on every aspect of bird life and showed how well she had researched her subject — helped, no doubt, by her daily jottings.

Animal life at Elfin Cottage provided yet another topic for her weekly column. She wrote at length on the toads, rabbits, hedgehogs, stoats and mice that passed through her garden, but in October 1926 she bought, for five guineas, the first of the domestic pets that from then on were to become such an integral part of her life and writings.

'Bobs', a four-month-old black and white smooth-haired fox terrier was introduced to readers of *From my Window* on November 10th:

> ... he takes cinders from the cinder box, has eaten a dozen staples, one curtain pin, a ball of silver paper, dead matches, a button from my coat and the manuscript of a Christmas story for *Teachers' World* ... and I shan't be able to help loving him as long as ever he lives.

Thereafter his adventures and misdeeds were regularly recorded. He appeared in numerous photographs with his mistress and when she began to write a complete weekly page for children in September 1929 the *Letters from Bobs* proved a popular feature and were eventually brought out in book form.

If Enid's contributions to *Teachers' World* and the other educational journals did much towards bringing her name before the staff and pupils of schools all over the world, her three-volume *Teachers' Treasury* and the six volumes that comprised *Modern*

Teaching — published by Newnes in 1926 and 1928 respectively — established her still further in educational circles.

'Let Enid Blyton help you in your work' ran the advertisement for *Teachers' Treasury* in *Teachers' World* and the editor, Mr. Allen, himself wrote the review of the book under the heading 'Classroom Riches' — despite, according to Enid's diary, showing some initial protest that she had undertaken such a work for a rival company. She had evidently smoothed over this disapproval, for the review was couched in glowing terms. Readers, he claimed, would need '. . . no elaborate analysis of Enid Blyton's gifts as a writer . . .' They had been able for some years to watch these developing —

> . . . branching out in new directions, in the story, in the verse, in the play, in Nature Study, and through all there has been the expression of a personality of great charm, one to which children turn as eagerly and expectantly as the flowers to the sun . . .

He ended his review by quoting some of the introduction to the book by T. P. Nunn, Professor of Education at London University:

> . . . In the training of the young there will always be a place, not only for tasks and enterprises which the little worker must face alone, under the watchful eye of the teacher, but also for activities whose educative value lies in the very fact that they are social . . . Miss Blyton offers to the right kind of teacher just the right kind of help in using these fundamental means of civilisation . . .

With the exception of the part dealing with handwork, written by Misses R. K. and M. I. R. Polkinghorne, Enid was responsible for every section. The first was devoted to six stories for the spring term, six each for summer and winter, and twelve 'for any old time'. Section II contained a graded series of preparatory rhythmic movements and dances for young children and the third consisted of 'Nature Notes', which supplied material for twenty-six complete lessons 'on simple things which the children know and can bring to class'. There were six of Enid's plays for the children to perform in section IV and twelve singing games and twenty songs, composed by Enid, appeared in V and VI. An anthology of thirty poems and twenty-one 'unfinished' stories for the children to complete, made up VII and VIII. Later in the year, Enid added two more chapters on geography and history and the *Treasury* became so popular that it was reprinted annually for the next three years.

Modern Teaching, of which she was general editor, offered '. . . practical suggestions for junior and senior schools' and included volumes on junior and senior history; geography; junior and senior English; nature study and science, art, handwork, housecraft and needlework — all written by experts in their field, commissioned by Enid. Sales of this work also resulted in several reprints and a four volume 'Infant School' edition was brought out in 1932.

But these educational books provided only a part of Enid's published work during her early years at Elfin Cottage. In 1926 she took on the editing of a new twopenny magazine for children — *Sunny Stories* — published by George Newnes, which was to grow considerably in popularity over the years and to be forever associated with her name. *The Play's the Thing* (Home Library Company), a series of musical plays for children with music by Alec Rowley, and a book about animals for Newnes were both published in 1927. *Let's Pretend*, a story book for Thomas Nelson, which Enid thought 'beautifully produced and very artistic' came out the following year. Her verses continued to be accepted by national periodicals and she maintained her flow of contributions to *Teachers' World*, many of which eventually found their way into book form. Among several full-page features for this magazine were accounts of her meetings with A. A. Milne and Marion St. John Webb, published in a special October 1926 supplement on *The Children's Poets*.

Enid greatly enjoyed these two commissioned 'interviews'. She was charmed by Mr. Milne: 'this writer of exquisite child poems and light-hearted lyrics'. She wrote:

He is just like you would expect him to be. Tall, good-looking, with friendly eyes and a whimsical mouth that often smiles. He is natural and unaffected, and is diffident to an astonishing degree, considering how suddenly and generously fame has come to him . . .

His son, Christopher Robin, she thought, looked 'just like the pictures by Ernest Shepard, except that he has much more hair'. When the interview ended the poet presented her with an advance copy of his latest book '. . . which has the most exciting title of *Winnie the Pooh*'. She was equally impressed by Marion St. John Webb, whom she described as a 'small and pixie-like woman'.

Enid was also featured in the supplement in a full-page article written by Hugh, under the initials 'H.A.'. He had, he wrote, found his 'hostess' in the garden of Elfin Cottage:

Imagine to yourself a slim, graceful, childish figure with a head of closely cropped hair framing a face over which smiles and mischief seem to play an endless game. A pair of merry brown eyes peep out at you . . . clever eyes, quick to appreciate all that is passing before them . . .

His final question was one he had been 'meaning to ask for a long time': why must she work so hard when she had a husband, home, happiness and peace? Enid had replied that 'so long as one child tells me that my work brings him pleasure, just so long shall I go on writing'. But she admitted, also, to another reason: 'and this is a secret — I'd love to write a novel . . . about children, and the jolly, happy things of life.' 'If the book should ever be written', commented 'H.A.', 'we shall have something worthwhile from this young understander of that which is in the hearts of all helpless things, be they children, animals, birds, or flowers.'

Hugh's article on his wife was read out in classrooms all over the country and this evidently endeared her still further to her readers for, from then on, her mail increased at an alarming rate. By 1927 she was replying, by hand, to an average of about a hundred letters each week and her Christmas post contained five hundred letters, two hundred cards and a hundred or more presents from teachers and children all over the world. Although by this time Hugh had persuaded her to use a typewriter for her manuscripts, she continued to answer all her correspondence by hand — a practice she was never to relinquish.

She had at first been reluctant to follow up Hugh's suggestion that she should learn how to type, but early in 1927 she decided to give it a try, though she recorded in her diary that, at the beginning, the method seemed to take her 'twice as long'. But with typical determination and Hugh's encouragement, she persevered and within two months, using only her forefingers, was typing as quickly as she could write in longhand. By the end of the year she was able to record: 'Worked till 4.30 and did 6,000 words — a record for me.'

She learned how to drive during the same year, but this did not prove quite as successful. The Pollocks had bought their first car at the beginning of March — a red and white Rover with a registration number that began YE — 'Young Enid' as friends laughingly called it. As neither could drive they began to take lessons and Hugh, rather to Enid's annoyance, made the quicker progress. She could not resist noting in her diary, after their instructor had pronounced him capable of driving on his own:

'Hugh went out by himself this afternoon and then took me out. Except for trying to start with the brake on twice, sticking on a hill and trying to start with the dynamo off, he was quite good.'

She did manage to drive eventually, but was always the first to admit that she was not very proficient and consequently limited her range of travel to within a few miles of home. The mechanism of the car always remained a mystery to her — as evidenced by an incident ruefully recorded by her later in the year. A mystified garage mechanic had been called after Enid had made repeated, unsuccessful attempts to start the engine. She remembered four days later, after the car had been thoroughly overhauled and sparking plugs renewed, that she had 'poured paraffin oil into the car battery instead of water'. She was, even so, very attached to the small car and made many happy excursions in it with Hugh. Most of these she wrote about in her column — without, however, mentioning the misfortunes that sometimes befell them *en ronte*. A holiday taken in Scotland gives an example of this.

She wrote in her newly-commenced *Letter to Children*, which replaced *From my Window* on August 31st, 1927, that she would shortly be travelling to Scotland in her small red car, with a bunch of white heather on the front. She hoped her readers would wave to her if they spotted her on the way. 'Here we go', she wrote, 'seeking adventure away on the white, high roads, up to the heather mountains away in the North!' They met with adventures, but not of the kind Enid had envisaged. In fact the holiday became something of a disaster. Much of it was spent in heavy rain, the car developed a puncture soon after they left home, another occurred seven miles out of Edinburgh and a third close to Oban. 'At the same time', Enid recorded in her diary, 'the clutch lever rod broke and we had to get a man to go to Oban and have another made.' Later in the week, when they had arranged to meet Hugh's family, the car again had a puncture 'which had to be mended six times and still went flat . . . It has been a hell of a day!' One can well understand this final comment and her relief on returning to Elfin Cottage two days later. Though she wrote very amusingly of this in her diary, her column gave a rather different story. According to this, the weather had stayed fine and she had done 'all the things' she had wanted to do — but she was also quick to add how good it was to be home again, and went on to describe her reunion with Bobs and her pleasure at seeing 'the old familiar things' around her once more. The minor disasters of the past two weeks were forgotten — or ignored.

But holidays, generally, were happy times for the Pollocks. Most Easters were spent by the sea in Sussex and their two weeks in the summer a little farther afield — though never outside the British Isles. Wherever they went, they were seldom away from each other for long. Neither sought the more sophisticated pleasures of the resorts. Instead they walked and swam together, lazed on the beaches or explored caves and castles — a favourite pastime of Enid, which also appealed to Hugh. Her notebook for jottings-and two diaries accompanied her everywhere and she faithfully recorded in her nature diary the changes in the weather and the bird, animal and plant life around her — just as she did each day at home.

Her life at Elfin Cottage had now settled into a regular pattern. If she were not travelling to London to visit publishers, her mornings began with breakfast at around eight o'clock. After seeing Hugh off to the station, she would feed her pets, give instructions for the day to her young maid and then begin writing. She usually wrote in the garden in the summer, or beside the fire in the dining room in winter, but always with her notebook or typewriter perched on her knees rather than on a table. She occasionally visited Mabel or other friends in the afternoon, but more often she would continue working until it was time to meet Hugh at Shortlands Station — either on foot or in the car. After dinner, work was put away and the evening was their own, for they entertained friends very rarely, though they would sometimes have an outing to the theatre or the cinema — 'Ben Hur,' Enid recorded after one such occasion, 'is the best film I've ever seen.'

Like most couples, they had their occasional disagreements and Enid's fierce temper would flare: 'Quarrelled with Hugh as he thinks I ought to like his mother and I can't ...' 'I went into the spare room [after another quarrel] but Hugh fetched me back.' However, none of the arguments lasted for long and to all who knew them during those early years together, they appeared ideally suited. Hugh was kind, considerate, and obviously very much in love with his wife. Immensely proud of her achievements, he wrote in another passage of the *Teachers' World* supplement that she was 'a constant source of inspiration to those around her ...' and he smiled indulgently at a publisher who introduced him at a Press dinner as 'Enid Blyton's husband'.

Enid's own feelings are expressed in her diary note for August 28th, 1926:

'This is the second anniversary of our wedding. I *am* glad I

77

married Hugh and I wouldn't be unmarried for worlds. He is such a perfect dear.'

Confident in his love, she felt free at last to be herself.

With most people she was, outwardly, what they expected her to be: the imaginative, clever young teacher; the capable, prolific writer; the nature-loving woman of simple pleasures; the dutiful wife. Hugh had seen her play all these roles but knew and loved her for the far more complex person she undoubtedly was, and went along with her every mood. He was her 'Bun' and she his 'Little Bunny', nicknames Enid had given them both early in their courtship and he indulged her occasional desire to act the part of a child with a beloved father, rather than that of a wife in her early thirties. Together they built snowmen in the garden on cold winter days; played French cricket until dark on summer evenings; took part in games of 'catch' against the house wall and collected chestnuts from the tree in the front garden for 'conker' matches — '... mine is an eighter', she recorded after one contest. Birthdays and Christmases were occasions for great celebration with the exchange of numerous gifts — 'Hugh gave me 42 presents and I gave him 25' — and Bobs and the other pets were not forgotten. She recorded on December 25th, 1926:

'Bobs had a stocking with two bones, two biscuits, one piece of chocolate, one comb and two clockwork mice. I also put out a little Christmas tree for the birds on the bird table, dressed with suet, fat, bread, biscuits and coconut. They loved it, especially the tits.'

But these festive enjoyments were marred as year followed year, by Enid's increasing fears that she might never be able to have a child of her own to share these happy times.

They had hoped, once they had settled in Elfin Cottage, that the baby they both longed for would be conceived. They were seemingly healthy enough, leading what appeared to be a happy and normal sexual life and there seemed no reason for the delay. Everything else she had aspired towards had eventually come her way, yet over this particular ambition she knew she had no control. It did not help that, by 1928, most acquaintances of her own age either had children already or were about to have them. Mary Attenborough was now married and had a young son and so had Phyllis and Felix. Hanly and his wife, Flossie, were the parents of a baby daughter, Yvonne, and Mabel's sisters and other relations were always bringing their latest offspring to visit her at the cottage. She wrote to and for children every day and thought of them constantly. 'Surely,' she confided to Phyllis, 'no one could be better equipped than I to bring up a family.'

Eventually in the late spring of 1928, she consulted a gynaecologist. His diagnosis was that Enid had an unusually undeveloped uterus — 'almost that of a young girl of 12 or 13,' she told Phyllis later. (Coincidental, perhaps, but this diagnosis does seem to indicate once again the far-reaching effects upon the thirteen-year-old Enid of the departure from home of her father all those years before.) The specialist suggested a series of hormone injections and these she stoically underwent — daily for a week and progressively less frequently for the following month. The Pollocks hoped, once the treatment had been completed, that results would quickly follow — but this was not to be. She tried to satisfy her maternal yearnings by seeing as much as she could of her young niece, Yvonne, and Phyllis's son, Barry, to whom she and Hugh were godparents. She also threw herself, with renewed effort, into her writing. This now included the preparation, with Hugh as co-editor, of a ten-volume *Pictorial Knowledge*, an illustrated 'Educational Treasury' for Newnes.

But something else was to occur, early in 1929, which soon occupied her mind in other directions. She wrote in her *Letter to Children* in *Teachers' World*:

I am rather worried lately because a great new arterial road is going to be made near Elfin Cottage. It may not come for some time, and perhaps it won't come at all ... but I am going to look for another little cottage, far away from anywhere busy, with a bigger garden than this one and where I can keep more pets than I have now ... I shall be so sorry to leave Elfin Cottage that I can hardly bear to think of it.

In fact, by the time her *Letter* had appeared in print, she had already found her new home. It was a large, rambling, sixteenth-century thatched cottage, close to the River Thames at Bourne End in Buckinghamshire. Her readers were thanked, in subsequent columns, for passing on information about houses they knew were for sale and might be suitable, and for their suggestions of names for her new cottage, after she had described it to them. These included Pixie Cottage, Ding-Dong-Bell Cottage, Pet Cottage, Fairy Cottage and Brownie Cottage — but, she told them, 'it is going to be called by the name it has had for a long, long time — "Old Thatch" '.

CHAPTER
VI

ENID AND HUGH MOVED TO OLD THATCH ON AUGUST 2ND, 1929.
'It is perfect, both outside and in . . .' she wrote in her diary, 'just
like a Fairy Tale house and three minutes from the river.' She
described it at some length in her *Letter to Children*. The house,
she informed her readers, was approached 'sideways on' through
an old lychgate which led into a lovely garden 'about nine times
as big' as that of Elfin Cottage. There were several fine old yew
trees and an orchard with apples and pears in abundance, a large,
somewhat overgrown lily pond, a rosewalk, a kitchen garden,
'with everything growing there that you could possibly want', a
small wood and a brook 'with a little bridge of its own'. There
was also an old well beside one of the two front doors. The
cottage had once been an inn and years later Enid wrote of how
she had always felt that people had been happy there — 'because
the whole place had a lovely feel to it — friendly, happy, wel-
coming . . .' She was to use the house and its setting many times
in her stories and it also figured largely in her new complete page
for children in *Teachers' World*, which began a month after her
arrival at Old Thatch.

The first *Enid Blyton's Children's Page* which included a photograph of Enid and her pets and a drawing of her new home, was
introduced by the editor of the magazine, Mr. Allen:

... We say no more about this than that the author is Enid
Blyton whose enormous following among children warranted

81

an extension of the space their favourite has hitherto been given . . .

Enid saw to it that this extra 'space' was used to the fullest advantage. In addition to her letter to the children and another, purporting to come from Bobs, the page contained each week a full-column story, a photograph (usually taken by herself) and a poem or competition. It says much for her astuteness and Hugh's careful guidance, that most of what she wrote for this page — and for *Sunny Stories* — was eventually re-used elsewhere, for the stories, verses and puzzles were all brought out later in book form by various publishers, and even Bobs' 'letters' were privately published in October 1933. The extent of Enid's readership appeal at that time is evident from the phenomenal success of these small booklets, sold direct from Old Thatch at threepence each, for within six days of *Letters from Bobs* being issued, sales exceeded ten thousand and subsequent editions went on to sell at the same rate.

Her other work for *Teachers' World* at that time also provided further material for book publication. *Tales from Arabian Nights, Tales of Ancient Greece, Knights of the Round Table* (all published by Newnes) and *Stories from World History* and *Round the Year with Enid Blyton* (Evans Brothers) were all written initially as weekly or monthly series for the magazine. But by far the most popular was her 'weekly course of seasonal nature study' — *Round the Year with Enid Blyton*.

This course of forty-eight lessons covered every conceivable facet of nature study from such things as weather observation to pond and insect life. Pupils were shown how to plant bulbs, stock aquaria, make school gardens and bird-tables and each lesson ended with *Things to Do, Things to Write, Questions to Answer, Things to Find* or *Things to Learn.* Throughout, Enid used some of the imaginative teaching methods that she had once applied to her own classes at Southernhay and the series, which was followed by children in classrooms all over the country and overseas, proved a resounding success. The editor received glowing letters from teachers including one from a headmaster in

Loughborough, who declared the course had been 'quite the most practical and finest' he had yet encountered throughout many years of teaching.

He went on to pay tribute to Enid's weekly page and wrote of revisiting a rural school in the east of England, which had long been a by-word for the poor quality of its work — due, he explained, to the extreme poverty of the surrounding area and the lack of interest and discipline among its pupils. This school had now undergone a 'miraculous change', brought about almost entirely through the regular reading of Enid's columns. All her suggestions had been followed through and the pupils now had their own flower garden, planted with the thirty-two different blooms she had recommended, a bird-table had been installed and a well-cared-for aquarium now stood in the classroom. The whole atmosphere among the pupils, claimed the headmaster, had been changed 'to one of happiness and an interested awareness of the things around them'.

There were certainly thousands of children and their teachers who knew that Enid had moved and that the name of her new cottage was Old Thatch. Most could describe the trees and flowers that grew in her garden and the birds and animals that frequented it — just as they had been able to do when she had been at Elfin Cottage. Many children living in industrial towns enjoyed a vicarious pleasure, through her pages, in the delights of rural life, for too often in those hungry 'thirties fathers were on the dole and there was barely enough money coming in to feed their families let alone provide for visits to the country. From her correspondence she was well aware of their yearnings and on one occasion suggested that country readers might like to send such things as budding twigs and wild flowers to their counterparts in the towns, and this suggestion met with such enthusiasm that she eventually had to recruit a 'go-between' to deal with the scheme. Children without pets gained the same kind of enjoyment from hearing about Enid's own collection which yearly increased in number with more pigeons, another tortoise, a pair of Siamese cats, their kittens, and Sandy, a mate for Bobs, who in turn also produced several puppies. But it was

Bobs, the little black and white terrier, who always remained the favourite.

A personality in his own right, this much-photographed dog received a hefty mail and hundreds of presents from young admirers. There was great concern about him when Enid told her readers of the floods that had swept through Old Thatch during her first winter and of how he and Patabang (the first of the Siamese kittens) had had to walk across planks in the dining room 'with seven inches of water below'. The children feared he might have caught cold as he had signed off his letter that week 'with a shiver and a splash'. They sympathised with him when he was in disgrace over his misdeeds, particularly on the occasion when he and Sandy were in trouble over 'a dirty little dog we often meet on our walks'. Enid had warned them, 'wrote' Bobs, not to go near this dog but they had disobeyed her and had picked up 'some nasty insects' which had meant a dusting with some 'very strong-smelling powder', isolation from the other pets and the fumigating of their kennel. Enid recorded this incident in her diary and it is interesting to see how she was able to turn it into a vehicle for a lesson on animal care, for Bobs' letter ended:

> I'm very sorry for that little dog. He told me that he had never had a bath in his life, that no one ever puts him out fresh water to drink, and he is never brushed or combed. Isn't it a shame? I don't know why people keep dogs if they can't look after them and love them, do you? Please do see that all your dogs are nice and clean, because if they're dirty and we meet them, good little dogs like us get into trouble.

When Bobs 'joined' the Tail Waggers Club, he urged other dogs to follow suit and hundreds of applications were received by the Club, resulting in a presentation to him of a silver medal in recognition of his 'splendid recruiting effort'.

With so many letters and packages to Bobs and his mistress, it was not surprising that the small village post office at Bourne End soon found that the mail to Old Thatch warranted a special delivery. The children enclosed all manner of items in their post. They sent posies of wild flowers or small insects in matchboxes and, on one occasion, even a dead bird was sent along for Enid to identify. She nevertheless took a delight in opening every package herself — even if it was, at times, with a certain amount of apprehension.

Some months before her move to Old Thatch, she had been forced to suggest that letters stood more chance of a reply if they came together from schools, rather than individuals. But even the 'school envelopes' soon contained between twenty and fifty separate letters and she decided to inform her readers that she would put 'a penny into a box for the Children's Hospital in London' each time she failed to reply. This resulted in 'quite a tidy sum' being passed on to the Great Ormond Street Hospital — the first of many contributions it was to receive as a result of Enid's writings in subsequent years.

In the early 'thirties, she asked the children if they would help to collect silver paper and foil for the hospital to sell and, within a few days, bundles of flattened paper and rolls of foil began arriving at Old Thatch. This continued for several years and one of her many daily tasks was to help her staff fill sack after sack, ready for forwarding to London. From time to time she wrote a progress report in her column on the number she had sent and the money that had been raised in this way 'to help sick children', and by 1935 she was able to tell her readers that they were the 'largest collectors' in the country.

Nothing, it seemed, was too much trouble if it was for a worthy cause. Her readers appreciated this and eagerly took up every suggestion she put forward. She happened to mention in a 1929 'letter' in both *Teachers' World* and *Sunny Stories*, that she considered the Pug Pups (Pick Up Glass and Pick Up Paper Society) was a very worthwhile organisation and gave the name of the founder — a Mrs. Jean Brodie Hoare. Within three weeks, much to her astonishment, thousands of children had joined the Society and the factory which supplied the badges had to work overtime to keep up with the demand. Four months later, Enid was able to report that twenty-five thousand badges had been ordered, seventy-five thousand Pug Pup postcards had been sent out and orders were still pouring in, many from overseas. 'It wasn't my idea', she wrote, 'but I wish it had been. Perhaps one day I'll think of a good society too, one really my own and we'll all belong together.'

At Old Thatch, Enid was moving in rather more sophisticated social circles than hitherto and her pattern of life changed accordingly. Bourne End in those days was a quiet residential area, consisting of a few shops and several large country houses, some of which were used as weekend retreats by businessmen from the City. Life was leisurely, with a plentiful supply of servants to help make it so, and Enid and Hugh soon found themselves drawn into the social round of cocktails, bridge, tennis and dinner parties. It was not long before she was persuaded to leave her writing for a few hours and play bridge for two and sometimes three afternoons a week. She took up tennis again and one of the lawns at Old Thatch was converted into a grass court, to which she invited her new friends for return matches. It was all 'great fun', she wrote in her diary, and in complete contrast to the quiet times she had enjoyed with Hugh at Elfin Cottage.

Even the pattern of their previously cosy evenings alone together had been changed, for a promotion from Newnes now meant that Hugh occasionally returned late and, with her own increased social activities during the day, Enid found she had sometimes to resort to catching up with her proof-reading or writing after dinner. Nor did she have the time to give much attention to the garden at her new home, although she managed to do some of the planting and sowing which she always enjoyed. The rest of the work she now delegated to her gardener-chauffeur, Dick Hughes. A young cook-general continued to relieve her of most of the household tasks, but there were several changes in this quarter during the Pollocks' early years at Bourne End.

Enid's rather unsympathetic conduct towards the young girls who came to work for her, many of whom were given notice after barely a month's work, is apparent from her diaries, and contrasts sharply with the warm-hearted, friendly personality projected by her *Teachers' World* columns:

'D . . . was still feeling bad so I had the doctor. He says it is just an ordinary cold but as she is feeling so sorry for herself she had better go.'

Another maid was given notice because the friend she had been out with the previous week had since developed scarlet fever. Enid commented:

'She is now isolated in her bedroom and I have had to put off all the Whitsun parties. The girl is a fool to run straight into danger as she has done . . .'

The young woman never did contract the illness but she was still expected to leave on the termination of the quarantine period. Enid was not, it appears, always the perfect employer, but her attitude was not an uncommon one in those days and she also had her share of dishonest and unsatisfactory maids. One young girl was arrested by a police superintendent in the drawing room at Old Thatch, after being discovered making off with the family silver and other articles. Enid recorded the episode with some relish in her diary and, like so many other incidents in her life, it was to re-surface many years later in one of her stories.

The move to Old Thatch certainly brought about changes in the Pollocks' life together and another, even greater, was not far distant when the pair embarked on a cruise to Madeira and the Canary Islands in October 1930. Some weeks beforehand Enid had informed her readers of her intention to make the voyage and had included a photograph of the ship — the *Stella Polaris* — on her weekly page. Her page of October 8th, when she and Hugh were already away on the high seas, showed a map of the proposed route, drawn by Enid, and once again the teacher in her could not resist the opportunity to give a minor geography lesson:

'I am going to tell you exactly where I am going and you can find all the places. Perhaps you can read a little about them in your geography or reading books . . .'

After writing that she would have to take a train to Southampton and then 'start out over the sea, past the jutting-out piece of France and across the Bay of Biscay' she suggested the children should find her first port — Lisbon. 'Do you see the river it is on...?' Madeira, Tenerife, Las Palmas, Casablanca, Gibraltar and the city of Seville were all placed and commented upon. The following week she caused great excitement in many a classroom for at the head of her page was written 'By *Air* Mail from Lisbon' and underneath was a photograph of the port.

She was, she wrote, hundreds of miles away on the blue Atlantic:

'England is now only a little island somewhere in the North and Old Thatch and its birds and animals nothing but a lovely dream which will come true when I return home again...'

The rest of the page was taken up with describing the beginning of her voyage: how small tugs had pulled their Norwegian ship out of Southampton, passing the *Mauretania* — 'one of the fastest afloat' — and the *Armadale Castle*: 'one of the ships that takes the letters to Cape Town. I am sure my little friends in Port Elizabeth know her very well.' There followed a description of her cabin and then she told of how sea-sick she had been in the Bay of Biscay.

The second of the four columns devoted entirely to her cruise, was sent from Las Palmas and was headed 'The Cruise of the good ship *Stella Polaris*'. Once again she described the events of the previous few days, including how, at Lisbon, she had twice been 'almost killed by the world's worst driver' and she had sharp words for the treatment of animals in Portugal:

'The dogs and horses looked thin and ill cared-for, not a bit like ours... Bobs is lucky to be an English dog instead of a Portuguese one, isn't he?'

She was, she wrote, much taken with Madeira: 'the prettiest place you can imagine — flaming red creepers, trees with pink and purple flowers and houses painted white, pink, yellow and blue.' She had ridden in a bullock sleigh through the cobbled streets and a photograph of a 'carro' was included for the children to see. On the way to the Canary Islands she had seen some sharks and flying fish 'looking like very big and beautiful dragonflies'. 'I wish,' she finished her column, 'that I could stuff a bit of this glorious sunshine into the envelope for you.' Morocco and Seville were the subjects for her final despatch from the *Stella Polaris*. In this she told of how she had bargained with Arabs in the bazaars of Casablanca over the price of their wares. 'The natives love it, so do I! It is great fun!' She drank mint tea 'sitting on carpets and bales of fine silk with Arabs looking like pictures of Ali Baba in the story of the Forty Thieves.' Seville, with its orange trees and a shop that had 'eight thousand different shawls' was described with her usual flair for detail that she knew instinctively would appeal to her young readers.

Her 'letter' on the closing stages of the cruise stretched over three columns and Bobs' contribution was reduced to telling only of his pleasure at having his mistress home again. The children were told how she had won 'two prizes in the sports competitions' and of how rough it had been through the Bay of Biscay:

'... My soup flew out of my plate, my glass turned a somersault, my bread disappeared, and there were crashings and smashings all round ... I couldn't help thinking how much you would have enjoyed it all ...'

The whole holiday, she wrote, had been 'glorious' —

'... but I hadn't seen any countryside anywhere that I thought was lovelier than England's. I had seen no animals nicer than ours, and no children that I liked better than English children ... and I know that, no matter where I go or what I see in other countries, I shall always love England best ...'

That she broadened the horizons of hundreds of her readers with her travelogue there is no doubt. But it seems a pity that her own rather insular attitude, by no means uncommon in England at that time, should also have crept into so many of her despatches — even her final summing up. Only once did she set foot out of the country again, and that was many years later, in 1948, for a short holiday in America, yet this single cruise in 1930 was remembered by her so vividly it provided her with nearly all of her foreign settings for subsequent stories.

Back home at Old Thatch, Enid was soon caught up again in her round of writing, bridge parties and other entertainments. It took her some weeks to read the hundreds of letters which had accumulated while she had been away. A special mailbag had to be collected by her from the small local post office where it had been held, pending her return — along with several more bundles of silver paper. But, unusually for Enid, her mind was not entirely on her work.

She had not felt well since returning from the cruise and on November 14th she called in the doctor. Considering all that had gone before, her diary entry on his diagnosis seems surprisingly unemotional: '... he thought perhaps I was going to have a baby'. Without further comment she went on 'I worked till tea, then wrote letters and read till bed.'

Perhaps she hesitated over showing any excitement until she knew for sure that her longed-for child was on the way — though a similarly matter-of-fact entry appeared a month later:

'The doctor came and examined me and said for certain I am pregnant, just about three months. I am so glad. That explains the horrid sickness. Hugh and I went shopping in Maidenhead. Back to tea. Read 11 p.m.'

No plans. No mention of Hugh's reaction. No hint even at any suppressed emotion.

Except for visits to the doctor and increased periods of rest, her days were spent pretty much as before. But the pregnancy was not without its uncertainties. On a visit to Mabel at Beckenham, she called in to see her old doctor who, it appeared, disagreed with the proposed date of the birth. According to her diary, Enid was surprised to be given between the 5th and 10th of June by one doctor and another set of dates — more than a month later — by the other. Eventually, however, both agreed that the baby would probably be born during the first week in July and in view of this she and Hugh decided to take an extended Easter holiday at Bournemouth.

On their return, Enid's excitement over the coming birth was more apparent and she set about making baby clothes. She was clever with her needle and usually made most of her own lingerie, with fine lace insets and embroidery. Now she turned this skill into smocking the tiny garments and stitching and embroidering pillow cases and linen for the nursery. She was, however, rather apprehensive over the actual birth itself as the time drew nearer. Dick Hughes' wife was also expecting a child and Enid confided to her that she was frightened that the birth might not be easy for her because of her age. She was almost thirty-four years old.

At the end of June the local midwife, Nurse Lane, moved in and Enid prepared for the baby's arrival. From then on, each day appeared to follow a similar pattern for, according to her diary, she either 'went for a walk with Nurse and rested until tea' — or she read, sewed, talked or 'did Children's Page'. On July 15th, however, there was a very different entry:

'Gillian was born at 6.30 this a.m. — $8\frac{3}{4}$ lbs. in weight, $21\frac{1}{2}$ inches in length, a lovely child. Hugh is delighted. A very easy confinement all over in five hours. Dr. Poles delivered baby and Dr. Bailey gave chloroform. I came round about 7 feeling very hungry and comfortable. Baby sucked as soon as she was put to the breast. Hugh went up to town in afternoon.'

The child the Pollocks had so long awaited had arrived and yet another new chapter was beginning for Enid.

CHAPTER

VII

BECAUSE OF THE IMPENDING BIRTH, ENID HAD WRITTEN SEVERAL of her children's pages in advance so it was not until August 26th, 1931 that her *Teachers' World* readers were told of the baby's arrival. She began her letter:

> A lovely new pet has come to Old Thatch. Some of you have heard the news already, but I know a great many of you have not, because the pet arrived in the holidays. You can have three guesses — what is it? I am sure you are nearly all wrong, so I must tell you. Well, the new pet is a little baby girl! As many of you know I am not really *Miss* Blyton, because I am married, and I am so pleased that a baby has come to live with me, because you all know how much I love boys and girls — and it is lovely to have one that really belongs to *me* and not to some other mother and father ...

There then followed a description of 'Gillian Mary' — of her eyes 'like two pieces of deep blue sky', dark brown hair 'such a lot of it', a 'funny little smiling mouth' and a pointed chin 'like a pixie'. Even Bobs referred to the 'new pet' in his letter. 'I do hope the Mistress won't forget to love *me*, her oldest pet, now ...'

As was to be expected, hundreds of letters arrived following upon the announcement and Enid was forced to apologise some weeks later for not answering all of them 'because, as you can guess, the new pet takes up rather a lot of time at present'. It was taking up a great deal more time, in fact, than Enid had anticipated.

She had started off happily enough, feeding the baby herself — 'I love it' — and attending to most of its needs, but within a month Gillian had been weaned on to a bottle and once the midwife had left for her own home, the repetitive round of bathing, feeding and changing the baby had began to pall. She enjoyed the long afternoon walks along the country lanes and by the river, wheeling her daughter out in her pram, the dogs at her side, but she found there was little time left in her busy day for writing and even her diaries were neglected. It was all she could do to keep up with her commitments for *Teachers' World* and bridge and tennis were now quite out of the question.

Towards the middle of September, she took a day off from her maternal duties and met Phyllis Chase in London. She told her friend of the difficulties she was having and Phyllis came up with a possible solution. She had living with her a young girl, Betty, who had helped to look after her son, Barry, but — as she pointed out to Enid — she was hardly more than a child herself and by no means a trained nanny, so any help she could give would only be very basic. However, if the girl was willing and Enid would like to take her over on that understanding, at least she could keep an eye on Gillian for part of the day and give Enid a chance to get her writing done. Betty was duly invited down to Old Thatch to talk things over and by the end of the month she was installed.

Within a few days of her arrival it is apparent from Enid's diaries that Betty was put in full charge and was entrusted with the baby for most of the day — and night too, for she also slept with Gillian in the nursery. Enid took up her writing and social life once more and although she gave periodic progress reports and photographs of the baby to the young readers of her page, she only took full charge of her daughter on the days the young nurse took time off. By November she was writing harder than ever and recorded in her diary that she had 'worked all day long at getting ready six readers for Evans Brothers' and as time went by, even 'played with Gillian at teatime' became a less frequent entry. It was not that Enid did not love her daughter but, during this — to her — rather uninteresting stage of her child's development, other matters seemed more absorbing.

The new year of 1932 had scarcely got under way before she was involved with an exciting new project — her first full-length adult novel. This was something she had long wanted to attempt and her excitement was difficult to conceal even within her diaries and from the book's commencement on January 6th, she referred to its progress daily. By the 15th she had completed a third and on the 25th she recorded that she had written some seven thousand words during the day, only stopping for a midday meal. By February 5th — just under the month from the time she had begun it — she recorded: 'Finished my novel! About 90,000 words. It's called *The Caravan Goes On*.' A few days later, while in London for a business lunch with the directors of Evans Brothers, she left the novel with the literary agent, A. P. Watt. Within a fortnight, however, there was another of Enid's inadequate and tantalising entries in her diary: 'Watt sent my novel back.' There was no further explanation and Enid was never to mention it again. Her family have no recollection of ever having seen this manuscript but, as Enid was never one to waste anything over which she had spent time and effort, it seems likely that the novel eventually reappeared, in a shortened form, as a children's book. The title suggests it may well have been transposed into *Mr. Galliano's Circus* (George Newnes, 1938) which contained several strong, adult characters — unlike most of Enid's other books in which children figure in the dominant roles. The agent's comments when he returned the novel must remain a matter for conjecture, but the only stories she ever wrote from then on were for children. She put aside her disappointment and set to work on several new commissions for Birn Brothers, Newnes and Evans.

With Betty to look after the baby the Pollocks' life together appeared orderly and happy. They were both immensely proud of their pretty, fair-haired daughter and on her first birthday several of the neighbours' children were invited to Old Thatch for a party. Enid was in her element and organised games after

94

tea, including 'fishing in the aquarium'. But there were soon to be changes in the nursery.

A month or so after the party, Enid recorded that she was 'very upset' because she had heard that Betty 'had let Gillian fall from her cot'. She was quite unharmed for the fall had been in no way serious, but the young nursemaid was given instant notice — despite her pleading to stay with the child she had loved and cared for almost since its birth. The intervention of Phyllis Chase, who had been aware for some time that Betty was getting more than her fair share of work, did not alter Enid's decision, and her intolerant attitude all but lost her a friendship she had valued for some years. But once her mind was made up there was never any going back and within a few weeks the nursemaid had gone, a new nanny had been engaged and life at Old Thatch continued pretty much as before, with Enid somehow finding time to take on a multitude of extra activities.

Early in 1933 she decided to keep chickens, ducks and turkeys and, once again, her readers heard all about it, for there were few happenings in her busy life which she failed to store away for use in one way or another for her writings. Even over the bridge table, she was quick to pick up other players' gossip about the escapades of their children and these, along with the doings of her own young daughter, often triggered off ideas for stories or articles. Everything she saw on her occasional walks with Gillian and her nanny was also retained in that fertile brain for use later.

Her readers heard how she and Gillian had watched the new-born lambs on the farm near their home and fed the ducks on the river and she studied and delighted in the little girl's reaction to each new experience. The pram on these occasions was also often used as a means of transporting to the local post office sacks of silver paper bound for Great Ormond Street, or dozens of tobacco tins filled with pondweed — requested by schools for their new aquaria and collected and packed for them by Enid herself.

When she started a vivarium, during her writing of the *Round the Year* nature series, she enlisted the help of Dick Hughes, her young gardener, in hunting for the necessary frogs, toads and other small garden creatures. So carried away was he by her knowledge and enthusiasm that he soon began to take a fresh interest in the bird, animal and plant life around him and before long was keeping, at her suggestion, a daily record of his observations. These he would periodically pass over to her for comment and her further encouragement led him into taking a diploma course in botany and zoology at his local technical college. But Enid also benefited from his studies for, together with his daily jottings, they provided her with many ideas for regular features and for her new monthly *Country Letter*,* which appeared during the twelve months of 1935 in *The Nature Lover* magazine.

Dick Hughes was the only member of the staff to remain with the Pollocks throughout their nine years at Old Thatch. He was in his early twenties and newly married when he took on the job and, by the time he left, four of his six children had been born in the small, two-bedroomed cottage they occupied in a corner of the garden. He was originally engaged as a chauffeur-gardener, but was soon turning his hand to a host of other jobs around the house and garden. He saw to the pumps which operated the water system — for there were no mains at Old Thatch in those days — fed the animals, painted and decorated and carried out most of the general repairs.

When a bedroom and dressing room extension was built on to Old Thatch, he used the left-over timber, brick and other materials to build a miniature house for Gillian in the garden. This delighted all who saw it and prompted Enid to write about it at length on her children's pages. It had a tiled roof with gables, a brick chimney and fireplace, latticed windows — which opened and shut on miniature latches — and a front door complete with knocker, doorknob and lock. It was furnished with 'a blue rug, a round table, two stools, a blue teaset, two pictures on the walls, a little lamp hanging from the ceiling, and a tiny carpet-sweeper, so that she can keep the house clean . . .' It looked, Enid wrote, 'just like a fairy cottage — so small and quaint!' From then on, her young daughter spent most of her summers playing with her

* See Appendix 4.

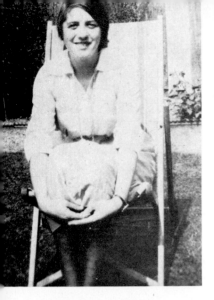

Enid during her kindergarten training
at Ipswich High School

Seckford Hall, Woodbridge, Suffolk

Mr. and Mrs. Hunt and daughter Marjory with Mabel Attenborough and Enid
at Seckford Hall

Enid, aged twenty-two

Mabel Attenborough

Bickley Park School group—centre, Mr. and Mrs. R. Brandram, Enid left

dolls in what came to be known to Enid's readers as 'Dilly's Cottage' — 'Dilly' being Gillian's own name for herself.

But life for the occupants of Old Thatch was not always as idyllic as Enid's writings would sometimes have her readers believe. The house's proximity to the river often meant heavy flooding during the winter months and the consequent dampness taxed even Enid's normally robust constitution, resulting in her being confined to bed on several occasions with severe colds and throat infections. This did not prevent her from seeing to it that her page went in on time, for she told her readers how, during one such illness, she had been writing her column sitting up in bed with her head swathed in bandages. Although she passed off what she termed her 'booming ear' very lightly, she had really been seriously ill with a painful ear infection, which necessitated the calling in of a London specialist. But nothing, it seemed, could stop her from honouring her writing commitments. Conscientious almost to a fault, she expected the same devotion to duty from her staff which explains why, when they became ill themselves, she brooked no malingering. Her readers were told of this illness and of the household's adventures during the floods, but there were certain other incidents about which she made no mention.

When Dick Hughes first pointed out to her that Bobs was showing signs of age, she refused to discuss it — or to believe that he was failing. The old dog dragged on for several months in pain and when he died, in November 1935, although she made a short mention of it in her diary, she refused to speak of his death to anyone or to let Dick and Hugh, who had buried the dog in the garden, mark his grave. For her, Bobs still lived on. His letters continued to appear for as long as she wrote her page and her readers were kept unaware of his death.

They were also unaware of another incident — not quite in keeping with the Arcadian pattern of country living so often portrayed within her columns — an invasion of Old Thatch by a horde of scavenging rats. Rats were a species of wild creature that Enid had always detested and when Dick told her that they were coming up the stream and forming colonies all over the garden, she thought he was exaggerating and that normal methods of control would soon drive them away. In her *Country Letter* in *The Nature Lover* magazine she was writing:

'My adult cats earn their keep well, for no rat is ever allowed to creep in under the thatched roof, as often happens in old cottages. Even a kitten will kill a rat as large as itself.'

Yet her animals were unable to cope with such an army and it was not long before the rats were carrying off a bushel of apples or a sack of vegetables in a single night. They got into the house, running beneath the floorboards and inside the sixteenth-century wattle and daub walls, on their way to the attic to reach the fruit stored there — and the traffic to and fro kept the whole household awake. Ordinary poisons also failed and eventually Hugh decided on more drastic methods and instructed Dick to set a day aside to conduct an all-out war, by gassing the animals out of their underground eyries. Enid took Gillian away to friends, the pets — with the exception of Bobs and Sandy, who were sensible enough to be of help in the hunt — were shut up out of harm's way and battle commenced. By midday, close on a hundred had been killed by Dick, Bobs or Sandy and by evening, the pit the young gardener had dug for the bodies was filled and Old Thatch once again returned to normal. Enid must have been aware of what had taken place, but she never spoke to Dick of his sterling work while she had been away. As far as she was concerned the matter was closed, and such an unpleasant episode was best forgotten. Protective as always, Hugh instructed Dick — as he was later to do over Bobs' death — that he was never to mention the matter to his mistress again.

But not so easily put aside was the household's increasing awareness that all was not well with Hugh.

Early in 1933, he was more than usually busy at Newnes. There were several notable authors under his aegis at that time, including those producing 'part-works' — abridged books published in weekly or fortnightly instalments and eventually bound into volumes. Winston Churchill's *The World Crisis* was one such work to reach a wider public in this way and Hugh was delighted to be responsible for its production. He was always intensely patriotic and admired the politician for his forthright views. He greatly enjoyed his periodic visits to Chartwell to discuss illustrations, or minor revisions and additions to the original script — but his involvement was to have another, less pleasant side. As they discussed many of the major battles in which he had taken part as a young man, Hugh found himself reliving some of the traumatic experiences of that time which he had tried to forget. The volume and pressure of his other work at Newnes only added to his stress for, always something of a perfectionist, he was finding it increasingly difficult to keep up his commitments without a lowering of his own standards. Even at home it was difficult to relax for all too often he returned, physically and mentally exhausted, to find that Enid had arranged a bridge or tennis party, and the pair seemed to be spending less time alone together than ever before. It was therefore not until the early summer that Enid came to realise what Dick Hughes had been aware of for some time — that Hugh was on the verge of a breakdown.

Dick had a great respect for Enid, but it was always to Hugh that he gave his allegiance. He recognised in his employer something of the disciplinarian, expecting the same high standards from his staff — in or out of the office — that he imposed upon himself, but he was also aware of the keen sense of humour and old-world charm and courtesy that earned Hugh the respect and devotion of all who worked for him. During their drives to and from Taplow and the London train, Hugh would encourage his young chauffeur to talk about himself — and in return would tell something of his own life: of his strict but happy boyhood in Scotland, of the friends he had lost in the war and his life in the trenches. At other times he would suggest books he thought might interest Dick, or discuss improvements he had planned for Old Thatch and its garden and, after a while, it was easy for the young man to gauge the nature of his employer's mood by the brevity or otherwise of their conversation. By mid-May it was apparent to Dick that something was seriously wrong. Hugh was looking tired and ill, was morose and silent in the car and, on some of his now frequently late return journeys to Old Thatch, it was evident that he had been drinking.

Like many another who had experienced the horrors of the war and had found temporary relief in alcohol, Hugh was still prone to turn to the same palliative in times of stress. Whether Enid suspected this at the beginning of their relationship is doubtful, but the happiness of their early years together possibly removed any worries she may have had. By July she was forced to acknowledge what was now apparent to the other members of her household, that Hugh was sick and in need of care. She made no reference to this in her diary, but in her weekly *Teachers' World* letter wrote: 'Gillian's Daddy has been working very hard and I want to take him as far away from London as possible.' Gillian and her nurse were sent to a residential nursery in London, and Enid and Hugh took a few weeks' holiday on their own in Scotland — but even there he could not leave his working cares behind. He spent a whole day at an Edinburgh printing works and made a flying visit back to London on 'urgent business'. Nevertheless, the holiday appeared to ease the pressures for them both and they seemed more relaxed and happy on their return to Old Thatch. They had a joint celebration of their birthdays a few days later and presents were exchanged as usual — though Enid's gift to Hugh came as something of a surprise. As she could never bear loud noises of any kind, particularly when she was working, complaining if Dick Hughes so much as whistled or Gillian was too noisy at her play, both Hugh and her staff were astonished when she gave him, of all things, a set of drums, something he had always wanted.

If she had intended the present to serve as an alternative safety valve for his tensions, it was a brave try, for he spent many hours after that playing by himself to the music of dance bands on the radio, or as an accompaniment to his own whistling of Scottish reels, and for a while he seemed his old self. But her worries were not over. After several references in her diary to his late or 'very late' homecomings, there appears on December 30th, another of those cryptic entries which gives cause for speculation: 'Wrote a letter to Hugh all p.m.' As he was at home at the time, it is reasonable to assume that this was Enid's way of communicating something to her husband about which she had to give great thought and care. Again no mention is made of its contents, nor of how it was received by Hugh — her only note the following day being an account of the New Year's Eve Ball which they had attended with publishing friends in London, and their journey home in the fog.

But whatever the contents of the letter, 1934 appears to have begun happily enough and Enid's early diary jottings refer only to her writing or social engagements — and her daily 'playtimes' with Gillian. These now included first lessons for her young daughter in reading, writing and 'number puzzles' and Gillian made good progress under her mother's expert tuition. She writes often of having 'gardened with Dilly' — and no doubt these sessions, greatly enjoyed by both, prompted her to write *The Children's Garden*, published by Newnes the following year. This popular book, which instructed children on how to grow their own flowers and vegetables and make them 'feel very proud indeed', went into several reprints and prompted many of its readers to seek further advice from the author on the management of their own small gardens. But her happy times with Gillian did not lessen her renewed anxieties over Hugh when, in the early summer, it was apparent that his old troubles were returning.

Editing the further volumes of *The Great War* — as Churchill's revised book was entitled — continued to take up much of his time, without any lessening of his other work and the familiar stress symptoms reappeared. It was during the latter half of May, while his mother was staying at Old Thatch, that Enid mentioned for the first time in her diary that Hugh was not well and that the doctor had been called in. She makes no reference to the nature of his illness, but a change was evidently prescribed, for she writes of him having journeyed back to Scotland with his mother the following day for a short holiday in Ayr. A further diary entry two weeks later seems to indicate that he was still not fully recovered when she went to meet him at the station: 'He drove home and we nearly had several accidents!!' But apparently he felt well enough after a few days to join the rest of his family in the small furnished house at Seaview, on the Isle of Wight, that had been rented for the summer.

Although Enid continued to work at her writing commitments and Hugh had to make one or two hurried visits back to his London office, they enjoyed this quiet time together: bathing with Gillian, building sandcastles on the beach, taking boats out and picnicking on sunny days. By the end of the holiday, Hugh seemed to be very much refreshed — and overjoyed by the knowledge that Enid was once again pregnant. Both hoped that this time it might be a boy, and eagerly looked forward to the birth. They were bitterly disappointed when she miscarried a few months later — but this was soon forgotten when early the following year she conceived again.

CHAPTER

VIII

THE SILVER JUBILEE YEAR OF KING GEORGE V IN 1935 DAWNED full of promise for the Pollocks. Enid's great national pride prompted her to write a poem for *Teachers' World* in honour of The Royal occasion and on May 6th, the day of the Jubilee, she noted: 'Sir Robert Evans [*the Chairman of Evans Brothers*] wrote to say the King is to see my poem!' Entitled *The Helmsman*, her tribute to the 'Sailor King' appeared on the cover page of the special Jubilee edition of the magazine:

His was the Ship of State; he could command,
Dictate with all the pride of race and name,
Or, like a lesser monarch, could have planned
A life of ease and leisure, kingly fame;
Nothing of this he asked, nor did he force
His will, his wishes, on a loyal crew;
He merely held his ship upon her course,
A Helmsman, firm of purpose, steadfast, true.
Through mutinous, bewildering seas of foam,
Through storms of war, through thickening mists of dread,
He steered our ship and brought her safely home —
True Sailor King, a helmsman born and bred.

A year later she was to write sadly of the King's death and on May 12th, 1937, she was called upon by *Teachers' World* to write another poem to mark the Coronation of George VI.

A casual observer of Enid during that Jubilee year would have thought that everything was now going her way and that any troubles she may have had were at an end. She had a devoted husband, an engaging young daughter and an attractive, smoothly-run home with ample staff to keep it so. Above all, with every year that passed, she was establishing herself still further as a popular writer for children. Eight books were due for publication during 1935, other work had been commissioned for the year following and, despite her pregnancy, these extra commitments did not deter her from continuing to write her weekly *Teachers' World* page, edit her *Sunny Stories* magazine and take on the monthly *Country Letter* feature for *The Nature Lover* magazine. She also found time to work on another commission — writing the introductory chapters for and editing T. A. Coward's *Birds of Wayside and Woodland* (published by Frederick Warne the following year).

Pressure of work had eased a little for Hugh as the year progressed and once again the family took a house in the Isle of Wight for a month's holiday in the summer. This time there was added excitement as it coincided with the Jubilee Review of the Fleet at Spithead, which gave her yet another topic for her page.

The family returned to Bourne End in good time for Enid to complete her preparation for the baby's birth in the autumn and she looked forward confidently to its arrival. But she was to have a longer wait than she had anticipated. The estimated date came and went without any sign of the child making its appearance and as time went on she became progressively more frustrated and difficult. It was never easy for her to accept that however carefully she might plan and organise other aspects of her life, over events such as this she had no control. As each new method prescribed for the hastening of the birth failed she took out her frustration and disappointment on her husband and staff. Midwives were engaged and given notice, or left of their own accord within a few days of each other, and the house was in a turmoil. It was a relief to all concerned when Imogen Mary finally arrived on October 27th: '8lb 6oz, a sweet little baby', Enid recorded in her diary. *Teachers' World* readers learned some weeks later that another 'new pet' had arrived: '. . . a tiny sister for Gillian . . . so now there are three Marys at Old Thatch — Enid Mary, Gillian Mary and Imogen Mary.' But someone else had joined the household at the same time who was also to make a deep impression on Enid's life from then on.

Dorothy Gertrude Richards was the last of the nurses engaged by Enid for Imogen's birth. Unmarried and one of a large, closely-knit family, she had trained at St. Thomas's Hospital in London and was a skilled and efficient nurse, well-balanced and outwardly calm in any critical situation. She also possessed a charm of manner that enabled her to handle even the most awkward of patients and this, with her other qualities, meant that she was usually in great demand. As chance would have it, she was between cases when a friend rang her from a nursing agency and begged for her help over 'a very difficult case' at Bourne End, who had been making repeated demands for an 'efficient' midwife. A trifle reluctantly, Dorothy agreed to take the case on, if only temporarily. On her arrival, however, she found that the baby had already been born the previous day and was agreeably surprised to discover that her new patient was not only amenable, but appeared also to have an intriguing and interesting personality. Enid for her part took an instant liking to this slim, dark-haired person of her own age, whose quiet efficiency gave her a deep feeling of security. 'The new nurse is sweet,' she wrote in her diary on the first day of their meeting and, later in the week, 'the new nurse is awfully nice and I like her very much'. The pair discovered they had many interests in common and by the end of November, when Dorothy left to take on another case, they were on Christian name terms and their friendship had become firmly established. Enid telephoned and wrote frequently and Dorothy soon became a regular visitor to Old Thatch.

One of the qualities which drew Enid to her from the start was the air of serenity which her friend seemed to transmit to all with whom she came into contact, and Enid was curious about the source of this seeming inner strength. She liked to appear self-sufficient, but she knew in her heart that she was not. Childlike in so many respects, demanding the attention of all around her, she still needed to cling to the guiding hand of someone she could trust. For a time it seemed that Hugh had provided her with the security she needed, but the events of the last two years had brought about a subtle change in their relationship. No longer did she turn to him for guidance over all her affairs, or feel she could fully rely on him to act as a buffer against the cruelties of life. He had proved himself to be as vulnerable as she — and Enid despised what she considered to be his weakness. But the physical side of their partnership was happy and satisfying and this, with Hugh's deep love for her, held their marriage together.

In the course of one of their many long talks together, while she was tending Enid at Old Thatch, Dorothy had revealed that she was a convert to Roman Catholicism. This so intrigued Enid that she questioned her friend closely on how she had come to make such a decision and continued the probing later in a series of lengthy letters. The first, written early in December, began:

I feel I want to discuss this spiritual business with you at great length. I can't tolerate you thinking that I am materialistic. I am not as materialistic as I may appear — the things I think about, the deeper side of life I have not very much discussed with anyone, because I have met very few people who either bother to think for themselves or, alternatively, can only think in the terms of the Church in which they have been brought up. Now you must be different — because you actually chose your religion when adult, and you are serious about it — though you don't try to force it on anyone. I do believe in God, though perhaps not your idea of God. I do trust him in that I believe that there is a real purpose and love behind everything and I do want to serve and love the highest — whatever and whoever that may be.

I would like a personal God like yours, but I find it difficult to believe in one that you can talk to as you do . . . I am not entirely without belief as you see. I do truly want to be as decent as I can and would like help to be, if it's possible . . . it is because you get it, I do want to know and I don't mind learning from you.

There then followed what, for Enid, was a rare and honest piece of self-analysis, which gives an insight into her character which would, perhaps, have surprised many of her regular readers at that time:

> Deep down in me I have an arrogant spirit that makes me a bit scornful of other people, if I think they are stupid or led by the nose, or at the mercy of their upbringing and environment — unable to think for themselves. I keep it under because I want to be charitable, but I have at times been horrid and contemptuous — really I have. I am usually the one who puts forth my opinion in most company I meet with and I am listened to, which is very bad for me. You said I was bossy — well I am — more than you think. In my mind I like to *dominate* even though I don't appear to be doing so! I want to hear all you have to say even if I argue at first and go all round things . . . I don't want to belong to a definite church — not yet, anyhow, but you might tell me a few things . . . I don't know exactly what I am looking for — something a little more than I seem to have found in religion up to now — I may be chasing a will-o-the-wisp, for all I know . . .

Dorothy was evidently not convinced of the seriousness of Enid's search for spiritual guidance, for Enid's next letter, early in January 1936, tried to reassure her:

> You can say anything to me. I want you to. I will be willing to be taught by you because I respect you and believe in you, in a way I have never felt for anyone else. I never thought for one moment that I could come to you for help like this a few months ago . . . I would like to know, love and serve God all the days of my life. *But* the God I thought of wasn't exactly the same as yours — not a personal one . . . my idea of loving, knowing and serving him was empty to me as a desert . . . I suppose that was really serving him blindly not loving and knowing him. It was mainly your example that has got it back — your somehow so certain knowledge and your beliefs and your prayers . . .

Enid's diary at this time makes no mention of this intimate correspondence or of any change in the normal pattern of her life. She wrote only of domestic and social matters — a change of maids, bridge parties, commencement of dancing classes for Gillian, Imogen's progress and an almost daily note that she had 'worked till tea'. Although she recorded having 'talked all morning and afternoon with Dorothy' during her friend's frequent visits, she never referred to the subjects of their talks — but presumably they must have been on similar lines to the letters.

In April, Dorothy returned to Old Thatch to take charge of the two children while the nanny went on holiday. While Dorothy was with them, Enid, who normally only spent an hour or so a day with her children, now extended this to most of the day and only worked at her writing in the mornings. In the evenings she again devoted so much time to her friend that Hugh, always inclined to be possessive, became — in her words — 'very grumpy'. But once Dorothy had left, Enid soon returned to her usual daily routine and went back to work with such vigour that, within a week, she was writing between five and six thousand words in a day.

But the correspondence with Dorothy continued and in June Enid wrote:

I have always wanted to be good and do good as much as lay in my power, and I did think that so long as anyone thought that and practised it that was all that mattered. I had dipped into this and that, read things here and there ... Hugh has often said that if your religion has helped to make you what you are, it should be worth going into ... I felt I would have to find out about you and your beliefs, not condescendingly, but humbly ... I did think that I had gone into things enough and had a lot of knowledge of these things and had come to conclusions far in advance of any likely to be held by you (please don't think I am being too horrid) — I told you in one of my letters that intellectual pride was the sin that really did hold me back — I thought so much of myself and my opinions and now I know I was wrong. I shall never be so high and mighty again ... I was baptised when I was 13 but had no real idea why, except that I became a member of the church. I did meddle with other beliefs out of interest more than *sheer urgency* — and I read a lot, and out of it all I came with some very poor ideas and no knowledge at all of the meanings of any of the things you know so well . . .

These letters appear to be sincere, but it is difficult to gauge the exact depth of Enid's spiritual thought and search. There is no evidence of any change in her choice of reading matter at this time and nothing fresh in her writings to suggest that she was undergoing a period of spiritual rethinking. Her short stories had always put forward a certain code of behaviour for her young readers and although she did eventually write many books of a religious nature, the first of these *The Land of Far Beyond*, based on *The Pilgrim's Progress*, was not embarked upon until almost six years later. Nor did she regularly attend any form of church service, either during or after this time, and despite her alleged wish to learn more of her friend's religion, only twice did she accompany her to Mass. The first occasion was during that same summer when Dorothy joined the family for their annual holiday in the Isle of Wight: 'We all went to the Roman Catholic Church, Gillian too . . .' Enid recorded and then dismissed the event with — 'then we went home and bathed and went for a picnic to Alum Bay'. Dorothy stayed for a further three weeks, but the experience of church-going was evidently not repeated and when Enid returned home, Sunday continued to be what it had always been for her up to then — a day for making up accounts and dealing with correspondence.

In later years she told Gillian that she had decided against Roman Catholicism because she had felt it was 'too constricting' and that she could not bear a tight rein over anything without 'chafing and fretting'. She also confided to Imogen that her 'spiritual arrogance' had always held her back from forming any strong attachments to a particular church. The God of her childhood had been one of vengeance and she wished he had not been, for she badly needed to be sure that he was all-loving. She had, she told her daughters, always tried to live her life according to Christian ethics and although she rarely attended church services with them she saw to it that both were baptised into the Anglican faith, taught to say their prayers and attend the local Sunday School.

After the Isle of Wight holiday together, Enid continued to meet and write to Dorothy as frequently as before but religion was no longer the main subject for discussion between them. This was particularly so by the latter half of 1936, for by that time Enid's thoughts were directed more towards a new project which Newnes were planning to launch early the following year.

She had been discussing for some months with Herbert Tingay, the company's managing director, the possibility of bringing out *Sunny Stories* weekly, under a new format, and on January 15th, 1937, the first of this series was launched with an introductory 'Letter from Old Thatch':

> I hope you will be pleased when you know that these little stories are going to come out every week now! There will be a new one for you each Friday. I am going to write your stories for you just as I have always done, and you shall have all sorts of extra things too — funny pictures — puzzles — competitions — prizes! What fun we shall have . . .

Apart from a page devoted to poems or puzzles sent in by the children, Enid was responsible for the entire contents of every issue.

The first of her long serial stories for the magazine, *The Adventures of the Wishing Chair*, was brought out in book form by Newnes at the end of the year, after (according to Enid's weekly letter) her readers had written asking her to put all the adventures 'into a proper big book', because they had enjoyed the serial so much. Correspondence of this kind proved invaluable to Enid in assessing the popularity or otherwise of her stories. She invited the children's comments on everything she wrote — and received replies by the hundred. She had no difficulty in gauging the appeal of her second full-length serial story for, from the first, it proved a sound favourite with most age groups and was the forerunner of many other 'family adventure' books. *The Secret Island*, eventually published by Basil Blackwell in 1938, told the story of four children who ran away together to a secret island

and the adventures that befell them. In reviewing the book, *Teachers' World* commented:

> Another example not only of Enid Blyton's ingenuity as a story writer, but her incomparable gift of knowing just how young children like a story to be.

She was to have the same kind of success with the serial that followed — *Mr. Galliano's Circus* — again destined to be the first of another well-loved series of books, which this time she based on life in a circus. Popular, too, were the short stories and poems for the magazine, which Enid later used — with slight variations — in many of her annuals and 'Bedtime' books.

Among the tales particularly enjoyed by Gillian were those written around her own rag doll — 'Naughty Amelia Jane'. This large, dark-haired doll had been given to Gillian on her third birthday and had been a favourite ever since the day Enid had 'brought her to life', a year or so after Amelia Jane had arrived in the nursery. Dorothy had been staying at Old Thatch at the time and she and Enid had joined Gillian and her nanny for tea. Enid had been in a playful, happy mood and had grasped the floppy, ringlet-haired doll under its red-spotted dress, and made her perform like a puppet. Much to Gillian's delight, and the others' amusement, Amelia Jane was made to pick up sandwiches and lumps of sugar and hurl them on to the floor 'talking' all the while in a squeaky voice, while Enid admonished her in stern tones. Her mother's superb clowning was such a success that Gillian would constantly demand repeat performances. When *Sunny Stories* appeared, other children were able to read of Amelia Jane's misdeeds and eventually these popular tales also found their way into a book.

As with her *Teachers' World* page, the *Sunny Stories* 'letter' was a way of introducing several worthwhile ideas to her readers. In one case she suggested that lonely children might like to write in to 'The Pillar Box' section, telling of their hobbies and pets, and whether they came from town or country, so that they might be put in touch with one another. She reported in a later issue that this suggestion had been followed up and dozens of new 'pen-friends' were now corresponding regularly.

Bobs, that lovable black and white terrier — who had died some two years before, but was still kept very much alive through his weekly *Teachers' World* 'letter' — appeared yet again in the new *Sunny Stories* magazine. This time he figured in an illustrated strip piece, *Bobs and his Friends*, which also incorporated the 'schoolgirl' Gillian, 'baby' Imogen and other members of the Old Thatch household.

With so much of her writing in both magazines now based on her home and family, it is not surprising that this cosy domestic world — free from the more unpleasant and irksome aspects of the daily round — should occasionally become more real for her than the reality. She tried to spend as much time as possible with her two young daughters. As often as she could, she took Imogen in the pram to meet Gillian from the small private school she now attended and usually played with them for an hour or so after tea, but found that her increased writing commitments prevented her from seeing as much of them as she would have liked, although her columns suggested that she did. Even her relationship with Hugh was not as happy as it had once been — before Dorothy came into their lives.

It had not escaped Hugh's notice that Enid had become less dependent upon him and more on her friend and he resented what he considered to be Dorothy's intrusion into his marriage. Now that Enid appeared to be gaining more confidence in herself and her abilities, with the acquisition of a certain amount of fame and fortune on her own, he was also beginning to feel that their roles in the household were being reversed and that he was fast becoming superfluous to her affairs. It was unfortunate that he should suffer additional stress at this time because of other broader issues at stake — outside the narrow confines of Old Thatch — which he was convinced would soon involve them all.

The outbreak of the Spanish Civil War and other inflammatory situations in Europe during the late 'thirties, confirmed Hugh's belief in Winston Churchill's warnings that the world was on the brink of another war. The more depressed he became over the

With the Thompson boys, John Terry and Mollie Sayer—first pupils at Southernhay

CHILD WHISPERS

PHYLLIS
CHASE.

By ENID BLYTON

Enid's first book, 1922—jacket design by Phyllis Chase

possibility of such a catastrophe, the easier he found it to fall back on his old means of consolation. But fearing that Enid would suspect his motives and despise him the more if he drank openly, he took his bottles into a small cellar under the stairs, only accessible through the maid's bathroom, and out of sight from the rest of the house. Only Dick Hughes knew what his employer was about, for periodically he was entrusted with the key to the cellar so that he might clear away the empty bottles. It was, therefore, not until Hugh became seriously ill in the early summer of 1938, and some of the undisposed-of bottles were discovered, that the rest of the household became aware of what had been going on.

Despite a heavy cold that had troubled him for some weeks, Hugh had stubbornly refused to take to his bed, but one evening he returned to Old Thatch on the point of collapse and Enid called in the doctor. His diagnosis, that Hugh was seriously ill with pneumonia and would have to be moved without delay into the local cottage hospital, came as a considerable shock to Enid. She had always had a fear of illness — and hospitals in particular — and had never known Hugh to be physically ill before. When he was put to bed in the ward, it was almost more than she could bear to see him lying pale, helpless and breathing with difficulty in such alien surroundings and she felt herself totally inadequate to cope with such a situation. Dorothy was away on a case and for the first time in her life Enid could find no release from unpleasant reality through her writing. Her stream of creative thought, normally so active, appeared to be stemmed and she found it impossible to get down to work.

Hugh's condition worsened and his brother was summoned from Scotland. For a few days, while the fever was approaching its crisis, no one was sure of the outcome. Dick Hughes, meeting Enid on the doorstep one morning and asking for news, was disturbed to see the normally bright and imperturbable Mrs. Pollock bury her head in her hands and, between sobs, admit that she was frightened and did not 'want anything to happen to Hugh'. But by the next morning the crisis had passed and Hugh began to recover.

Although this period of deep anxiety was short-lived, the experience seemed to bring back to Enid the happiness of her early years with Hugh, and the realisation of what she might have lost if he were no longer there to share her life. She looked again at the attractive setting in which they played out their joint lives and, in her own way, showed that she recognised her good fortune. Her *Teachers' World* letter for June 22nd, written shortly after that crucial day — and probably the first piece of work since his illness — described how she had woken up early, pulled back the curtains of her room and looked outside:

> The sun is low, and its beams come slanting through the waking trees, giving them long shadows towards the west . . . There is a blackbird talking away to himself slowly and melodiously in the pear tree nearby — and a chaffinch is carolling in the pink hawthorn . . . The big scarlet poppies are shining like red lanterns by the tall blue lupins. I can see Gillian's little garden in the distance, her Virginia stock a thick green mass and her cornflowers growing tall . . .

She went on to tell of how she had listened to her doves cooing to each other, her dogs, cats and other pets waking and, as breakfast time approached, the 'two little voices' that meant Gillian and Imogen were also awake. 'It's lovely,' she wrote, 'to see the world looking so fresh and new.' She made no mention of Hugh's illness at that time but the following week she wrote:

> Gillian's Daddy has been very ill indeed and I have had to keep staying near him . . . I am sure you will be glad to know that he is getting better now — but it is a dreadful time when daddies or mummies are ill, isn't it?

When Hugh returned home he was very weak from his illness but happy to be with his wife and two small daughters again and he looked forward to a holiday at the seaside to convalesce. Even the arrival of Dorothy, who had been engaged by Enid to act as his nurse, did not dim his happiness, for he had come back to a seemingly loving and attentive wife. Their marriage appeared to be all set for a new, brighter phase and in this mood Hugh and Enid set off on holiday.

She informed her young readers, as usual, that she would be going away: 'Gillian and Imogen have already gone with their nurse, but I am waiting till their Daddy is well enough to go too . . .' — but it was not until a week later that she gave them the surprising news that, this time, the family would not be returning to Old Thatch.

CHAPTER

IX

THE POLLOCKS HAD FOR SOME TIME BEEN LOOKING FOR A LARGER house for their growing family and staff, but both had been reluctant to leave Old Thatch and its delightful setting. Although they had extended it once, they felt that further additions would only spoil the character of the cottage and make it, in Enid's words, 'neither old nor new — just a hotchpotch'. But the house that eventually replaced their old home and was to be associated with Enid for the rest of her life, was not of Hugh's choosing. Dorothy and Enid had decided upon it together, weeks before Hugh's illness — a fact which had further aggravated the situation existing at that time between husband and wife and possibly accounted for Hugh's dislike of the proposed new home from the start.

The house was some thirty years old and was built of red brick with black and white half-timbered gables. It had eight bedrooms, several large reception rooms and stood in two-and-a-half acres of grounds in a pleasant, tree-lined road in Beaconsfield, a small Buckinghamshire town about twenty-five miles from London. Much to Hugh's dismay, for he was a countryman at heart, it was situated in less rural surroundings than Old Thatch and, in his view, the house itself had little character. But it was close to the station and shops and with Gillian now at school and Imogen soon to follow, Enid felt it would be altogether more suitable for the family. There were bitter arguments at first over her choice, but she was adamant that it was the house she wanted and Hugh, as always, eventually let her have her way. A buyer was found for Old Thatch and plans for the move were already well advanced when Hugh became ill.

But despite her determination to make the change, as the time approached for leaving the house that had been her home for close on ten years, Enid began to realise just what a wrench it would be. Several of her *Teachers' World* columns beforehand extolled the beauties of the cottage and garden and she wistfully wrote in her letter of July 27th:

> 'I know you will be sad that Old Thatch is no longer going to be our home, because you know it so well — I am sad too because it is a beautiful place, and we had made the garden so lovely . . .'

There was no going back on her decision by that time, however, and she set about convincing her readers that her new house would be as appealing to them as the old:

> '. . . But I am sure you will love our new home and garden. I want you to think of a name for it. It has a bigger garden than Old Thatch, very sheltered, with a great many little lawns surrounded by green yew hedges . . .'

It was, she wrote, a very 'happy-looking' house with its roof of deep red-brown tiles, many casement windows and tall chimneys. Gillian was to have a small bedroom to herself and on her recent birthday had been given presents towards its furnishing. There was, as yet, no pond, but the new garden had two rockeries, an orchard and a large vegetable garden 'that seems to grow prize vegetables'. Gillian and Imogen were to have 'one of the little hidden lawns' for themselves — 'their own secret place', for their gardens, swing and sandpit.

Enid's request for names for this new home met with an enthusiastic response. Hundreds of children wrote to her in the weeks that followed and she quoted their suggestions in her columns. Eventually she revealed to them that although she thought Sunny Corners, Red Roofs, Tall Chimneys, Cherry

Trees and many others, were all 'charming', one name in particular — Green Hedges — had appeared more frequently than any other. It had been first choice for close on three-quarters of her readers and she had decided to use this for her new home. From then on her page in *Teachers' World* and her letter in *Sunny Stories* always carried 'Green Hedges' at its head — a house-name which was to become synonymous with Enid for several decades. But she did not entirely dismiss the other names that had been suggested for many subsequently appeared in her stories and books.

There was still a considerable amount of decoration needed before the family could move in, so it was not until the end of August that Enid was able to tell her readers that she was actually living in her new home and that she had written a poem to mark the event:

GREEN HEDGES

What shall we call you, little new house,
With your chimneys red and tall?
Your leaded windows and cosy nooks,
Your sunny corners and smiling looks,
And your creepers all over the wall?

I think we shall love you, little new house,
With your big trees all around,
And your quaint green hedges and secret bowers,
Your hidden lawns and your glowing flowers,
Your daisies all over the ground!

Will you shelter us well, you little new house,
And welcome my family here,
And love my two little girls at play,
With their birds and animals happy and gay,
For many and many a year?

We'll call you Green Hedges, little new house
It's just the right name for you,
We'll be like the birds for they build their nest
In the hedgerows high that they love the best,
And *we'll* build in Green Hedges, too.

Perhaps Enid and Hugh intended to 'build' and strengthen their marriage in their new home. On the timber beam of the front doorway, a former owner had carved *Pax huic domui* and Enid decided the inscription should remain there for, as she explained later, on describing Green Hedges in her autobiography, 'all homes should be happy, peaceful places . . .' — but for Hugh it was to be associated with one of the unhappiest periods of his life.

The first autumn at Green Hedges got off to a bad start when the whole family developed influenza and once again Hugh had a bout of pneumonia — though not as serious as during the summer. In the meantime, war clouds had been gathering and after the Munich crisis Hugh was even more sure of the eventual outcome. Enid, however, dismissed his fears as groundless, and refused to believe he was serious when he expressed his willingness to be called up as a reserve officer should the need arise. She never liked to have the pattern of her life disturbed and, at that time, everything seemed to be running smoothly. She now had room in the house for a cook as well as a general maid and it was easier than ever to delegate all her domestic affairs, the management of her daughters and the care of her pets and concentrate fully on her writing. The large garden was tended by a new gardener, a Mr. Tapping, for Dick Hughes had been left behind at Old Thatch.

Many of Enid's friends were also 'left behind' at Bourne End, for she only kept in close touch with one or two after she moved house. Dorothy was one of the few people whose friendship she really valued and their close relationship had remained unchanged over the years. Since his illness, Hugh seemed more willing to accept that Enid needed both of them to ensure her happiness: Dorothy to provide a stabilising influence and Hugh to be father to her children and a husband upon whose deep love and affection she knew she could always rely. At no time would she let herself believe that events outside this small, cosy world might change the course of all their lives.

By the beginning of 1939 she was working harder than ever. In addition to the regular items for *Teachers' World* and *Sunny Stories* — both read by 'hundreds of thousands of children', according to one critic of the time — she was compiling school readers, books of plays and putting many of her serial and other stories from her magazines into book form. She tried to interest the B.B.C. in broadcasting some of her work but nothing came of this, despite the fact that both she and Hugh repeatedly sent in material they considered suitable for the children's programmes. But she had few rejections elsewhere, for most publishers seemed only too willing to take what she had to offer.

Her routine day began early and the pattern had changed little over the years. Soon after breakfast, if she was at home and not consulting publishers in London, she would first give instructions to her cook on the family's meals and then start writing on the verandah overlooking the garden, or in an armchair by the fire, with her typewriter poised, as always, on a board across her knees and her red silk Moroccan shawl close at hand. She liked to have red near her for the colour acted, she thought, as a 'mental stimulus'. She had usually written between six and ten thousand words by five o'clock, with only a short break for lunch on a tray, during which she would read one of the many books she obtained weekly from two libraries. Then it was time for the children.

This was the hour her daughters enjoyed most during the day, for Enid would play games or read stories with them, all the while listening carefully to what they had to tell her. On summer evenings they would go out into the garden and play with the animals or listen for and try to identify some of the birds round about. Both girls liked to hear about the stories she had written during the day — particularly if they included Amelia Jane, or one of the family pets. Enid was quick to note that Gillian's and Imogen's favourite stories were often those which were eventually to prove the most popular with her other readers, and it is interesting to note that as the years passed, so did the proportion of books for their age group increase. As the girls grew older they were sometimes entrusted with reading proofs and earned themselves a penny for every mistake they spotted.

Hugh's return home was usually the signal for the 'playtime' sessions with her daughters to come to an end and Hugh and Enid would then have a quiet dinner alone together. Afterwards she would set about answering some of her vast correspondence, which still ran to hundreds of letters each week. Occasionally she would take an evening off for a game of tennis or bridge or to visit a cinema or theatre with Hugh. But they generally retired early, for Enid always maintained that her active brain needed plenty of sleep to keep the story line flowing.

She would allow little to interfere with this strict, daily pattern which she had set for herself and visitors were often made to feel unwelcome if they brought about any change in her routine.

In the early summer a new maid arrived at Green Hedges. Mary was an attractive, auburn-haired Austrian girl, who had been forced by the crisis in her country to leave her comfortable home in Vienna and seek safety and work in England. Although Mary had never undertaken any form of domestic work before, she was bright, intelligent and willing and was soon helping with all manner of jobs around the house. She assisted the cook, stood in for the nanny on her day off — even did a little typing for Enid on occasions — and after a while became more friend than servant to the whole family.

Enid was at her best with people she liked and she went to endless trouble to ensure that Mary's stay at Green Hedges should be happy, for she realised that there were times when her young maid felt very lost and homesick. She managed to get a letter through to Vienna to let Mary's parents know that she was in good hands and would be well looked after. She also wrote to the Home Office to say that she would take the responsibility of looking after Mary's parents should they decide to come to England — but by the time both letters had been received, the rest of Europe had been plunged into war. Mary never forgot Enid's kindness at this time and remained a loyal friend throughout the stormy and eventful years that were to follow. After she left the family in 1945, Enid based 'Greta, the Austrian maid' in *House at the Corner* on this young woman who had a special place in the family's affections.

Enid and Bobs both broke the news to their readers of *Teachers' World* that their country was at war. Bobs 'wrote':

'Did you know we were at war with the Germans? Well, we are. Gillian told me . . .'

Enid's letter was more explicit about the changes that were now inevitable. Many of her readers had been evacuated into strange surroundings and these children received her special attention. For a while, she told them, her page would not be quite so large and she would have to cut down on her weekly story:

'. . . The war is making all our lives different and until things shake down a little, we will put up with them cheerfully . . . Some of you have left your homes and are in the country. You will now be able to see all the things I write about — how lucky you are!'

She continued in the same vein, the following week, having heard through her correspondence of the problems that were being encountered:

'. . . you will be able to see, hear, smell and enjoy all the loveliness of the countryside and you will make the most of your stay there. You are guests of the kindly country folk and will do your best to help them . . .'

There followed a description of some of the poisonous fruits the children might come across on country walks, and she finished her letter with a gentle reminder to all her readers:

'We have a little underground shelter in our garden . . . Gillian and Imogen call it "Bunny Burrow" . . . When the sirens go they are as obedient as soldiers and do exactly as they should. I am sure you are the same . . .'

In a later column she wrote of the 'many happy letters' she had received from town children who were now living in the country:

'. . . and how they love the country! Well I knew they would and I only wish that we had big camp-schools for children, so that we might always have all our children in the country going home for weekends and holidays. Perhaps we shall some day.'

Her mail in war-time did not appear to decrease — rather the contrary. Evacuated teachers and children wrote in their hundreds asking for advice on country matters and many schools took up her suggestions for contributions to the war effort. By early 1941 Enid had already distributed to the Red Cross and other organisations over three thousand blankets, made from squares knitted by her readers. These were usually sewn together by the teachers but Enid made up many of the blankets herself with the help of any members of her household who happened to be available. In the spring of that same year she wrote of having received during the past few weeks — in addition to the usual quota of blankets:

'. . . face flannels made out of old bits of towel . . . hot water bottle covers, babies' vests, gloves and socks of all sizes . . . khaki and Air Force blue stockings, oiled stockings for sailors, and hospital stockings about two yards long! . . . and an enormous supply of scarves . . .'

She encouraged the children to 'Dig for Victory', as Gillian was doing by having vegetable gardens in place of flower beds. Sacks of silver paper and used stamps for the Red Cross continued to arrive at regular intervals. Among the many packages that arrived, several were intended for Enid herself. She had only to mention that her doves were short of seed, or that she was having difficulty in obtaining pet food, for wild seeds and recipes for making dog biscuits or cat food to be sent to her by every post during the week that followed.

She was often called upon to open school fund-raising activities and at one of these — a War Weapons' Week sale — she found herself presented with an assortment of small packages to take home, the contents of which suggested that the pupils and staff were regular followers of her columns. There were bones for Bobs and biscuits for the other dogs, tins of sardines for the cats, seeds for her pigeons and chickens and sweets for Gillian and

Imogen. There were also a tin of peaches and home-made cream for Enid herself and two sacks of silver paper. In return she donated three of her Siamese kittens and there was great competition for their ownership.

When her fox terrier, Sandy, disappeared from Green Hedges early in 1941 and she mentioned the fact to her readers, a teacher sent a black, white and brown smooth-haired terrier as a replacement and from then on the mischievous 'Topsy' was featured regularly in both her *Teachers' World* columns and *Sunny Stories*.

There had been no great changes at Green Hedges during the very early months of the war, for Hugh was at that time still working at Newnes and Enid's domestic staff remained the same. Her cook, whose husband subsequently died on active service, was allowed to have her small son, Kenneth, living in with her at the house and after a while his exploits, too, were described at length in her columns, along with those of Gillian, Imogen and the pets. With a full household, she was able to tell the billeting officer that there was no room at Green Hedges for evacuees, and that she needed her staff to allow her to carry out what she considered to be her own particular form of war work — writing for children — and there was certainly no let-up for her in this direction.

After the invasion of Norway, newsprint was rationed and even typing paper was not so easily come by. Publishing houses were struggling for existence at that time and crucial decisions were having to be made over which publications were to be retained. But, for Enid at least, this presented no problem. The managing director of George Newnes was still the shrewd Herbert Tingay, who had long ago gauged her worth to his company, and it was his decision that ensured the continuation of *Sunny Stories* throughout the war years. *Teachers' World* — along with its regular weekly feature from Green Hedges — was also retained by Evans Brothers and Mr. Allen, who continued as its editor, accepted any other contributions Enid cared to make to his magazine. The stories from both these publications were still reproduced in book form at the same rate as pre-war, and other publishers appeared only too happy to add Enid's name to their lists.

During 1940 alone, eleven books were published under her name, including: *The Secret of Spiggy Holes* (which like its forerunner, *The Secret Island*, had previously appeared in serial form in *Sunny Stories*): *Twenty-Minute Tales* and *Tales of Betsy May*, both collections of short stories for Methuen; *The Children of Cherry Tree Farm*, published by Country Life, and a story book annual for the *News Chronicle*. The remainder were brought out by George Newnes, who continued as Enid's main publishers. In addition to those listed by the company under her own name during that year were two others — *Three Boys and a Circus* and *Children of Kidillin* — which appeared under the pseudonym of Mary Pollock. This subterfuge, however, was to have unexpected and amusing consequences. So popular did these books become that one reviewer was prompted to remark that 'Enid Blyton had better look to her laurels' — but the children who read these stories were not deceived. They very quickly realised that the two authors were, in fact, the same and wrote letters of complaint to Enid and the publishers. The whole matter led to such confusion that it was eventually decided to reissue these and two other subsequent 'Mary Pollock' books under her own name.

Despite the shortage of paper, she had no difficulty in obtaining further commissions for her work, for the publishers had long since realised that a book by Enid Blyton was usually guaranteed to sell almost as soon as it left the presses. But the accolade for the most enterprising idea for making use of her talents and of what little paper was available during those early war years, must surely go to Brockhampton Press and its managing editor, Mr. E. A. Roker. It was his brainwave to use previously scrapped off-cuts, from the highly popular *Picture Post* magazine, to produce child's hand-size cartoon booklets, measuring about three by six inches, and he engaged Enid to write the first script. She suggested, at their meeting in bomb-scarred London, that a mouse might provide a good central character and within a few days had completed outline stories. By late 1942, ten thousand copies of *Mary Mouse and the Dolls House*, printed in two colours and selling at a shilling each, were on the market. The whole project proved to be a resounding success, for its very Lilliputian size endeared the book at once to young children and other titles quickly followed. The popularity of this format was such that eventually several reprints and new titles were printed at the same time so that the publishers could keep up with their readers' voracious demands. By 1966 the sale of books in this series had run to more than a million and one parent complained that her child so loved one particular book she had refused to be parted from it and it was now worn down to 'three-quarters of its normal size'. Other companies took up the lucrative idea and similar strip picture books, written by Enid, were put on the market.

Hugh had put his name on the reserve list of officers prior to the outbreak of war, despite Enid's protests, but it was not until the early spring of 1940 that he was once again in uniform — if only in a part-time capacity at first. With events across the Channel forcing the British Army into retreat and his beloved country in jeopardy, Hugh could not ignore Anthony Eden's call to civilians to take up arms and he was soon organising — and was finally put in command of — the local battalion of the Home Guard. After this had been running efficiently for a few months he agreed to take up other duties elsewhere, but Enid did not take kindly to this decision. She could see no reason why Hugh should have decided to leave both herself and Newnes, particularly when, in spite of the war, everything seemed to be going so well for them both. She pleaded and cajoled but to no avail. At length she realised that, this time, her husband was not to be swayed by words or tears. She felt rejected and unhappy and, surprisingly, very much alone without him beside her at Green Hedges. Even Dorothy could offer little consolation, for now her nursing services were even more in demand and meetings between the two friends consequently became fewer as the war progressed. There seemed nothing for it but to continue to work at her writing, and the stories that were generally set in a less troubled world, undisturbed by wars and separations.

Hugh meanwhile had rejoined his old regiment — the Royal Scots Fusiliers — and was soon posted to Dorking in Surrey as

Commandant of the No. 1 War Office School of Instructors for the Home Guard. His prime function was to organise weekly courses for officers of the South Eastern Command on the use of small arms and, as with everything else he undertook, he gave himself wholeheartedly to his task.

After a few weeks, Enid became more reconciled to his absence — especially now that she was able to tell her readers that he, too, was 'serving his country' and she commented, as far as she was able, on his movements to and from Green Hedges:

'Our Daddy gets home once every week now, did I tell you? So we are always pleased when Thursdays come. We are lucky to have him stationed near enough to see us. He comes home in the most enormous army car I have ever seen. Really it hardly gets in at the big gates . . .'

During that hot summer of 1940, the German air raids started, and although no bombs fell close to the house at Beaconsfield, the family at Green Hedges could hear the noise from the anti-aircraft guns and other activity coming from the direction of London. One of her columns told of how, during a particularly noisy night, she had taken her daughters into the air-raid shelter at the back of the house and, 'much to their delight', had tucked them up on the seats there, with blankets and rugs, until the morning. Many of her readers' experiences at that time were not so happy — as was evident from some of the letters she was receiving from teachers, telling of the long hours their young charges were having to spend in cold, damp and poorly-lit shelters. The time was often whiled away with stories read out by their mothers or teachers — and Enid's books were often first choice among these children. 'I like to think I am with you in that way, when you are waiting underground for the all-clear to go . . .' she wrote, commenting on these letters, in a December column. 'I only wish I could come myself and tell you stories — that would be fun for you and fun for me, too!' . . . But her main source of amusement by that time came from another quarter.

Imogen and Gillian were now both at school during the day

and after they had gone to bed Enid did not always feel like taking up her work again and the evenings seemed to pass slowly, with neither Hugh nor Dorothy there to keep her company. There were still several unattached men living in the neighbourhood and it pleased her that one or two in particular appeared to seek out her company. Although she was used by this time to a certain amount of adulation over her work, it was a boost to her morale, with Hugh away, to have members of the opposite sex paying court to her and she did not discourage their attentions.

Hugh was also not without alternative company at that time. While on a visit to the War Office in the late summer of 1940, he had chanced upon Ida Crowe — a novelist he had first met at Newnes — working in the Records Office. As he was in the process of recruiting staff, he had asked Ida if she would care to join him at Dorking and she had readily agreed.

With two such highly-strung, possessive people as Enid and Hugh, such a situation was bound to prove inflammatory and the tinder appears to have been ignited during Hugh's first Christmas leave.

No one knows exactly what passed between the Pollocks at that time. Enid had seemed excited about his homecoming, and for several weeks beforehand had told her readers that he would be back at Green Hedges for a week and would be able to 'put up the Christmas decorations as usual' — but she made no reference to 'our Daddy' in any of her subsequent columns.

After the breakdown of a marriage, recriminations on both sides are commonplace and it is always difficult to gauge the truth, but Hugh told Ida years later that one of his staff at Green Hedges had given him disturbing information about the way his wife had been entertaining men in his absence — and to someone whose previous marriage had come to an end through similar circumstances during the First World War, such news must have come as a great shock. On the other hand, Enid also confided to Dorothy at a later date that she had been upset by an anonymous telephone caller whose only words had been: 'Don't let Ida crow over you' — a pun worthy of Enid herself. But, whatever the truth of the matter, their relationship reached a crisis point that

Christmas, from which it was never to recover. Hugh returned to Dorking in a thoughtful and depressed frame of mind and told Ida, although he gave no reasons at the time, that it had not been a 'good' leave. Enid plunged back into her work and sought consolation from one admirer in particular, who seemed only too willing to provide the diversion she needed.

But the marriage might, perhaps, have been saved even then, if Dorothy had not had a few days' holiday during the spring of 1941 and, unwittingly, been instrumental in introducing Enid to the man who was soon to replace all others in her affections.

Dorothy had arrived at Green Hedges to find, to her dismay, that her friend appeared to have become deeply involved with a rather dubious and unscrupulous character — more interested in Enid's money and position than in the woman herself. To get her away from what she felt to be an impossible and dangerous situation, and hoping that a change of scene might bring Enid to her senses, Dorothy suggested that they should both take a few days' holiday with her sister Betty at Budleigh Salterton in Devon. Some doctor friends from Betty's prc-war days at Twickenham were also there on a golfing holiday and they were invited over one evening for a game of bridge. With them was a middle-aged surgeon from one of the London hospitals, Kenneth Darrell Waters, and from the moment of their meeting, Enid knew that there was now no chance of any reconciliation with Hugh, and all interest in the other man she had left behind at Beaconsfield faded.

There is little doubt that the attraction between them was immediate and mutual. Kenneth was captivated by the vibrant dark-haired woman whose quick brain and witty exchanges so enlivened the evening for everyone, and Enid was flattered and excited by the obvious attentions of the tanned, good-looking doctor sitting opposite her at the bridge table. They arranged to meet the following day and the rest of the holiday was spent in each other's company. From then on, events moved quickly. Within a few weeks of returning home, they were meeting regularly at a London flat which Enid had rented under Dorothy's name, and Kenneth became a frequent visitor to Green Hedges in Hugh's absence.

After the disastrous Christmas leave, Hugh had also become romantically involved with Ida Crowe, but he continued to come home from time to time — despite Enid now having put his clothes into the spare room and the relationship between them being anything but happy. The young Austrian maid did her best to cover up for her mistress when Hugh returned home unexpectedly, but it was not long before he discovered the real reason for his wife's frequent overnight visits to London and he told Enid that he proposed to start divorce proceedings against her. Enid, however, had also become aware of Hugh's own involvement with Ida in Dorking and, after much discussion between them, it was agreed that the position should be reversed and Enid should be allowed to present the petition against him. Hugh later told Ida that he had consented to this on the understanding that after the divorce there would be no animosity between them and he would be allowed free access to his daughters. Meanwhile, Kenneth's wife was also obtaining a divorce and Enid was careful to ensure that she would not be implicated.

Her divorce decree was granted in December 1942 and made absolute in June of the following year, by which time Kenneth was also free to re-marry. The wedding took place on October 20th, 1943, at the City of Westminster Register Office — six days prior to Hugh's marriage to Ida at the City of London Register Office. For the past year, Hugh had been in the eastern United States as an adviser on static defence and had not seen his two young daughters since his departure from England in June 1942, when Gillian had walked with him to the station at Beaconsfield, hating as always to say goodbye to the father who loved her so dearly and whom she so closely resembled.

There was nothing unusual about fathers being away from home during those war years and Enid had given no hint that anything was amiss, so the first her elder daughter was to hear of the true situation was a few days before her mother's marriage to Kenneth, when she made a special visit to Gillian's boarding school to break the news. Imogen was told later, in the nursery, with her nanny. Both girls were upset at the time, but they loved and respected their mother and, as they had not seen their own father for some time, it was not long before 'Uncle Kenneth' was accepted as Hugh's replacement. They accepted also, Enid's later decision to change their surname to that of Darrell Waters 'so that we can all be one family'. But this, and her repeated refusal to allow him to visit his children, was something that Hugh was never to forget or forgive.

The war was driving more trivial matters from the notice of the Press and it was easy for Enid to slide into her new life without any hint of the divorce reaching her wide readership. By the time the feature writers were again taking note of her activities, 'Enid Blyton' was already firmly established as the devoted wife of a London surgeon, living with their two young daughters at Green Hedges — an image which was soon to become well known throughout the world.

CHAPTER

X

KENNETH WAS FIFTY-ONE YEARS OF AGE ON HIS MARRIAGE TO ENID. An active, virile man, he was fond of the open air and many sporting activities, all of which he entered into with vigour and enthusiasm. His enjoyment of these was in no way marred by an acute disability which must have been a considerable handicap to him in his career. An exploding shell at the Battle of Jutland during the First World War had permanently impaired his hearing, but his skill as a surgeon had taken him to his position as senior consultant and Deputy Medical Superintendent at St. Stephen's Hospital, Chelsea.

There were no children by his first marriage, but he readily accepted Enid's as his own and the understanding and kindness which he showed them did much to bring about their acceptance of him as a father. He had long been a familiar figure to them both, for he had already spent holidays with them at Swanage, taken Imogen's tonsils out in the nursery at Green Hedges in the spring of 1942, and stayed at the house so often prior to the wedding that it seemed to make little difference to their lives when he moved in permanently. By the time Imogen had joined Gillian at boarding school some twelve months later, the household was beginning to settle down into its new pattern — though for a while Enid and Kenneth were still in the process of adjusting to their new marital state.

Enid had for some years now been used to getting her own way and running her life as she chose. Kenneth was also a man accustomed to being in command and he, too, wanted a say over affairs in which he considered he had a part, and during their early married life, heated, stormy exchanges between them were commonplace as each sought to dominate the other. When Enid eventually realised that her husband could be as stubborn as herself, she found a better way of overcoming his obstinacy than trying to counteract it with harsh words. By using all her feminine wiles and coaxing, she was soon able to manipulate any situation her way — all the while letting him believe that he still retained the upper hand. She brought him more and more into her affairs and found, to her surprise, that not only did he enjoy this, but that it was a relief to have him share some of her problems. She knew that in Kenneth she had a devoted husband upon whom she could always rely and with him beside her as an ever-willing prop to her confidence, she felt she could achieve anything.

But Enid also brought a considerable happiness into Kenneth's life. He was immensely proud of her achievements and grateful that she loved and appeared to need him as much as he did her.

One of the most rewarding facets of their relationship from their first meeting was that in Enid he had found someone with whom he could freely converse. His hearing aid, in those early days, was of the primitive, trumpet type and he found it difficult to follow conversations with most people, but Enid's clearly enunciated speech — something she had acquired during her teaching days — he was able to pick up instantly. They would talk together for hours in the evenings and on those days when she had been on business trips to London he would always look forward to her return and the perceptive and hilarious accounts of her meetings there. She was a talented mimic and on these occasions would put on such a superb solo act for his benefit, impersonating the voices and actions of those she had seen, that he would invariably finish up laughing until the tears ran down his cheeks.

They shared many interests in common, including gardening — which was just as well, for during the first summer of their marriage they found themselves without a gardener and had to tackle all the work themselves. There was always a great deal to do for it was a large garden and during the months when the war-time 'double summer-time' gave them extra daylight hours, it was not unusual for them to be seen working out there in the evenings from eight-thirty until midnight. Such strenuous activity for Enid, however, was brought to an end in the early spring of 1945 when she discovered she was pregnant.

They were both overjoyed at the prospect of a child and were bitterly disappointed when, five months later, following a fall, she miscarried. 'The tragedy is,' Enid wrote later to a friend, 'it would have been the son Kenneth wanted so badly.'

One of her happiest discoveries about her new husband was that he was genuinely interested in her work. Each evening she would read out to him what she had been writing during the day, and after a while he took to opening a bottle of champagne on the completion of each new book. He never ceased to marvel at the apparent ease with which she handled her business and private affairs but, as a doctor, he was also concerned lest she overtax her obviously active brain. In addition to her regular features she was producing during the late 'forties and early 'fifties some twenty books a year, and he felt his worries over her were justified when she confessed to being unable to sleep each time she embarked upon a new story. While her characters were being established, she told him, they would 'walk about' in her head, take over her dreams and give her little rest until she had got back to her typewriter the following day.

She frequently attempted to analyse the formation of her stories and described the creative process, as far as she was able, in a protracted correspondence with psychologist Peter McKellar,* during the researches for his book *Imagination and Thinking* (Cohen and West, 1957):

> I shut my eyes for a few minutes, with my portable typewriter on my knee; I make my mind a blank and wait — and then, as clearly as I would see real children my characters stand before

* See Appendix 9.

me in my mind's eye... The story is enacted almost as if I had a private cinema screen there...

She would know the names of the characters that appeared almost at once, and though she might see them beside an old house or at the seaside, she was never certain at this stage how the story would progress. Once the first sentence had been put to paper, however, the rest unfolded 'like cotton from a reel'. But occasionally, if she had been interrupted, the thread would break and she would have to go back and begin the sequence again. Enid's staff also knew that noise of any kind distracted her and that if her strict working routine were to be disturbed her quick temper would flare and everyone in the household would suffer. Kenneth, perhaps more than anyone, made allowances for her temperament and the pressures under which she worked and did what he could to ease the tensions, but others were not prepared to be so tolerant — as was evident by an episode, a few months after Enid's marriage, which resulted in a ten-year break in her long and intimate friendship with Dorothy.

Although Dorothy, for religious reasons, had been upset by Enid's divorce and remarriage, and had not attended the wedding, there was still a deep bond of affection between them, and it was Enid whom she rang up, in some distress, when she and four members of her family were bombed out of their London home early in 1944. On the telephone Enid had seemed only too willing to have them all stay at Green Hedges but when they arrived her manner towards them changed. She made little effort to disguise her annoyance over the upheaval the five extra people were causing, both to her household and her writing, and thereafter made their life so unpleasant that within two days they decided to pack their bags and leave. Enid made no apology for her behaviour and Dorothy, who had never before sought her help, could not easily forget the treatment her relatives had received, at a time when they particularly needed the sympathy and understanding that Enid always professed to have. Over the years Dorothy had never failed to come to Enid's aid when summoned — whether to give reassurance and counsel over emotional matters or to help in moments of domestic crisis, when she would stand in for cook, maid or nanny. She was used, by this time, to her friend's uncertain moods and understood something of the heavy burdens her writing life imposed upon her, but on this occasion she felt Enid had gone too far.

There were no further meetings after that until 1954, when some bonds for Gillian and Imogen, over which Dorothy had acted as trustee, matured, and having re-established contact, they took up their friendship again, but it was never to return to its previous intimacy. A curious aspect of this affair is that Enid should have thought the ill-starred visit of Dorothy and her family worthy of a mention in her *Teachers' World* column. Apologising for not answering her correspondence that week she wrote:

'I have had such a busy week. Five people who had been bombed out of their house suddenly came to me with their kitten, so, as you can imagine, I have not had much time to do anything beyond getting beds for them and looking after them . . .'

As she was unlikely to have done much of either — for her household staff would have coped with such an emergency — perhaps Bobs' letter of the same date was nearer the truth of the matter:

'We have had a houseful of people this week and everywhere I went I bumped into somebody . . .'

Enid could be very convincing in explaining away actions which she knew did not show her to advantage and Kenneth seemingly accepted whatever explanation she gave for the family's sudden departure. As far as he was concerned, his wife could do no wrong and he brooked no criticism of her or jokes at her expense — as many recipients of solicitors' letters in the years that followed were to discover.

A notable example of this was his strong complaint to the B.B.C. in January 1952 over some lines in the comedy series *Take*

It From Here. Actress Joy Nichols had observed that her little boy
was never happier than when he was 'curled up in front of the fire
with Enid Blyton' and Dick Bentley, as a schoolboy, had retorted:
'Ah, now that whacks reading any day. We got a kitchen maid
here who always . . .' Schoolmaster Jimmy Edwards had interrupted: 'Hey, you're not supposed to know about the kitchen
maid . . .' Kenneth subsequently received an apology and the
offending lines were deleted from the script. But his remarks at
the time that he and his wife had been 'disgusted' to hear her
name mentioned in such a context when she was, after all, a
'world famous children's author', were quickly taken up and
widely quoted by the national and overseas Press.

Throughout his life he continued to be as protective over her
as Hugh had been, shielding her from much that was unpleasant
and placing her wishes — and welfare — above that of his own.
When he retired in 1957, he would have preferred to live in a
warmer climate for health reasons, but Enid did not like the idea
of leaving England and her publishers, even for holidays, and the
couple remained at Green Hedges. Only once did they travel
abroad together and that was in the late autumn of 1948, when
they joined friends for a three-week semi-business holiday in New
York, sailing out on the *Queen Elizabeth* and back on the *Queen
Mary* — an experience which Enid, as usual, put to good use as
background material for stories.

The Mystery Island — the American version of her *Island of
Adventure* (published by Macmillans in 1944) — had won a Boys'
Club of America award for one of the six most popular junior
books published in that country during 1947, and her New York
publishers used the occasion of her visit to introduce her to book-
sellers, librarians and reviewers at a large cocktail party given in
her honour. The *New York Times* of November 14th described
her as 'a bright-eyed, breathless Englishwoman' who, 'between
gasps at the reckless speed of the Manhattan taxicabs', had explained how she managed to turn out fifteen to twenty children's
books a year: '. . . All it takes, really, is imagination.' The
American Press, generally, was not as tactful or as kind to Enid
as their British counterparts had been up to then and the holiday

was not altogether a success. In a letter to a publisher friend shortly after her return, she had nothing but praise for American business efficiency:

'I learnt more in ten days over there than I would have learnt in ten years here ...'

But she had not been so impressed by her agent in New York, whose services she had dispensed with on the spot:

'I walked out and he was very angry. But I could place my books far better in America myself, now I know the ropes, if only I were there long enough ...'

She told her daughters later that, although she had enjoyed certain aspects of her visit, she had been 'deeply shocked' by the pace and toughness of the American scene generally. She never again ventured overseas for business or pleasure, and holidays from then on were usually spent playing golf with Kenneth in Dorset.

Kenneth had always encouraged her to join him in a variety of outdoor activities for he felt that, whether working in the garden together or playing tennis on the court at Green Hedges, she was away for a while from the pressures of her writing life. A year or so after their marriage he had introduced her to golf — his own favourite method of relaxation — and she had taken up the game with characteristic enthusiasm. Under Kenneth's expert tuition, for he had at one time been a scratch player, she soon achieved a handicap of twenty-six and later managed to reduce this to eighteen. They played regularly once or twice a week at the Wentworth Club in Surrey until 1951, when they decided to acquire their own eighteen-hole course at Studland Bay, close to the sea and set among the Purbeck Hills in Dorset. This was an area in which they had spent many happy holidays together and something of her feeling for this beautiful part of Dorset is expressed in a poem written during one of her spring holidays in later years.* Kenneth no doubt saw the investment in this club

* See Appendix 1.

138

as yet another means of getting Enid to relax. To a certain extent he succeeded, for although she usually allotted some part of each day to her writing, she always enjoyed her thrice-yearly golfing holidays and returned to Green Hedges feeling refreshed.

Purchasing the lease of this club was one of the first business transactions to be dealt with under the name of Enid's own company — Darrell Waters Limited — formed the previous year to help co-ordinate her increasingly complex publishing and financial interests. At the time of her marriage, she had employed neither agent nor secretary, preferring to deal direct with her publishers, and she handled her affairs shrewdly and competently. She insisted — even when the paper shortage was still acute after the war — that most contracts should contain a clause guaranteeing a minimum first printing of twenty-five thousand copies, and quoting her own terms with regard to rights. By the late 1940s, however, she was contracted to more than twenty British publishing houses apart from those overseas, and it was apparent that some other arrangements would have to be made to help her over the intricacies of her business affairs. She was advised to form a limited company specifically for this purpose and the inaugural meeting of Darrell Waters Limited subsequently took place at her solicitor's office in Bolton Street, London, on March 31st, 1950. Enid was in the chair and her board of directors consisted of Kenneth, their financial and business adviser, Eric Rogers, accountant John Basden and solicitor Arnold Thirlby. The formation of this company did much to lessen the strain of managing her already very considerable monetary assets, but she insisted that she herself should continue to handle the actual manuscripts with the publishers.

She had learnt much over the years, from both Hugh and her other editors, about book production and was by this time treated with enough respect by the majority of her publishers for her to be granted a say over the illustrators for her stories and the layout of her books. She insisted always on wide margins, good line spacing, large, clear print and plenty of pictures. She particularly favoured all-round jackets for, as she wrote to one of her publishers:

'It does give an artist a chance to get at the heart of a book and display it on his jacket.'

The appearance of the spine she also felt was important:

'If you have an attractive picture underneath the title the book will immediately catch the eye of the child for, after all, that is what is usually seen first . . .'

Of Eileen Soper, who illustrated many of her books over a period of some twenty years she wrote — to Noel Evans, of Evans Brothers in 1949:

'I don't need to see roughs of *any* of her sketches. She and I have worked together for so long now and I have always found her accurate and most dependable — in fact excellent in every way . . .'

This credit where she felt credit was due was typical of Enid at all levels, for publishers were surprised and pleased when she thanked them for their part in a 'good production'.

All her business matters with her publishers were discussed either in person or through her distinctive, hand-written letters — by now very well known to all who had regular dealings with her. The recipients never failed to be astonished when they discovered that she kept no copies of these letters, but could usually rely on her extraordinarily retentive memory should she have to refer to the contents again. George Greenfield, who eventually became one of her literary agents in 1954, described Enid at that time as having a 'card index' mind, for he had known her to ring up and refer to certain paragraphs of letters she had written six or even twelve months previously — and she could always remember the terms under which she had signed contracts with editors and publishers.

Enid realised that she had been fortunate in being able to establish herself as a best-selling writer during the war years, despite the obvious publishing difficulties and that this was in no small measure due to the links with her readers of *Sunny Stories* and

Teachers' World, and the faith of her publishers in her eventual sales. Even at the most deperate period of shortage it was rumoured that one house allotted sufficient paper for the printing of some hundred and fifty thousand copies of a single title in a popular series and others set aside enough to print between twenty-five and a hundred thousand copies of each of her new books. This certainty over her selling powers was evidently justified for no sooner were most of these on the market than they were out of stock — as her readers would continually inform her. She commented on this in several war-time editorial letters in *Sunny Stories* and went on to suggest that if the children could not obtain the books they wanted, they should either try the public libraries for other titles or borrow from their friends: 'I'm sorry I can't help you more,' she wrote in March 1944, 'but I can't get the books myself, sometimes! You shall have as many as you like after the war.' Once the restrictions were over, she soon set about keeping this promise and the relinquishing, in the autumn of 1945, of the column she had written for *Teachers' World* for almost twenty-three years, gave her the opportunity she needed to widen still further the range of her writing activities.

She decided to wind up her column on the retirement of Mr. E. H. Allen, who had taken her first contribution to the magazine and had continued to follow her career with friendly interest throughout his editorship. Enid disliked changes not of her own making, and did not feel inclined to fall in with any fresh ideas that a new editor might bring, and her last 'Letter from Green Hedges' appeared on November 14th, 1945:

I think the time has now come for me to stop writing these long letters to you each week. We have had some lovely times together, and I have made thousands of boy and girl friends, and hundreds of teacher friends too. We have hunted for flowers together, watched the birds, looked for twigs and berries, collected all kinds of things. You have learnt all about my many, many pets and I have heard about yours. We have been very good friends, and we always shall be. Although I shall not be writing *to* you anymore, you know that I shall be writing *for* you! I shall write you many books, you will have your *Sunny Stories* and some of you will read my tales in many papers. You can always write to me if you want to. Go on doing all the things we have done together, won't you, work hard, be kind and just, be my friend as much as ever. I shall be here at Green Hedges just the same, with my children, my pets and my garden — writing books for you all as hard as ever I can . . .

Seven years later Enid also withdrew from *Sunny Stories* after twenty-six years as its editor — though this time there was no letter of farewell. She had already circulated teachers, librarians and educationalists and advertised widely in newspapers and other periodicals that she would soon be starting up her own fortnightly magazine. It would be, she told them, the only one from then on to be written entirely by herself and to contain 'all the stories the children love best'.

The first edition of this *Enid Blyton Magazine* appeared on March 18th, 1953 — some two months before the Coronation of Queen Elizabeth II — a circumstance which Enid was quick to follow up with a six-part serial *The Story of Our Queen*, and a special photographic competition with seats to watch the Coronation as first prize. In a later issue she suggested readers might like to send their own personal Christmas messages of affection and loyalty to the new monarch. This resulted in a special leather-bound volume, containing a letter from Enid and twelve selected greetings from the hundreds received, being despatched to the Queen.

The new magazine, which was published by Evans Brothers, contained an editorial letter, puzzles, competitions, a nature-lovers' corner, and serials, short stories and strip cartoons featuring characters already well known to Enid's regular readers. As with her previous publications, the *Enid Blyton Magazine* was also used as a means of encouraging children to help with several worthy causes and regular news was given of four clubs specifically formed for this purpose.

In a 1957 article describing these sponsored clubs, Enid wrote that she felt young people *should* help animals and other children:

. . . they are not interested in helping adults; indeed, they think that adults themselves should tackle adult needs. But they are intensely interested in animals and other *children* and feel compassion for the blind boys and girls, and for the spastics who are unable to walk or talk . . .

Membership of her clubs, she explained, did not merely mean the wearing of a badge, it meant 'working for others, for no reward' and from all corners of the world she received hundreds of letters each week enclosing money and information on the many ingenious ways it had been raised. These children wrote of how they had saved their bus fares, helped with odd jobs, organised concerts, sales and fêtes and the publishing of these letters acted as a further stimulus for other readers to do likewise.

The oldest and largest of the four clubs involved, was the Busy Bees — the junior section of the People's Dispensary for Sick Animals. Enid had been interested in this society since 1933, when she first started writing articles and short stories for its publications. She had frequently mentioned the work of the P.D.S.A. in her *Teachers' World* columns and when she became 'Queen Bee' of the Busy Bees in 1951, she encouraged membership still further through her letters in *Sunny Stories* and monthly contributions to its own magazine, *The Busy Bees News*. When she decided to give information about this club's activities in the *Enid Blyton Magazine*, some hundred thousand readers joined in less than three years.

The Famous Five Club originated through a series of books about the 'Famous Five' — four children and a dog — the first story of which was published by Hodder and Stoughton in the autumn of 1942. So popular did this series become that Enid was commissioned to write a fresh title each year and the *Fives* created such a following that regular readers of these books asked if they might form some kind of 'fan' club. Enid agreed, on the condition that the club should also serve some useful purpose and suggested that it might help raise funds for a Shaftesbury Society Babies Home in Beaconsfield, on whose local committee she had served for several years.

This home had been founded by a group of wealthy Beacons-field residents to house convalescent, deprived children from the East End of London, but when it was taken over by the Shaftes-bury Society in 1921, it was used mainly for boarding out pre-school infants in need of special care. Enid had first been introduced to the Home in 1945 and had subsequently taken to visiting it occasionally with toys and sweets for the children. When she became a committee member in 1948 she also began giving considerable financial help and interested herself still further in its activities. In 1950 alone, she made over by deed of gift her accumulated royalties on *Before I Go To Sleep* (Latimer House, 1947) — amounting to several thousand pounds — and other cheques followed once the Famous Five Club got under way in 1952. Despite her busy writing life, she made a point of visiting the Home regularly and always attending the monthly committee meetings, and was thus able to report in her magazine on the children's progress and how the money raised by the club was being spent. In time, members provided funds towards such amenities as the furnishing and equipment of a special 'Famous Five Ward', a paddling pool, playground, sun room, summer house and a host of other extras, including visits to the pantomime and contributions towards Christmas and birthday celebrations. Enid became chairman of the committee in 1954 and remained so until the closure of the Home in 1967, but the Famous Five Club, with a membership approaching two hundred and twenty thousand — and still rising steadily at the rate of some six thousand each year — has since provided a special Enid Blyton bed at Great Ormond Street Hospital and a mini-bus for disabled children at the Stoke Mandeville Hospital, near Aylesbury in Buckinghamshire.

Soon after launching her new magazine, Enid had visited one of the Sunshine Homes for Blind Babies — another cause in which she had always had a special interest — and mentioned the visit to her readers. She suggested that they might like to help her form a society to help raise funds for these blind children and asked for their assistance in choosing its name. Although 'Lamp-lighters' was the choice of many, Enid preferred 'The Sunbeam Society'

Hugh Pollock and Enid at the Attenborough house on their wedding day

Beside the pool at Elfin Cottage, their first home

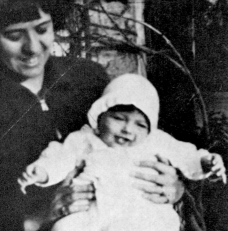

Enid and baby Gillian

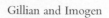

Gillian and Imogen

Gillian's miniature house
built by Dick Hughes

Beside the well at Old Thatch, with Bobs

for 'Sunbeams light up the dark places and bring joy and delight to everyone'. Within six years of the society being formed, its yellow badge — depicting the head of a blind child turned towards the sun — was worn by, according to Enid, 'over 22,000 of my warmest-hearted and generous readers'.

The main object of the Enid Blyton Magazine Club was to help the young spastic children, who daily attended a special centre in Cheyne Walk, Chelsea, London. This centre had been the subject of a Week's Good Cause broadcast appeal made by Enid in May 1955 and, once again, the response from her readers to the suggestion of forming a club on the centre's behalf was overwhelming. Ten thousand requests for membership were made within the first month and by January 1957 the club had recruited its hundred thousandth member. Evans Brothers decided to mark the occasion by inviting Enid and some of the children who had worked for the club to a celebration party at the magazine's headquarters at Montague House in London's Russell Square. There was a special cake and Enid was presented with an initialled and dated gold replica of the Magazine Club badge. Funds raised by this club eventually helped to furnish a hostel attached to the centre and to provide various other extra amenities. Enid broadcast two further appeals on behalf of these spastic children and in 1960 was elected a Vice-President of the Friends of the Centre — by which time the Club's membership had increased to around a hundred and fifty thousand.

When she decided to close the magazine in September 1959,* Enid was determined that this would not mean that her clubs would also cease to function without their 'headquarters'. With the exception of the Famous Five Club, which was then handled by the books' publisher, all were kept alive through the organisations they had helped — and by the Enid Blyton diaries (first published by Collins in 1950) which continued to give news of all four and the charities they supported. Monetarily, they had contributed between them around £35,000 during the magazine's six years of life — in those days a sum which, Enid told her

* See Appendix 5.

readers in her last editorial letter, 'even grown-ups would find difficult to raise'

But the charities supported by the four clubs were not the only causes to benefit through Enid's interest. She made mention from time to time in her magazine of other organisations needing help, often following up in her 'letter' any broadcast appeals she had made. After one such appeal on behalf of a home for retarded boys, the secretary wrote: '. . . To us, whose children are usually at the tail end of public sympathy, the response was nothing short of miraculous . . .'

Enid's attitudes, generally, had by this time become well known. Each new year she would urge her readers to make 'Be kind and love one another' their resolution for the coming twelve months; '. . . kindness of heart means you cannot possibly do or say anything that would hurt anyone or upset them . . .'

She had for some years made regular visits to exhibitions and large bookshops and stores to talk to groups of children and she would invariably weave a moral into the stories she told them on these occasions. Such was her personal magnetism and charm that even the most unruly bunch of youngsters — sometimes numbering a hundred or more — would within moments of her appearance be quietened down into a well-behaved, adoring audience, listening and absorbing all that she had to tell them. This effect upon those she met was by no means confined to children only, for even cynical adults at other gatherings (such as the Foyle's Literary Lunch of 1947, at which she was a guest speaker) were won over by her personal charisma and left in no doubt as to her sincerity over everything she professed and her dedication to her young readers.

Her letters and articles, giving her views on a variety of topics, appeared regularly in the national press and she was frequently being quoted — both at home and overseas — on anything pertaining to children and their care. At the opening of an exhibition of mothercraft at the Central Hall, Westminster in November 1949, she was widely reported for her criticism of the Government's call to married women to work in factories as she felt this would mean 'abandoning children to the care of others', and in all her interviews both on the radio and with the Press, she stressed the need for a secure home background and the part a mother should play in achieving this. She wrote of her own family in *The Story of My Life* (Pitkin, 1952):

> We all have a sense of humour. We are all (thank goodness!) good-tempered. Nobody sulks, nobody complains, nobody is unkind. But that, of course, is largely a matter of upbringing. Spoilt children are selfish, complaining and often conceited. But whose fault is that? It is the mother, always the mother, that makes the home. The father does his share, he holds the reins too — but it is the mother who makes a happy, contented home. She is the centre of it. She should always be there to welcome the children home, to see to them and listen to them. I was lucky to have a gift that could be used at home. I could not have left my husband or my children and gone out into the world to make my career. All true mothers will know what I mean when I say that . . .

In a church magazine of the early 'fifties, she answered a reader's question about the necessity of religious teaching in bringing up a child:

> . . . He can certainly be brought up without it — but not 'properly' . . . Religious teaching provides a moral backbone throughout life; it gives a child invincible weapons with which to fight any evils, any problems he meets . . .

In early editions of the *Enid Blyton Magazine*, she encouraged readers to follow a daily course of Bible readings, either through the International Bible Reading Association or the Scripture Union, and she put her name to special issues of Coronation and Christmas Bibles — stocks of which very quickly ran out. This apparent interest in the spiritual welfare of the young, together with her already popular books of prayers and Bible stories, resulted in further commissions from ecclesiastical journals and an invitation from a church in the Midlands to preach a sermon at a special children's service.

She made visits to juvenile courts, commenting afterwards on what she had seen and heard; wrote a booklet in story form, *The Child who was Chosen*, to help adoptive parents tell their children 'how and why they were adopted', and by the late 'fifties, there were few situations relating to children which she had not covered in one way or another through her writings or talks. Even her views on child murderers were expressed in a poem written during Government discussions over the abolition of capital punishment* and she let it be known in no uncertain terms in a *Church of England Newspaper* article in the autumn of 1950, how she felt about those who corrupt the young:

> I want to take up the whip that Jesus once used when he drove out from the Temple the polluters of holiness and goodness. I want to whip out those who pollute the innocence and goodness in the hearts of children . . .

She deplored that violence was so often depicted in 'American type' comics and on the cinema screens, and wrote at length, in the same *Church of England Newspaper* article, on the need for more films to be made specifically for and about children:

> . . . It cannot be said too often that the cinema is one of the most formidable powers for good or evil in this world, and most especially for children. Its great danger lies in the fact that it can make evil so attractive, so tempting and irresistible. Adults are mature, they can resist the attraction portrayed if they wish to. But children are not mature, they are credulous, they believe whole-heartedly what they see. As the twig is bent, so the tree will grow, and the false world portrayed in many adult films must have warped great numbers of developing young minds . . .

The 'best writers for children' did not deal in murders, rapes, violence, blood, torture and ghosts — these things did not belong to the children's world — and it was 'perfectly possible' to write any amount of adventure, mystery or 'home' stories for children

* See Appendix 6.

without them and yet keep a child 'enchanted and absorbed for hours'. She summed up the 'books that children love most' as those containing first-rate stories, well and convincingly told, with plenty of action, humour and well-defined characters — with animals as their friends or companions: 'Children find it easy to identify themselves with animals, and love them in their books'. These stories always contained 'absolutely sound morals' and it was a very heartening fact that the writers who held these convictions 'were the ones whose books the children clamoured for most'.

That her own books fulfilled all these requirements, she had no doubt, as is clear from a letter to Mr. S. C. Dedman, which was reproduced in the Library Association Record for September 1949* and by the introduction to her *Complete List of Books*, privately published in December 1950. In this she insisted that she did not write merely to entertain, 'as most writers for adults can quite legitimately do'. She was now aware of her responsibilities as 'a best-selling writer for children' and she intended to use the influence she wielded wisely, no matter if, at times, she was labelled 'moralist' or 'preacher':

... my public, bless them, feel in my books a sense of security, an anchor, a sure knowledge that right is right, and that such things as courage and kindness deserve to be emulated. Naturally the morals or ethics are *intrinsic* to the story — and therein lies their true power . . .

Although her two hundred school readers, teaching encyclopaedias and manuals are not included in this impressive catalogue of two hundred and fifty of her published works, this *Complete List of Books* shows something of the variety of her work up to that time. There were collections of short stories and annuals — which were mostly made up of items she had used previously in either *Sunny Stories* or *Teachers' World* — books of plays and poetry, a religious section of 'simply told Bible stories and prayers', and several titles under the headings of 'Farm', 'Circus',

* See Appendix 7.

'School', 'Family', 'Mystery', 'Adventure' and 'Nature'. In her Foreword Enid explained her reasons for writing so many books:

> It is not usual for one author to produce such a number of books, nor is it usual to produce such a variety. Authors tend to keep to one subject, and, where children are concerned, to one *age* of child only ... But my difficulty is, and always has been, that I love all ages of children from babyhood to adolescence ...

As she was also 'interested in all the things they love', it was inevitable that she should write 'every kind of book there is for children of all age groups'.

CHAPTER

XI

FOLLOWING THE SUCCESS OF HER FIRST FULL-LENGTH CHILDREN'S adventure story — *The Secret Island* — in 1938, Enid had written a second book involving the same characters: 'Jack', 'Mike', 'Peggy', 'Nora' and little 'Prince Paul', and this proved as popular as its predecessor. She had by this time realised from her readers' letters that these fast-moving, exciting tales, woven around familiar characters with whom the children could identify, had a far wider appeal than she first supposed and she set about writing other full-length stories on similar lines. These proved so successful that each developed into series, whose followers were soon demanding that she should produce annually fresh 'adventures' or 'mysteries' for one or another of their favourite characters. Among those destined to remain most popular were *The Famous Five* (Hodder and Stoughton); *The Secret Seven* (Brockhampton Press); the *Adventure* series (Macmillan); the *Mystery* series (Methuen) and the *'Barney' Mystery* books (Collins). All these consistently sold many thousands each year, both at home and overseas, and went into several reprints, including paperback editions, and some of the characters were taken up by commercial concerns to market toys, games and stationery.

By far the most successful of all the 'family adventure' books were the twenty-one stories Enid was eventually to write about 'Julian', 'Dick', 'Anne', 'George' and the dog 'Timmy' — *The Famous Five*. When she began this series in 1942 with *Five on a Treasure Island*, she only meant to write six books, but her readers had pleaded with her to increase this to twelve. Even this number, however, did not appear to satisfy the children and they wrote in their hundreds clamouring for more. By the time she had written the last book in the series — twenty-one years after the first — close on six million *Fives* books had been sold and this figure continued to grow with each year that passed, as a fresh generation of children began following the adventures. When paperback editions were brought out these alone increased sales still further by some sixty thousand on each title annually. Overseas the series proved equally successful. Within the first two years of Hachette publishing the books in France, a million copies had been sold there, and other countries — particularly Germany, her first overseas market — reported similar successes. A stage play, *The Famous Five*, ran for two Christmas seasons — at the Princes Theatre in London during 1955-56 and at the London Hippodrome the following year. Two books were made into films for the Children's Film Foundation: *Five on a Treasure Island*, produced by Rank Screen Services, was filmed on location in Dorset and screened throughout the British Isles and overseas in the late 'fifties. *Five have a Mystery to Solve* was made by Rayant Pictures Limited in 1963 and a Danish Company, Dimension Productions, filmed yet another two stories, some ten years later — *Five Go Adventuring Again* and *Five Get Into Trouble*.

Enid always acknowledged that 'George', the main character in this series, was based on a 'real person, now grown up', but only once did she reveal the true identity of this girl 'who so badly wanted to be a boy and acted as if she were'. The 'real' George, she wrote in *The Story of My Life*, had been 'short-haired, freckled, sturdy and snub-nosed ... bold and daring, hot-tempered and loyal' — and, like her counterpart, had also been sulky on occasions. At the head of the same page in the autobiography appears a clue to the true origin of George, though the description of her physical appearance would seem to belie it. Beside a photograph of Enid with her spaniel, Laddie (also portrayed as 'Loony' in another series), is a similarly posed drawing of George with her dog, Timmy. Was this a wry joke on Enid's part — or was she unaware of this photographic implication?

No one knows. But it was only in an unguarded moment, many years later, while discussing the *Fives'* popularity in France, that she eventually confessed to Rosica Colin, her foreign agent, that George was, in fact, based upon herself.

She did not always draw her characters or situations from life, but would sometimes find, after she had completed her story, that her 'undermind' (as she termed it) had unearthed long-forgotten memories of people and places, or she would recognise someone she knew in a character she thought she alone had created. Bill Cunningham (or 'Smugs' as he preferred to call himself), who appeared in all eight books of the *Adventure* series, was one example of this. She had met the original at an hotel in Swanage the summer before her marriage to Kenneth, and had found him amusing company She had laughed when he jokingly suggested that she put him into one of her books — just as he was, ,bald head and all' — and call him 'Bill Smugs of the Secret Service'. But when she came to write the first of a new series for Macmillan — *The Island of Adventure* — she found, to her surprise, that this engaging man had somehow appeared in her plot, along with four children — Jack, Philip, Dinah and Lucy-Ann — and Kiki, a talking parrot she also recognised from her childhood. She never saw the real Bill Cunningham again, but the fictional version became an important character throughout this popular series.

A jovial Police Inspector — Stephen Jennings — who first came into contact with Hugh during the organisation of the Beaconsfield Home Guard, little guessed when he was introduced to Enid that he, too, would soon become well known to millions of her readers as Inspector Jenks of the *Mystery* books. After meeting him she had, from time to time, sought his advice on plots which involved police procedure and when she began writing *The Mystery of the Burnt Cottage* in the late autumn of 1942, she asked if he would mind being brought into the story as the kindly, shrewd Inspector, who was a friend to the five main child characters. He had cheerfully agreed and from then on appeared in every one of the fifteen books that made up the series. He was amused to discover that when he was promoted, first to Chief Inspector and then to Superintendent, Enid saw to it that his fictional counterpart was similarly elevated. His only criticism to her of the stories was that he felt she had rather 'overdone' her portrayal of the other, entirely fictitious, policeman involved — the rather pompous and stupid Mr. Goon — all too often outwitted and sneered at by the 'Five Findouters': Fatty, Larry, Daisy, Pip and Bets.

Enid's ideas for stories came from countless sources, but a great many were undoubtedly sparked off by hearing of the exploits of real children — either from themselves or their parents. Ewart Wharmby, of Brockhampton Press, happened to mention to her, soon after their meeting in 1949, that his four children had just formed a 'secret' society, with very firm rules and a password designed to keep intruders from their ramshackle 'headquarters' — a shed at the bottom of the garden. She was greatly amused by his story and was quick to follow it up by a letter to his eldest son asking for further details, which he duly supplied. With her usual intuitive skill over the handling of such matters, she enclosed money along with her letter of thanks — 'to defray expenses' — and was delighted to hear later that this had been spent on a feast of 'jelly and chips' for the Wharmby secret society. But the rewards for Enid and Brockhampton Press were far more substantial, for out of this idea was created the first of the fifteen *Secret Seven* books, woven around the adventures of seven children and their dog, whose popularity both at home and overseas has only been surpassed by that of the *Famous Five*.

Other series with less 'adventurous' themes were more than holding their own by the early nineteen-fifties, particularly those written around a family, farm or school. Enid had chosen the unusual setting of a progressive, co-educational boarding school for a story about *The Naughtiest Girl in the School*, which she wrote during the early war years. Her readers' approval of both the serialisation of this in *Sunny Stories* and its later publication in book form prompted her, in two more books, to take Elizabeth, her main character, through to her final form at 'Whytleafe'. It also decided her to take up the suggestion of Alan White of Methuen that she should write other girls' school stories with a more conventional background. This resulted in two series for Methuen, centred around St. Clare's and Malory Towers, which Enid maintained were made up of a mixture of all the schools she had known 'a bit of one, a piece of another, a chip of a third!' Memories of her own schooldays and incidents related to her by her daughters 'of the games of lacrosse, hockey and tennis, the little spites and deceits of school life, the loyalty and generosities of friendships, and the never-ending impact of one character on another' were all recalled and transposed into what were to become immensely popular books, not only in her own country but overseas — and in Germany in particular.

Enid had a special reason for always remembering the writing of *Six Cousins of Mistletoe Farm* — one of her many successful 'family' books, for it was to be associated with an event within her own family which caused her great anxiety at the time. She had begun her initial negotiations over the book in April 1947, on an optimistic note, writing to Noel Evans of Evans Brothers:

> . . . It will be easy to have it in a country setting, of course — most of my books are, anyway. I will do it for ages 11-15, though I expect you realise that children of any age from six upwards will buy it! That's the snag about my books — no age limit really applies. I will write it for both boys and girls as I might as well get both markets . . .

She could not, she explained, start writing the story until the autumn — 'because I have so many *series* on hand at the moment . . . it's a pity I have no ghosts or I could set one or two at work!' But the book was destined to be delayed still further and her tight working schedule altered by a happening which, if only temporarily, halted Enid's writing activities. On October 12th, Noel Evans received a shorter letter than was usual from Enid to a publisher:

> . . . About the new book. I have had rather a shock. My little girl, Imogen, has developed infantile paralysis — yesterday. I had a specialist down and we took her up to Great Ormond Street Hospital late last night, poor child. She was very good

and brave but it was heartrending. There is paralysis of the left leg so far, but I am praying that it will not spread any more. This all means that I shall simply have to put my work on one side for a few weeks and be with her morning and afternoon in her private ward till I see how things go. So I must warn you that I do not see my way at the moment to getting the book done as soon as I hoped. I am dreadfully sorry, but I do feel a bit knocked over at the moment — it's so awful to see one's own child attacked like this — though I am hoping it will be one of the milder attacks and that it has been diagnosed early enough for us to prevent any desperate damage ...

Imogen made a good recovery but was in hospital for some months. When the danger had passed, Enid began work again and, knowing her twelve-year-old daughter's love of riding, suggested she might like to describe and name all the horses in a book she had just begun. This was *Six Cousins of Mistletoe Farm* and when it was despatched to the publishers just before Christmas, Enid requested that it should be dedicated to Imogen and mention should be made of her part in its writing.

In an article for *The Author* in 1958, Enid wrote that there were a 'dozen or more different types of stories for children — including adventure, mystery, fairy, school, nature, religious, pony and family' and she had tried them all, but her favourites were those centred around a family which, 'if told in the right way, would always sell as fast as any adventure . . .' But this could equally well have been said of anything she cared to tackle during those golden days of the 'forties and 'fifties. Her stories for young children, particularly those told in strip form like *Mary Mouse* and *Bom the Drummer*, were just as popular with the under-sevens as most of Enid's tales written for their older brothers and sisters. But topping the popularity poll among all her characters for the younger age group, from the moment he first made his appearance, was a friendly little fellow with a nodding head, whose name and Toyland adventures were to bring not only further fame and fortune to his creator, but a storm of criticism and controversy.

Early in 1949, David White of Sampson Low, Marston and

Company Ltd., the publisher of Enid's successful *Holiday Books*, was hoping to interest her in another series recently launched by his company. These books were dependent upon strong, central characters of a 'Disney-like' type, and David White was searching for an artist of sufficient calibre to carry such a series through with Enid. He happened to be looking through a batch of sample drawings, submitted to him by an agent, when he came across a sheet of what he later described as 'fantastically lively little people, beside tiny houses in the lee of bluebells as proportionately big as trees'. On making further enquiries, he discovered that not only had the drawings been submitted entirely by mistake, but they were already being used to illustrate booklets given away by a jam manufacturer, and were the work of a Dutchman — Harmsen Van Der Beek. Undeterred, and convinced of the potential of this artist, whose unique style had so impressed him, David White lost no time in summoning him from Holland and arranging a meeting with Enid.

From this first encounter, it was obvious to everyone present that the proposed collaboration was destined for success. Through an interpreter, for Van Der Beek's English was not good, David White explained that he would like to use the artist's unusual, continental-style toys and small people, with their distinctive houses and shops, as a visual background for a new series to be written by Enid — and from that moment writer and artist took over.

The first sight of Van Der Beek's drawings had excited Enid immensely. This tall, thin, rather mournful-looking man seemed to understand her own pictorial imagination and his vivid expressive illustrations both captivated and inspired her. She immediately described the central character she had 'seen' emerging from a background that she felt '*must* be Toyland' and the Dutchman, with a curious, palm-uppermost style of drawing, sketched in pencil a quaint, toy figure with long ball-topped hat over tousled head — exactly, Enid claimed, as she had visualised. Enthralled, she suggested other characters which were taken up by an enthusiastic Van Der Beek and by the time the meeting came to an end, both had a clear idea of the form the new series would take. On Monday, March 21st, 1949 — four days later — a small package arrived on the publisher's desk with the following letter:

. . . I have finished the first two Little Noddy Books, and here they are. I have written them with a view to giving Van Beek all the scope possible for his particular genius — toys, pixies, goblins, Toyland, brick-houses, dolls houses, toadstool houses, market-places — he'll really enjoy himself! I don't want to tell him how to interpret anything because he'll do it much better if he has a perfectly free hand — but as Noddy (the little nodding man) Big Ears the Pixie, and Mr. and Mrs. Tubby (the teddy bears) will probably feature in any further books, and will be 'important' characters as far as these books are concerned, I'd be very glad if he could sketch out these characters and let me see roughs. (He said he would do this for me.)

Now about the general title — at the moment this is 'All Aboard for Toyland', and I imagine we might have as a 'motif' a toy train rushing along crowded with passengers — going all round the jacket top, sides and bottom or something like that — to give the books a 'series' look. The specific titles (which will all be different of course) will each contain the name 'Noddy'. In the end, if they are very successful, they'll probably be referred to and ordered as the 'Noddy' books. What do you think about it?

David White's delight over the stories was matched by that of Van Der Beek. Within a few weeks of the Dutch artist's receiving them, he had replied to Enid's request for more detailed sketches of the main characters, with a letter which bore at its head the first fully-coloured illustrations of Noddy, Big Ears and their friends:

. . . Herewith I have the honour to present to you in pictures little Noddy, Big Ears, Mr. and Mrs. Tubby and some other characters from your stories, which reached me through Mrs. Sampson Low some days ago.

I have thoroughly enjoyed reading them and think they are

extraordinary (*sic*) amusing, especially for an illustrator, because every line gives new inspiration for an illustration. I sent to Mrs. Sampson Low a series of sketches of the characters as above and I sincerely hope that you'll like them. When you possibly have any particular ideas in your mind please let me know, as I can always make some alterations. I would be greatly pleased if my collaboration would contribute to the success of your books. Yours sincerely, Harmsen Van Beek.

The first story — *Little Noddy Goes to Toyland* — was published later the same year and its sales exceeded all expectations. Children were instantly attracted to Van Der Beek's distinctive drawings and seemed to identify themselves with Noddy — the little toy man who always meant well, but invariably ended up in trouble of one kind or another and had to seek help from his Toyland friends. Other *Noddy* books of various sizes and types followed in rapid succession and Enid also contracted to write a daily strip series for the London *Evening Standard* — all of which Van Der Beek insisted on illustrating. He was a lonely man, whose artist wife had died during the German occupation of his country, and the success of his new venture seemed to give his life a fresh purpose. But the sheer physical pressure of producing the eighteen-frame newspaper strip each week — enough for any artist on its own — in addition to his other work, proved too great and he once confessed to David White that at times, when he was working through into the early hours to meet a deadline, 'Little Noddies' would appear from everywhere and crawl all over his desk. He died suddenly in Holland in 1953, but his characters lived on as he created them. By that time they were so well established, other artists were able to perpetuate their appeal — with the aid of a special pictorial 'Noddy dictionary', prepared by Sampson Low. This carried details of all the Toyland characters and a map of the village, which marked the houses, shops and 'places of interest' mentioned in Enid's stories.

The 'dictionary' also served as an aid for the many British manufacturers who had been quick to realise Noddy's potential selling power and were already using 'this best-loved children's character' — as one described him — in a variety of ways. By the middle 'fifties, the range of 'Noddy' products had become so wide that a walk through any large store at this time would have revealed one or another of the Toyland characters displayed in almost every department. There were 'Noddy' toys and games of every description, toothbrushes, soap, stationery, chocolate, clothing, cutlery, pottery and furnishings. During the Christmas season, large Noddy replicas, with 'bobbing' heads, were used as part of the decorations or as a means of collecting for the four main Enid Blyton charities. Meanwhile, the book sales alone were enough to keep Noddy before the public eye, for by 1956 these had already reached almost unprecedented figures. By the end of the decade with the character's regular appearances on stage and television screen, well over twenty million copies of his books had been sold in England alone.

Enid was very excited when she heard that her 'little nodding man' had been chosen to feature in one of the first puppet series to be shown on the new British commercial television channel. She loved experimenting with new media and was delighted when Norman Collins, one of the original A.T.V. directors, suggested she might like to help him select the type of puppets and the puppeteer to be used for the Noddy series. She enjoyed this experience immensely and later amusingly described how they had all prostrated themselves on the director's carpet, in his newly-acquired Queen's Square office, in order to get a clearer 'worm's eye view' of the puppets' action. It was typical of Enid that before the first of this successful series had been completed, she had acquainted herself thoroughly with all the processes involved in its screening. She devoted the same meticulous care over the production of another new venture embarked upon some months before, which had also been built around Noddy and his Toyland friends.

Early in 1954 Enid rang up her agent, George Greenfield, and asked if he thought she could write 'a kind of pantomime for children'. Several people, she told him, had approached her with a view to using one or another of her books as the basis for Christmas plays and she had refused, preferring to leave it until such time as she could tackle the work herself. She had written

Dorothy Richards at Old Thatch

Enid, 1930s

With Kenneth Darrell Waters at
Green Hedges

In the garden, war years

The swing seat, Enid's favourite place to work in summer

several short scripts in the past for *Teachers' World*, but had never before attempted anything quite so ambitious and was wondering if it would be worth her pursuing the idea. George Greenfield was by this time well aware of Enid's capabilities and encouraged her to try, commenting 'I reckon that if you put your mind to it, you could write pretty well anything' — an opinion which was amply justified by the arrival on his desk, a couple of weeks later, of the finished script.

But despite the speed at which the play — *Noddy in Toyland* — had been produced, the writing at the beginning had not been easy. In her correspondence with psychologist Peter McKellar* she described her difficulties and how she eventually overcame them. At the close of the pantomime's first season, in January 1955, she wrote:

. . . You may have seen that I have had a play for children put on at the Stoll Theatre in London. (It was a great success I am thankful to say!). For the first two days I endeavoured to use the same process of writing as I use for my books — finding characters and settings and then using the 'cinema screen' in my mind, on which the whole story seems to be projected from beginning to end without any active volition from me. This method was a *complete* failure for the writing of the play. It was very odd. I stumbled over the writing. I laboured, I could not draw on my imagination at all. Then like a flash I seemed to discard the old way of writing, and instead of needing to see characters in their story setting and using the 'cinema screen', into my mind came the stage itself, all set with scenery. And then in came the characters on this stage, singing, talking, dancing — and once again something went 'click' and the whole writing of the play went out of my hands and was taken over by my imagination again. I no longer stumbled, puzzled, tried to invent. There were the characters, all dressed for their parts, there were their houses and their 'props' (car, bicycle, etc.) and on they came, talking, dancing, singing . . .

Many that appeared she recognised from previous books and

* See Appendix 9.

stories — Mary Mouse, Mr. Pinkwhistle, the Saucepan Man and Silky the pixie — and somehow these, and other favourites of her younger readers, seemed to belong quite naturally in Toyland along with Noddy and the others. Even the songs they sang were in keeping with her original conception of their characters. She wrote some thirty-three lyrics in all — far more than were eventually needed — and the music, she told Peter McKellar, 'came' to her in the same way:

> . . . I worked a good bit with the Musical Director (Philip Green) and although I did not tell him — I was afraid he would think me unduly conceited — in many cases the melodies were much the same, the rhythm *always* the same, and in some cases the key was the same — notably in one instance where I heard the song in E minor — rather unusual — and the composer actually set it in the same key! . . . In one day we had more or less worked out all the music — and this for a play lasting two-and-a-half hours! I was, of course, very lucky in my composer, scenic designer and so on, which helped to make the play the success it achieved in four weeks — the audience's response and participation was extraordinary — the children took over the play at times and even held up the action . . .

The play, which was produced by Bertie Meyer and directed by Andre van Gyseghem, broke all attendance records during its first season at the Stoll Theatre in London, and in a later letter Enid was able to inform the psychologist that the pantomime was 'now to be an annual, like Peter Pan'. In the meantime she had written a second play for older children — *The Famous Five* — which would also be produced in London the following Christmas:

> . . . The second play did not take me as long as the first one — and except for some ridiculous rhymes which one of the characters suddenly recited, there is no verse — and no lyrics. It is a straight play of adventure and mystery. One interesting thing about this is that the man who designed the scenery (quite a genius, Richard Lake, who did the Noddy scenery too) managed to produce designs that exactly fitted my own

visualised conceptions, in particular some dungeon scenes —
which I had not even explained to him in detail . . . I was
amazed when I saw them and could not keep from exclaiming . . .
It was almost as if he had seen into my mind and drawn what
was there . . .

Now that she had established the format for playwriting, she
felt confident to produce other scripts. None, however, was to
achieve the success of *Noddy in Toyland*, which continued to play
to packed houses in London, the provinces and overseas during
the nine years that followed its first performance. A later film of
the pantomime proved equally popular wherever it was shown.

Noddy's impact generally — whether in book, film, play or
television puppet form — was phenomenal. He became the
subject of music hall jokes and sketches, pet rabbits were named
after his pixie friend 'Big Ears' and many a British policeman was
referred to — a shade derogatorily — as 'Mr. Plod'. Before the
decade was over 'Enid Blyton' and 'Noddy' had become household names — and to many the two were synonymous, despite
the continued popularity of her other series. But troubled under-
currents were already beginning to cause ripples on the surface of
Enid's seemingly happy, successful life.

CHAPTER
XII

ENID ALWAYS FOUND IT DIFFICULT TO UNDERSTAND THOSE WHO criticised her work. She sincerely believed that she was providing her young readers with enjoyable, exciting — but never frightening — stories, that at the same time laid down certain moral codes of behaviour. Librarians and educationalists did not always agree. They questioned her involvement in the actions of some of her main characters who, they felt, too often displayed petty, spiteful, vindictive — even cruel — behaviour towards their adversaries, who were usually of a different nationality or social background to her predominantly middle-class English heroes or heroines. They disliked her style with its limited vocabulary 'drained of all difficulty until it achieved a kind of aesthetic anaemia' as one critic put it. Others considered her work 'too mediocre' to even give it mention and ignored her very existence.

Her reply to them all was that she took no note of critics over twelve years of age and that no one could deny her immense, universal appeal among the children themselves. Half the attacks made on her work she claimed came from jealousy and the other half 'from stupid people who don't know what they're talking about because they've never read any of my books...' Her stories were read 'in palaces as well as in working-class homes' and 'whatever the child's mental capacity' were equally well enjoyed. Reluctant readers found her books easy to read and this gave them an incentive to experiment further, while other children, who required more mental stimulus, 'took hold' of her stories and set their own imaginations to work over the characters and the settings.

But the main target for the anti-Blytons throughout the 'fifties and early 'sixties was undoubtedly Noddy — 'the most egocentric, joyless, snivelling and pious anti-hero in the history of British fiction', according to one critic of the time. Colin Welch, in a five-page feature in the January 1958 edition of *Encounter*, went further: 'If Noddy is "like the children themselves" [*Enid's own description*] it is the most unpleasant child that he most resembles'. He always had to have somebody to run to, to whine and wail at, and 'the machinery of benevolent authority (Big Ears) or the state (Mr. Plod) could always be invoked to redress the balance between cowardice, weakness and inanity on the one hand, and vigour, strength and resource on the other.' In some respects, the writer commented, the Noddy books left the impression of being 'an unintentional yet not wholly inaccurate satire on — or parody of — the welfare state and its attendant attitudes of mind'.

Mr. Welch's article, 'Dear Little Noddy — A Parent's Lament', was well received and widely quoted, particularly by those who wished to impose sanctions on Enid's works. Several librarians had already removed her books from their shelves completely, giving a variety of reasons for so doing. The main complaint against her stories appeared to be that with such a prolific output (still increasing at the rate of a dozen or more each year) it was quite possible for children to be introduced to one or another of Enid's books at the age of two or three and read no other author until they progressed 'if ever, on such a spoon-fed diet' to adult literature. Stories of greater depth and characterisation, of which there was now a wide range, were thus being ignored.

The anti-Blyton — and, more particularly, anti-Noddy — campaign gathered momentum and by the end of the 'fifties scarcely a day passed without one newspaper or another giving publicity to the banning of Enid's books by librarians — not only in Britain, but in New Zealand, Australia and elsewhere. 'Murky undertones' were claimed to have been found in some of Noddy's adventures: his relationship with Big Ears was 'suspect' and Enid's 'racial discrimination' was shown by her use of black golliwogs as the villains in one of the Toyland tales. She countered the latter by saying that she had written far more *good* golliwogs into her stories than bad and gave, as an example, *The Three Golliwogs* in which they appeared as the 'heroes' throughout:

> Golliwogs are merely lovable black toys, *not* Negroes. Teddy bears are also toys, but if there happens to be a naughty one in my books for younger children, this does not mean that I hate bears!

So wild did some of the accusations become that it was inevitable that the balance should eventually be redressed by such articles as that written by Roy Nash in the *Daily Mail* of February 7th, 1964. Entitled 'As Big Ears Said to Noddy Yesterday' the piece was written in the style of a typical Noddy story and followed the banning of his books by yet another library:

> One day Noddy came home quite tired out. He really had had a very busy day. He had gone all the way to Nottingham in his little car. And when he got there a nasty man called Librarian had kicked the poor little car very hard. He had also told Noddy that he would never be allowed back there again because he was just not grown up enough for all the boys and girls in Nottingham.
> 'Oh I am so sorry, poor little car,' said Noddy, stroking the steering wheel.
> 'Parp-parp,' said the little car, painfully.
> 'Hallo, Noddy,' called a voice over the fence. It was Tubby Bear.
> 'What's a vocabulary, Noddy? That grumpy Librarian at Nottingham says you *have* got a very limited one. And he thinks you're awful bad for the little boys and girls.'
> Noddy was so worried that he hurried off to see Big Ears. He had never seen his old friend looking so cross.
> 'We'd better face it,' said Big Ears, sternly. 'You and I and all the rest — and that goes for Mr. Plod, the policeman, too — are like Librarian says, caricatures. And what is more, we are members of the intellectually under-privileged class.'
> Noddy could not believe his ears.

'B-b-beg pardon,' he stuttered. Big Ears sounded just like the fierce Librarian.

'We're redundant in Toyland,' said Big Ears, angrily. 'Do you really think that children want us and our stories any more? We've got to do what the man says. All these little what-nots are going to be specialists by the time they're nine. You've got to catch up on Thermo-dynamics and the Economic Position... Children want literature now. Literature with a capital "L".'

Big Ears began to be quite worked up and so frightened Noddy that a little tear ran down his cheek. He rushed away and ran all the way home. As he went through the gate he fell right over the poor little car and BUMP!

With a big start Noddy woke up. It had all been a nasty dream, after all. And everything in Toyland was all right and always would be until Blyton knows when. And what is more, the kiddies went on loving Noddy and they didn't give a parp-parp for Librarian and all those big words.

Enid had long since discovered the truth of Roy Nash's final comment. Whatever the action of the librarians, Noddy's popularity continued and his stories, along with her other books, were taken up and read as fast as they appeared on the market. Far from reducing the numbers of her young readers, the disappearance of her books from library shelves resulted in increased sales, particularly when the first of her cheap, paperback editions were brought out in the early 'sixties. Children could now afford to buy the books for themselves and a certain one-upmanship developed, in some quarters, over the collection of complete 'sets' of her series.

Although she had been distressed at first by the withdrawal of her books from the libraries, Enid was far more perturbed by other persistent rumours, which had begun circulating in the middle 'fifties, that she was not responsible for the writing of all her stories. In June 1955, she wrote to her solicitor, Mr. Arnold Thirlby:

...I announced in my magazine last Wednesday that it had been reported to me from South Africa that I did not write my own books but merely put my signature to them and asked any child to tell me at once if they heard such a rumour so that I could immediately put it right. I put in this announcement because I have had several extremely rude letters from South Africa, from children, pouring scorn on me for being such a fraud! (I don't wonder the children felt like that, really — to believe in a person and then to find she has apparently deceived them for years is a blow to a worshipping child!)

She went on to explain how she had heard only that day from the mother of one of her readers, who had attended a parents' meeting at her daughter's school at which the speaker, a young librarian, had implied that all the books bearing the name 'Enid Blyton' were not necessarily written by the author herself.

> ... This is very damaging, not only to my books, but to me. I am such a public figure now, and well trusted, as you know, and run many clubs and societies which bring in money, that I absolutely *must* have these rumours cleared up — for who is going to believe I am honest if I don't even write my own books! ... In the last month or two we have had rumours from Australia that I am dead and someone else is writing my books. Rumours from S. Africa that I am dead and no longer write my books and rumours, also from S. Africa, that I am alive, but do not write my books and now here is a librarian with the same slander ...

The solicitor pursued the matter and proceedings were taken against the librarian, which resulted eventually in an apology to Enid in open court in the spring of the following year. For a time, the reports of this affair helped to scotch some of the rumours, but stories that Enid ran a 'company' of ghost writers still circulated, for the cynics refused to believe that one woman could produce such quantities of work on her own.

They could, perhaps, be forgiven for their incredulity for, in 1956 alone, she had turned out her usual quota of books and articles; continued to write for her *Enid Blyton Magazine* (overseeing the four clubs involved — and making occasional visits to their respective charities); recorded some of her Noddy stories for H.M.V.; supervised a second Noddy puppet series for I.T.V. and Australian television and the casting and staging of another season of *Noddy in Toyland* and *The Famous Five*. She was still answering a vast correspondence without any secretarial help and making her usual public appearances at bookshops and exhibitions.

Her regular rounds of golf with Kenneth continued, either at the local club or on their own course at Swanage and, during that same year, she also embarked on a new venture with him — the purchase of a farm at Stourton Caundle, near Sturminster Newton in Dorset. She was greatly interested in this project and eagerly took part in all the subsequent discussions over its renovation and eventual occupation by a manager. Yet in the midst of all this activity, she still managed to complete, in May, her first attempt at a full-length play for the adult theatre, which she hoped might help to disprove the criticism of those who thought her only capable of writing for children.

All the preliminary negotiations over the play, she instructed those acting for her, were to be conducted with the utmost secrecy, for her fame in other directions must not be allowed to influence any decisions about the possibility of its production — and to ensure this, she used the nom-de-plume of Justin Geste. The play — *The Summer Storm* — was duly sent to several theatrical managers for consideration but it was apparent, even to those to whom the identity of the author was revealed, that as it stood it was totally unsuitable for staging. The over-dramatised theme was one of marital intrigue and mistaken parentage, set in an upper-middle-class background. It had ten characters,* required five different stage settings, and owed more to those playwrights of the 'twenties, who indulged in a world of sophisticated artificiality, than to the Angry Young Men of the 'fifties, whose stark dramas were beginning to fill the theatres at that time. But perhaps this was not surprising, as Enid had rarely visited the theatre since her marriage to Kenneth, for his deafness spoilt his enjoyment of any straight play. To produce *The*

* See Appendix 8.

169

Summer Storm for the London stage, which had been Enid's goal, would have involved drastic rewriting, great ingenuity over the changing of the sets and weighty production costs which, it appeared, no one was prepared to risk. Greatly disappointed, Enid put it aside and, characteristically, turned her thoughts to other activities. But those close to her noticed that she was showing increasing signs of strain, particularly by the spring of 1957, following the Christmas productions of her two children's plays which, highly successful as they were, involved frequent visits to London and additional public appearances.

Kenneth, who was about to retire, had been trying for some time to persuade his wife to take things more easily, by relinquishing some of her full-length books and concentrating instead on her magazine work and shorter stories. But with each post came more letters from children urging her to write 'just one more' of the series which involved their favourite characters and she found it difficult to ignore their requests. He knew how much Enid's work meant to her and that she was not really happy unless she had a new project on hand, but at the same time he was concerned about her health, and felt there was no reason why she should not ease up a little on her activities and join him in a well-earned retirement with, perhaps, occasional visits overseas.

There were certainly no domestic or financial reasons to prevent Enid from taking holidays wherever and whenever she pleased. After their schooling at Benenden, both of her daughters had gone on to university. Imogen was still reading economics at St. Andrews, but Gillian had been living and working away from home since she graduated some three years earlier, and there seemed every likelihood that Imogen would soon follow suit. Green Hedges continued to run smoothly and efficiently with its regular staff of cook, housemaid, gardener and chauffeur, and Enid's well-invested income alone (estimated at that time to be over £100,000 a year) was more than sufficient to keep up their present standard of living for the rest of their lives, without her writing another word. Not that either were over-lavish in their expenditure. Green Hedges was comfortably furnished but it could by no means be termed a 'luxury' home. They ran a Rolls-

Royce, a Bentley and a small M.G., lunched weekly with business associates at the Savoy, entertained friends from time to time and enjoyed their golfing holidays at Swanage, but in the main their tastes were simple and expenses modest. For Enid, the life they led together incorporated everything she had ever wanted — freedom to write, a happy companionship and, above all, a feeling of security that depended more upon Kenneth's love and devotion than financial considerations. Nevertheless, she was not prepared to make any drastic changes in her writing life — just because Kenneth wished to spend more time with her — and knowing how stubborn his wife could be once she had made up her mind, Kenneth ceased trying to persuade her. But the matter was shortly to be decided for them.

During a round of golf together on the course at Beaconsfield early in May, Enid suddenly complained of feeling faint and 'breathless'. Kenneth took her pulse and, not satisfied with the result, insisted on taking her back to Green Hedges, putting her to bed and summoning a heart specialist friend from London. When he arrived Enid was showing some agitation, for Kenneth's quick action in summoning the cardiologist had convinced her that she was seriously ill and memories of her father's fatal heart attack all those years before, which she had tried so hard to bury, resurfaced. She was sure that she had a condition similar to his and felt that the 'attack' was by way of a warning to her that she had, as Kenneth had often told her, been working too hard.

The cardiologist diagnosed that her discomfort and pain was due, not to a diseased heart, but to a digestive malfunction, brought on, he thought, by Enid's many long hours hunched over her typewriter. But despite his assurance that her heart was working satisfactorily, she did not believe him, and Kenneth, for reasons known only to himself, appears to have encouraged this self-deception. The specialist prescribed no treatment other than a mild sedative and certainly put no embargo on her work — which makes the events that followed even more curious.

Gillian and Imogen were both away at the time — Gillian in America and Imogen at university — and were disturbed to hear from Kenneth on their return a month later, that their mother had suffered a heart attack, and that she had been told to rest. She was to undertake no more 'rush' jobs or public appearances that might cause additional strain and there was to be a general easing up on all her activities.

Why Kenneth should have kept up such a pretence with Enid's daughters as well as herself is difficult to understand. It could be that, despite his friend's diagnosis, he genuinely believed that Enid had suffered a minor heart attack, but the most feasible explanation seems to be that he had already noticed certain signs in her behaviour which indicated a breakdown in her health in other directions, and sought to delay this in some way by curtailing her activities, without divulging his own fears as to the real nature of her illness. His concern convinced Enid even more that her heart was not sound and that the specialist had not told her the truth.

Despite the pressures under which she worked, she had kept remarkably well in past years. Except for a short, sharp bout of pneumonia in 1954 and a spell in St. Stephen's Hospital two years earlier — after Kenneth had repaired the injuries to her leg, which had been badly bitten by a stray dog — she had rarely had more than a few days in bed and had always been able to fulfil her writing commitments. She consoled herself by the thought that, as most of her magazine work was prepared well in advance and much of this was material that was later made up in book form, her publishers would not be kept waiting and need not be told of her illness — at least for the time being. But rest from her work did not appear to alleviate the situation. Instead it brought about other, more distressing, side-effects.

She confided to Imogen that, whereas previously she had always been able to ride disaster by 'keeping busy' she was now finding her thoughts 'closing in' upon her. It is easy to suppose that, now she was no longer directing most of her thoughts towards the fantasy worlds of her own creation, some of the harsh realities she had for so long 'put away' were at last rising to the surface — aided, perhaps, by the sedative drug she had been prescribed. So much of her life she had kept hidden from those around her, and what little she had revealed had been embroidered into stories she now half-believed herself. Perhaps with time now to brood over some of the unhappy events of the past, triggered off no doubt by the reminder of her father's sudden death, she may even have experienced certain feelings of guilt over her treatment of those once close to her — particularly of Hugh and her mother.

She had heard nothing from Hugh for some years. He had long given up his attempts to visit his daughters and was not prepared to take the matter further, but Enid must have known in her heart that she had not treated him fairly by going back on her original promise to him. Nor had she been fair in the much over-dramatised accounts she had given of his supposed misdeeds, both to their daughters and friends, in order to exonerate herself. But it was far too late for her to retract any of her stories.

It was too late, also, to effect any reconciliation with her mother, for she had died in a hospital at Maidstone in Kent seven years previously, after an illness lasting some years. Although she had sent occasional small sums of money towards her upkeep, Enid had not seen Theresa since the early 'twenties, despite her mother's pleadings — particularly during her latter years — to see the daughter from whom she had so long been estranged. Hanly found his sister's attitude towards the dying woman difficult to understand and repeatedly begged her to visit, but Enid's reply had always been that she was 'too busy' to make the journey — and this was also the reason she gave for not attending the funeral. Whatever the origins of her bitter feelings towards her mother it was impossible, it appeared, for her to put them aside. Gillian and Imogen knew nothing of their grandmother until after her death and neither Hugh nor Kenneth were ever given an explanation as to why they were never allowed to meet their mother-in-law. They had no reason to disbelieve Enid's story, also told to her daughters, that she had been 'brought up' by the Attenboroughs, having run away from home as a 'young girl'. With Carey overseas, it had been left to Hanly to bear the brunt of caring for an ailing and difficult mother throughout his married life and — for the past twenty years — for his two children and a sick and almost bed-ridden wife. There had been little enough contact between brother and sister before their mother's death and now there was even less, and Enid must have been aware that Hanly felt she could have given more help of a practical nature at a time when he already had more than enough to cope with at home.

When she was busy with her work, she could shut out any thoughts which conflicted with that of her popular image, but now that she was forced into an unhappy introspection of herself perhaps she did not like what she saw. She found it increasingly difficult to sleep and became even more depressed and irritable. Early in July, Kenneth thought a holiday at Swanage, with a chance to walk through the Dorset countryside she loved, might prove beneficial and refresh her in time for Gillian's wedding, which was planned for the middle of the following month.

Gillian was to marry a rising young television producer — Donald Baverstock — and Enid was determined that her daughter should have the kind of wedding that she herself had been denied. She had already helped to choose the wedding dress and those of the six bridesmaids, although Gillian had herself decided that the service should be held at St. James's, Piccadilly and, with Kenneth, was organising a reception at the Savoy Hotel. Leaving her daughter to work out the final arrangements Enid left for Swanage, hoping that her husband was right, and that she would indeed feel refreshed on her return.

She tried to rest in Dorset but the 'breathless' feelings returned and Kenneth telephoned Gillian after a few weeks to say that her mother had again had an 'attack' and been put to bed. Gillian was on the point of postponing her wedding, when he telephoned again two days later to say that Enid was much better and that everything could go ahead as planned. She returned in time for the wedding in a more cheerful frame of mind, but those among the guests who knew her well, noticed that she was looking tired and strained — though few outside her immediate family were told of any specific ailment. Less than a month later — on September 11th, 1957 — she wrote in her *Enid Blyton Magazine*, which had previously made no mention of her illness:

I know that a great many of you learnt that I had been ill, because I had so many anxious letters from you wishing me well again! Some of you reproached me for not letting you know about it in my magazine letter — and perhaps I *ought* to have told you instead of risking your hearing about it suddenly from the newspapers. But I did not want to worry you, as I was sure I would soon get better . . .

She was also afraid, she told her readers, that they would send more letters and she would not have been able to answer them. But she was better now:

I was allowed to go on with my magazine, thank goodness, but that was all and fortunately I am always well ahead with my work. I had been working much too hard — but as you know, I do so love my work for you children, and there was so much to do this year! . . . I shall be sensible in future and not work so hard, but it is going to be very, very difficult! . . .

By this time Enid had found herself swept up again into most of her writing commitments. She tried to cut down on the amount of work she normally tackled prior to her 'illness', but it was not long before she was once more involved in the casting and other preparations for yet another *Noddy in Toyland* production and plans for additional books for most of her popular series. Now that she was writing again, she seemed happy and more contented and Kenneth, although he tried to curb some of her more strenuous activities, let her go her own way, for by that time he had health problems of his own, with the worsening of an arthritic condition that had troubled him for some years.

As the months passed, both fought against the inevitability of their respective illnesses in their own way. For Kenneth, who had always been an athletic man, the progressive limitation of his physical activities was difficult to accept, but he refused to let the painful disease rob him of his regular games of golf and stubbornly continued to play, with the aid of an electrically driven 'caddy car' to take him around the course. Whereas he assessed every problem of his illness as it arose and tackled it accordingly,

Enid resorted to the means she had long used for banishing anything unpleasant. She pretended — both to herself and those around her — that she was now fit and well and tried to ignore the occasional bouts of breathlessness and other more alarming symptoms that Kenneth had already noticed and which were now beginning to make themselves even more apparent.

By the early 'sixties, however, she could no longer ignore the fact that her once active brain was refusing to function in its old 'card-index' fashion and that the memory upon which she had always relied was failing. She tried to cover up this unhappy situation, but this only resulted in further confusion over which she appeared to have no control. Throughout her life, her greatest fear had always been that she might one day be unable to govern the workings of her own mind. During her correspondence with Peter McKellar* she had written on May 13th, 1957:

'. . . Your mescaline experiences [*conducted during his researches*] must have been rather terrifying — they would be to me. I dread the feeling of losing my identity, of not being able to control my own mind! . . .'

To discover that this was now happening to her was more than she could bear. Kenneth helped as far as he could by taking over most of her business affairs, but as time went by she found it increasingly difficult to concentrate long enough to write coherently or to stop her fantasy world from spinning over into the reality of her day-to-day life.

By 1966 Kenneth's illness became worse and complications set in. He must have known from his medical training that he had not long to live, but even up to the last year of his life, he protected Enid from the harshness of the world outside and very few, apart from those close to her, were aware of the extent of her illness. He rarely left her side, prodding her memory or covering up for any deficiency in her dealings with her publishers and the public, and watching over her correspondence until she was unable to answer her letters even at his dictation. Occasion-

* See Appendix 9.

176

ally, she seemed to awake from the semi-dream world into which she had now drifted, particularly when her grandchildren came to visit her — something which she always enjoyed — or when there was discussion of her books or of the children who continued to write, begging for more stories in their favourite series. But these moments of clarity did not last for long and she soon slipped back into brooding thoughts centred around her own childhood.

It was early in 1967, during one of these rare journeys into reality, that she telephoned a surprised Hanly, who had not heard from his sister for nearly seventeen years, and begged him to visit her. Kenneth had been taken into hospital for a short period, her daughters were both away from home and she was, she told him, 'desperately lonely'. Realising, with some concern, that Enid was obviously a sick woman, he made the journey from Kent a few days later, only to find his sister quite unable to recall her urgent summons and barely able to recognise him. Once the realisation came that this 'strange man' was indeed her brother, she was obsessed with the thought that she must immediately return 'home' with him to Beckenham and 'Mother and Father' and this idea persisted long after he had left. She could remember only the happy times the little family had spent together before their father had left them, and all the pain of parting had mercifully been obliterated. Hanly continued to visit her from time to time and even took her back to Beckenham on one occasion, in an endeavour to prove to her that her old world no longer existed and that her life now revolved around Green Hedges, but the moment she returned to Beaconsfield the visit was forgotten and she talked once more of returning 'home'.

Yet in the midst of this childhood dream world, Kenneth still remained beside her, solid and reassuring. Sick man though he was, he recognised the responsibilities she had laid upon him and was determined not to fail the wife he had cherished for so long. When he realised that time was running out for him, he characteristically set about putting his own and Enid's affairs in order. He cleared her desk and burnt many of the documents it contained including, it is thought, most of her diaries. Only those prior to 1936, which Enid had stored elsewhere, and a few covering the last years of her life, remain. These later diaries are by no means complete but sadly show the confusion of mind under which she laboured at that time — which makes the one clear and concise entry for 1967 all the more poignant. She wrote on Friday, September 15th:

> 'My darling Kenneth died. I loved him so much. I feel lost and unhappy.'

The news of his death, at the London hospital where he had been for more than a week, had somehow penetrated the comforting wall she had built around herself and brought her cruelly back to the reality of her life at Green Hedges. For a few days she appeared to be in command of her actions and her thoughts were only of the husband she had lost, but after returning from his cremation at Amersham, she again relapsed into her old dream world and the desire to return to her childhood home once more obsessed her.

During the months that followed, without her beloved Kenneth beside her, she declined rapidly, both physically and mentally. She was cared for throughout this time by her faithful housekeeper, Doris Cox, who had been with the family since 1945, and other members of her staff who had also known Enid in happier days. Her daughters and friends visited her regularly, but by December 1967 Gillian and Donald and their four young children had moved to Yorkshire and Imogen, who had recently married, was living in Sussex with her husband, Duncan Smallwood. Both daughters did what they could for their mother, but her illness grew progressively worse and some three months after being admitted to a Hampstead nursing home, she died peacefully in her sleep on November 28th, 1968.

Only Enid's family and close friends were present at her cremation at Golders Green in North London, but her memorial service at St. James's Church, Piccadilly, on January 3rd of the following year, was attended by representatives of her many publishing houses and of the four children's clubs with which she had for so long been associated. The service was conducted by the rector, the Reverend William Baddeley, and included a reading by her eldest grandchild, ten-year-old Sian Baverstock, of Enid's own version of the Parable of the Sower. Paul Hodder-Williams, the chairman of one of her main publishing houses, spoke of Enid's incomparable gift for 'making friends' with children from all backgrounds and of several generations:

> ... She really loved children and understood instinctively what would interest them. It was with children that her gift of sympathy had its greatest flowering ... That is why they have loved and will continue to love the best of the books which she wrote for them and them alone ...

No plaque marks the place where Green Hedges once stood and other houses have now taken its place. But Enid Blyton surely needs no memorial other than her books. Several years after her death, despite her critics being as fierce as ever in the condemnation of her work, her stories continue to be bought and enjoyed by children the world over. To them — and to hundreds of her former readers — she remains the spinner of magical tales, almost without equal.

Many have tried to solve the mystery of her phenomenal success and apparently ageless appeal, but perhaps psychologist Michael Woods, who attempted to analyse Enid, the woman, from her books* came closer than most when he wrote:

> 'She was a child, she thought as a child and she wrote as a child ...'

For surely her secret lay not only in her extraordinary creative and imaginative gifts, her great vivacity and charm, her amazing capacity for hard work and shrewd business acumen — but also in her very ability to look with childlike wonder on to a world of constant enchantment and surprise, putting aside those things which were unpleasant and keeping only her dreams of life as she would like it to be.

* See Appendix 10.

But perhaps the last words should be from a South African girl of eighteen, who wrote to Enid in 1957:

. . . I am in the middle of my final Matriculation examinations and in four weeks' time will be starting my training as a nurse.

I suppose you are wondering what on earth this has to do with you and why I should be writing to you? I am just writing to thank you for all the pleasure your books have given me during my childhood. (I am eighteen now, so can afford to speak of the distant 'childhood' — I hope!)

Throughout you have educated me in your English way of life and I have learnt a great deal about your countryside — your nature books were the ones I loved best and from them I got my avid interest in biology.

Even when I graduated to adult literature, your books never lost their charm and fascination for me. When I was tired, and not in the mood for any serious book, a 'Fives' story would soon transport me into a wonderful world of adventure, where my mind could relax completely.

Another thing, all your characters in the many series are so fine and upright, always striving to right wrongs. Between the strong influences of American cowboys and your enthusiastic adventurers, my friends and I grew up with — I hope — well-formed characters ourselves!

I must thank you, too, for bringing me my finest glimpses of Fairyland. Grimm, Andersen, George Macdonald and you *made* my fairy world — especially your books, as there are so many of them! I can still feel the magic thrill whenever I think of the great Faraway Tree.

Your autobiography and magazine have really brought us into close contact with you, and I do think it is a fine gesture to run those different clubs, each working for such a noble cause. May God bless you in your work.

Once again, thank you for helping to make my childhood so extremely happy. I hope I can make my children as happy by introducing them to the magic, sunshiny world created by you . . .

Appendices

I Have —

by Maud K. F. Dyrenfurth

(In reply to *Have You* —? in the March 1917 *Nash's*)

I have heard the night-time silence full of mystic melody,
    And have seen and called that star you love so well;
I have heard the wind, a-weary, whisper all its griefs to me;
    I have heard the tale that flowers have to tell.

I have pressed my lips against the rose and longed for you to clasp,
    And have closed my eyes and dreamed you were my own;
I have felt the petals crumble in the burning of my grasp;
    I have waked to find that I was all alone.

I have dreamt of old-world gardens and of mystic midnight hours
    When the stars are shining all the night a-through;
I have seen the rambler-roses and the scented passion-flowers,
    I have seen them in the sunshine, wet with dew.

I have felt quite lonely sometimes in the bygone yesternights
    With the darkness, or the stars above to shine;
I have heard your tender promise echo somewhere in the heights;
    I have laughed for very joy that you are mine.

I have watched the moon come, timorous, from clouds she hid behind,
    And have seen the transformation and the light;
I have stretched my arms out bravely, hardly hoping what to find;
    I have sought you, yes! and found you — in the night.

The Poet

by Enid Blyton

(The Poetry Review (Poetry of Today) 1919)

A CHILD
Whose eyes at times see God
And all his angels,
Hid in some sunset cloud
Wherein *we* see
But shapes.

And lo,
Around and thro' the stars
He hears the song
Weaved from the rolling worlds —
While we but hear
The wind.

A love
He bears to all the world,
And to his God.
Beauty in all he sees.
Beauty we find
In him.

Dear heart
And soul of a child,
Sing on!

Things I Won't Forget

by Enid Blyton

(From *Silver and Gold,* 1925)

When I'm grown up I won't forget the things I think today —
I won't forget the sort of things I like to do and say;
I won't be like the folk I know, who seem so very old,
And quite forget the things they did when *they* were eight years old.

There's lots of other things, of course, that I'll remember too;
And then when I'm grown up I'll know what children like to do.
I'll know the things they're frightened of, I'll know the things they
  hate —
And oh! I *hope* they'll love me, though they'll know I'm long past
  eight!

April Day

(Enid Blyton's last known poem)

There is a copse I know on Purbeck Hills
That holds the April sun to its green breast;
Where daffodils
Are wild and small and shy,
And celandines in polished gold are drest.
Here windflowers dance a ballet full of grace,
And speedwell blue
Looks on with brilliant eye.
There, innocent of face,
The daisies grow,
And yellow primroses like children press
In little crowds together all day through.

Be silent, velvet bee,
And let me brood
At peace in this enchanted loneliness.
Chaffinch, take your merry song, and go
To some more distant tree.
'Tis not my mood
To have this silence stirred
By wing of bee
Or voice of bird.

Now, let me stand and gaze —
But ah, so lavishly is beauty spread
These April days,
There is no place to tread.
Then must I choose
To put away my shoes
And kneel instead.

On the Popular Fallacy that to the Pure All Things Are Pure

(*Saturday Westminster Review*, February 19th, 1921)

The Pure, I have found out from the thirty-three people I have met since last Friday, means the 'Really Good People'. The definitions varied in detail, but in the main trended towards those three words. I myself give no meaning; having been swamped by other people's opinions — but I do know that I feel relieved. The reason is this: I used to think with sorrow that I did not belong to the ranks of the Pure, being firmly convinced that margarine is not pure, nor our new silver. Therefore it followed that I also was not pure, nor one of the 'Really Good People'.

It is with joy that I realise (helped by the *Saturday Westminster*) that I may still attain Heaven. On studying the subject further I find that those to whom all things are pure must be either extremely undiscerning or hypocritical. This is a very grave decision, as I myself possess several relatives who professs to trust everybody, and to find no fault with anything. 'Everything', according to them 'has some good in it', and 'Evil cannot touch those who do not believe in it'. Of course there really is something in that — but it may lead to Christian Science, which is quite all right outside the family, but very uncomfortable in. Aunt Maria did not believe in measles herself, even when she had it, so that I thought it most unkind of her to pass it on to people who did believe in it. However, she could never see my point — she may do now that I am in the 'Really Good People' set.

A difficult point has come into my thoughts. How can we distinguish the *Pure People*, for the Impure also can often discern the difference between good and bad things? Of course, before we found out that the subject of our essay was a fallacy, it was so easy to point out the Pure. We cannot say 'To the Pure all things are pure if they are, and impure if they are not'. For one thing, it sounds silly, and for another, as I said before, it applies also to those who are *not* the Pure. Neither can we rewrite the saying, 'To the Undiscerning and Hypocrites all things are pure', since it is certain most of my relations (and yours) would rise in indignation and drive us from their doors.

How did this fallacious saying of Paul's become accepted? Is it possible that the thousands of people go about believing in it, and so cheerfully resign their claims to goodness, because they know they turn up their noses at the smell of cabbage cooking? Surely something deeper lies below — some hidden meaning I have missed; perhaps 'pure' could be replaced by a better word? But, no; our Problems Editor should know — he who separates the wheat from the chaff so many times a year. It would be so dangerous to find the fallacy fallacious. He would have to give prizes to everybody . . .

ENID BLYTON

(N.B. — This essay is not really obscure in meaning.)

'From My Window'

(Enid Blyton's weekly talk in *The Teachers' World*)

July 4th, 1923

FIRST COLUMN

Here am I embarked on the first column, and what shall it be about? Books? No. Nature? No. Children? Yes, because I have been with them all day, and my mind is full of them.

It has often struck me how like a child's mind is in its way of working to the mind of a genius. A compliment to children! some will say. I think it is a compliment to genius. A child's mind is wonderful in its simplicity, directness, and sensitiveness. The younger a child is, the more clearly these characteristics show. The older he gets, the more he learns to hide his mind from others, and in doing so, he loses in simplicity and naturalness.

I have been reading some lives of men and women of genius. Their characteristic attitude of mind was a questioning one. Why? How? When and where? they were continually asking. Just the words I have heard the children say to me all day. And then, too, like the genius, the child is always delightedly finding things which resemble each other. "Oh, isn't that piece of sorrel like a small red poplar tree!"

The genius works in the same way. The poet uses his lucid and beautiful similes, the scientist reasons by analogy, and a Linnæus minutely records the similar characteristics of a host of plants.

A young child is intensely original. He has not learnt to think as others think, nor does he know enough to realise he is ignorant. He thinks for himself, he imagines, he observes with a curiously thorough and penetrating eye, often with comical or embarrassing results. Genius also is tremendously original and independent, and observes with a child's own absorbed concentration.

And at last of all, as Froebel knew, a child is always seeking to express himself—to give out what he has taken in—and through the same need of expression, genius has given our greatest treasures.

The questioning, wondering mind, that analyses and puts together, that observes and records for itself, and that finally bursts out into an expression of the many impressions—there is a description equally applicable to mature genius, or to immature childhood. What is the explanation of the curious similarity? *Why does it in all but a few cases cease as the child grows?* Is it some fault of our education, that has not recognised the real trend of a child's mind, which is, surely, genius-ward in its simplicity and need for expression?

I do not think genius is a mysterious something with which one must be born. I think it is the natural result of using one's mind to the fullest extent, of loving beauty in any form and of directly expressing the powerful spiritual effects which clamour for release. If only we could train our children in the way that geniuses perforce have to train themselves, we should get a wonderful type of ordinary men and women.

I may be entirely wrong in my surmises, but the question is an intensely interesting one, and I, in common, I suspect, with many other teachers, would dearly love to hear the modern psychologist's reasoned solution of the problem.

February 27th, 1924

ON PRETENDING

I love children who pretend. I love grown-ups who pretend. I love pretending myself. There is no doubt about it, it is a distinct gift, and one to be used and cherished and developed. It is nothing to be ashamed of, nothing to hide and put away with other childish things. But though I think this with all my might, I am sometimes powerless to prevent myself feeling extremely foolish and babyish when I am accidentally caught by one of those admirable, practical, common-sensical people, who seem to pop up anywhere when one is doing something rather odd and unusual!

I think the "pretends" I like best are those I enjoy in the company of children. There is one rule about pretending which must never be broken — you must be absolutely serious about it. If you break this rule you can neither pretend yourself, nor will the children pretend in front of you.

Last week was quite a red-letter week. I had in the garden, at 11.15 every morning, two or three policemen, a frightfully bold and audacious burglar, one Indian, a Canadian express train, a goods train, two motor-'buses who had the exciting gift of changing into their own

189

conductor and driver at will, and last, but not least, a galloping horse, who said "Gee-up" and smacked himself at short intervals. He invited me for a ride, but (fortunately) I happened to be a stern Bedouin of the desert at the moment and therefore preferred camels for riding. The horse, before my eyes began to change into a suitable camel, but the school-bell rang before the metamorphosis was complete.

But I love pretending by myself, too. That is one reason why I love London so much. You can wander about in London pretending anything in the world that you wish to pretend, and no one is a penny the wiser.

I have only met one person so far who owned to me that he loves pretending, and does it shamelessly. Are there many others, I wonder, who pretend too, and hide it all away carefully? I would love to know. There ought to be a Society for Pretenders, to give us more self-confidence!

Of course, pretending has its drawbacks. One of the characteristics of real pretending is that it is practically impossible to become yourself again at short notice. If you *do* happen to go dreaming down the Strand, imagining yourself to be a sailor home from Mandalay after ten years' absence, it is almost impossible to avoid saying, "Avast there, mate!" when anyone bumps into you.

But a worse thing than that happened last Friday. I had spent the afternoon with someone who had told me about a thrilling journey in an armoured train to Bagdad. I was living it over again, and felt the heat of the East over me, and I was wondering if Arabs would hold up the train, and wishing we could quickly arrive at Bagdad. Suddenly the person opposite me leaned over and said, "Can you tell me if this train stops at Herne Hill?"

I stared at her scornfully. "First stop Bagdad!" I answered promptly and decisively, and then was covered with the direst confusion. My companion gave one straight look at me, and fled from the carriage at the next stop.

Yes, I certainly think Pretenders should wear some sort of badge. It is not nice to be thought mad, when you yourself know you are perfectly sane. But I'm going to be VERY careful in the future!

January 6th, 1926

LETTERS FROM TEACHERS

I want to write about something which has been growing in my mind for a long time, and that is, what I read in letters from teachers. I have written once or twice about the charm of *children's* letters, and I could quite easily write a whole book about them, especially just after

Christmas. I can't say a big enough thank you to those teachers who allow their children to write naturally to me. The gems I get in practically every letter are without price, and I long to see every child-writer, as I read his or her letter. "I am a very norty boy," says one frank letter, "so I don't egspeck you would like me, but I like you allrite." And I should love you, little norty boy, if only I could see you! I could quote a hundred other gems of literature, but I won't just now. It is the teachers I am thinking of.

The one big outstanding fact that strikes me always in the letters I get from teachers is their real love for, and understanding of the children. It may not be, and seldom is, written down in so many words, but it is there, unmistakable and distinct between the lines, and hidden in many naïve sentences. If parents could know the very real understanding that the great majority of teachers have of the children that pass yearly through their hands, they would marvel and admire. Naughty children, good children, clever children, dull children, and all the many degrees between, teachers know them all, and see into the minds of them all with sympathy, and wonder, and sometimes with pity and puzzlement. Many a teacher must, by her real understanding, have passed up into the world scores of children who, unknowingly, are indebted to her (or to him) for a straight outlook on life, a sense of humour, or perhaps an appreciation of beauty. Unless they are unusual children, they will never know, never realise, and never acknowledge their debt. That, to my mind, is the saddest part of a teacher's profession. Those teachers who really love their children feel an interest in them for always, but it is not in the average child's nature to remember — he changes and grows every year, and strips from him the years that are gone, with an insouciance and lightheartedness impossible to us of more mature years. It is part of the charm of childhood.

Most of the letters I receive have a delightful sense of humour, and an absolutely charming way of taking it for granted that I will be interested — as I always am — in the writer's children. "You would love my children" is the commonest sentence to be found in the hundreds of letters I have in my possession. Another gift that teachers always seem to have is the most fascinating one of drawing a child for me in a few sentences. Listen to this: "You would love Alfred Stevens. His front teeth project, and the dentist says it is because he whistles, and always has whistled far too much." There is Alfred, large as life in front of me, character and all outlined in those few words!

There are two things I badly want to do some day when my ship comes home. One is to go on a grand tour round the kingdom, and see all these fascinating children for myself, and the other is to enlighten the British public on the subject of teachers. The things I could tell would make a hundred thousand people sit up and say, "Good gracious! We must revise our views on teachers at once! Their profession is the greatest in the kingdom!

So it is. To deal with living, growing material is ticklish work, dangerous work, hazardous work. To form the minds and characters of countless eager, restless children is a task the dimensions of which no outsider can judge — a task demanding illimitable patience, unending sympathy, and a love that can never be broken.

February 24th, 1926

'THINGS I DON'T LIKE'

Somebody wrote to me the other day and said: "You always write of the things you love — are there *any* things you don't love or like? It would be entertaining if you told us a few."

I don't know about entertaining, but I'm quite willing to relate a few of the things I don't like, for it would be nice to find a few fellow-sufferers.

Well, to begin with, of course, I hate going to the dentist. I dream about it for nights beforehand. In vain I say to myself, "Don't be silly. The dentist is a very nice man. Think of how nice and bright and shining all his dear little instruments are. Think how nice it is to sit in a chair that goes up and down and backwards and forwards at any moment." There always comes a moment when Myself answers back and says. "Uugh! Don't talk such rubbish. I HATE going to the dentist!"

Then another thing I really dislike is walking in a crowd. I always have disliked it from a child, because it makes me feel I am in a dream, and not properly myself. It was only the other day I discovered why I got the dream illusion. When you walk in a crowd you can't hear your own footsteps — and you don't hear them in a dream either. Time after time in dreams have I gone down the street like a wraith, hearing never a footfall. Think of your own dreams — you never hear your feet walking, do you? And that, I think, is why I get the queer dream-feeling in crowds, and dislike it so much.

I don't like doing anything that makes people stare at me. I have a remarkable habit of getting into a bus which is going in the wrong direction. When I give the conductor my penny and say, "Charing Cross, please," and he says, "Aw, you're going the wrong way," and rings the bell with a jerk, I go as red as a penny stamp, and feel dreadful inside. Even when I get out of the 'bus, I feel as if everyone in the street must be saying, "Look! Look! There's the girl who got in the wrong 'bus!" And I determine fiercely never to do it again. But I did it yesterday, alas! — and I shall quite probably do it to-morrow.

The next thing I'm going to say is a very silly thing — but I don't like thinking about eternity. You think about time, and the end of time, and then you think what's beyond the end of time, and it gives you a sort of gasping-for-breath feeling. Lots of people never think these sorts of things at all, for I've asked them but *I* do sometimes, and I don't like it, it's too big and overwhelming.

I don't like hearing sad stories if I can't help to put things right. I can't bear to hear stories of the war. I once heard a Scotsman tell of a mortally wounded Turk whom he found two days after a battle, and to whom he gave some water. He couldn't get a doctor to him, but managed to visit him again after a further two days. He was still alive. The next time, the poor wretch was asleep. The Scotsman shot him out of pity. That story haunted me for weeks, and still does — and other stories too. The feeling of impotence that comes when a story of suffering is related, is one of the hardest things to bear, that I know. If you could go straight off and put things right, it wouldn't matter — but you can't in ninety-nine cases out of a hundred.

Oh, there are lots and lots of things I dislike a little or dislike a lot. But the reason I write so much more about the things I love is because love or liking is positive, and dislike is negative, and I give *my* vote to the positive things of life.

A Country Letter from Enid Blyton

(*The Nature Lover*, September 1935)

The old country folk are fond of quoting proverbs and rhymes, in which country lore is enshrined, picturesque and wise. Each month has its own store of sayings, September as much as any other. One of the quaintest and shrewdest is well known to us country-dwellers:—
"St. Matthew bids goodbye to summer, and St. Maurice shuts the door after him."

St. Matthew's Day falls on the 21st of the month and St. Maurice's is the day after — and, sure enough, we feel the first chills of autumn then and begin to talk of the days drawing in. We light our first fires and turn our backs on the golden summer months.

But we have many days of September before we need light our fires! September is a lovely month, quiet, peaceful and golden. The earth still contains great heat, and, after the first chills of the morning, the sun feels as hot as in the days of mid-July. The dews are very heavy, both in the morning and evening — each morning when my curtains are drawn and I look straight out on to my lawns (for my bedroom is on the ground level) I see a shining expanse of heavy silver — the dew on the grass. Where the sun catches the dew here and there it splits the silver light up into the seven colours of the rainbow, and miniature jewels sparkle brilliantly. But as the sun gains in power the dew dries, and the grass shows green again, losing its silvery lustre.

A Medley of Bright Colours

It is still very lovely in the garden, especially in one of my favourite places, an old teak seat set in the curve of a big rockery, facing due west. Behind me blaze the orange marigolds and the scarlet snap-dragons, which have now taken pride of place on the rockery, and in front of me is a round bed of gorgeous zinnias, a medley of bright colours, from deepest magenta to purest orange — a crude mixture, one might say, but most gay and delightful, nevertheless! I am always surprised that more people do not grow these tall, brilliant flowers, so splendid for cutting and so useful in the beds. I grow mine each year from seed, and they are truly bonny flowers.

In this favourite corner of mine hum many bees, and often the great gleaming dragonflies come darting here and there in the sunshine. There are two that I know well this month, for I see them every day, and I know they are the same ones. One is a yellow-bronze colour, and the other is a kingfisher blue. Both are enormous, at least five inches long, very different from the slender, bodkin-like dragonflies that hatch out much earlier in the year, and which infest the rushes by the long lily pond. I think these big ones come from the marshes behind Old Thatch, where there are many quiet backwaters, undisturbed year after year. They are magnificent creatures, and cause much excitement among the eager sparrows when they fly by. It is most amusing to watch the clumsy little brown birds dart heavily after the zigzagging dragonflies, only to give up the chase in disgust after a minute or two.

A Bird-like Moth

The vanilla fragrance of my big standard cherry-pie plants still draws many kinds of moths and butterflies. Once again the quaint, hovering humming-bird hawk moth has come to visit them. It stands in the air on its quickly vibrating wings savouring the scent of the heliotrope flowers, and then is off again in wide circles, a strange bird-like moth, not often seen.

The fruit harvest is a tragedy this year — not only at Old Thatch, but in all the district round, and in many other counties too. The great frost in May did its work only too thoroughly, alas! My fruit trees, of all kinds, number nearly a hundred, and few of them have any fruit at all. There will be no apple picking, and but few pears. Even our marvellous baking-apple tree, which has never failed us before, and has to be shored up year after year at fruit time, has no more than a handful of apples on its green boughs! Usually our apples last us from one harvest time almost to the next — this year they will barely last a week! We, however, do not depend for our livelihood on our fruit, as do many fruit-growers and market gardeners, and some of these folk are filled with despair at their bleak harvest.

But other things are good, as is always the way. The outdoor tomatoes are loaded down with great trusses of ripening fruit, and the cucumbers grown in a small glass frame with the sun's rays for heat, have ripened in dozens. They are easy to grow, and should find a place in every garden, set in some warm corner. A salad made of home-grown tomatoes, brought in warm from the September sun, a green cucumber cool to the hand, and a fresh curly-hearted lettuce cut from the lettuce row, is a salad fit for a king, especially if you pick all of them yourself!

Mushroom Ketchup

Then there are mushrooms, growing by the hundred in the fields around, big white ones, small button ones, all to be picked in the heavy dew of the sunrise. Have you made mushroom ketchup from mushrooms picked by yourself? I can assure you it tastes far better than any you can buy in the shops! It is well worth paddling about in dew-hung grass, getting your skirts soaked through.

There are swarms of different insects about now, all eager to enjoy the last few days of summer. The wasps forsake their nests and come to gorge on the new-made jam or the fallen pear. Daddy-long-legs, clumsy and ineffectual, drift over the fields, their legs hanging down in a bunch. The stable fly, unpleasant creature, comes into the house, and stabs our legs and arms. It is so like the ordinary house fly that we say in surprise and anger, "How strange! The flies are beginning to bite now!" But it is not the house-fly that is attacking us, it is its cousin the stable-fly.

Her Children are Precious

Running among the grasses in the lane I have seen two or three wolf-spiders. Each was carrying her precious egg-ball. If you have quick eyes, you may see her, too, in your garden or by the wayside. Soon the eggs in the ball will hatch out and the tiny spiders may be seen clinging to their mother's back, like small brown warts. It seems strange that such maternal care should be shown by this fierce spider. If she is forced to leave her egg-ball, she will hide and return to it time after time, to try and retrieve it. She will eat her husband — but her children are precious to her.

I am always amused with the woolly bear caterpillars in the month of September. There seems to be so many of them on the lane and on the high road, hurrying along fast as if they were late for an appointment. You cannot fail to see them if you look. Most of them are the larvæ of the garden tiger moth. Perhaps their food plant is dying or has been eaten up, and they are seeking fresh quarters. Whatever the reason they are always in a hurry, crossing the road like tiny furry snakes!

September's glory this year is her roses. The June roses were a failure — poor, frosted buds that showed none of the brilliance of summer. But the autumn roses are lovely. It is as if the bushes were determined to make up for the poor summer display. Now — glowing, prolific, brilliant — the roses, perfect in shape and colour, are rounding off the summer with a mass of gorgeous bloom. They may continue right into November if the weather is kind. There is something enchanting about a bowl of roses in the fire light of an autumn evening!

Enid Blyton Magazine

(Last issue, September 9th, 1959)

This is the last issue of our much-loved magazine. There are two reasons. First, all kinds of interesting work keeps coming along which no one but myself can do — making films for you — T.V. programmes — making new records, overseas radio programmes — *Noddy in Toyland* panto, now to be put on in other big towns as well as London — and new books of course! And going all the time is my magazine of which, as you know, I write practically every word myself (except the adverts). The second reason is to do with my husband, who, now that he has decided to retire, naturally wants me to go about with him a good deal, and share the things he loves so much — his farm in Dorset, golf and travelling here and there about the world. Well, I must be with him, and so with much sadness, I have decided to give up the thing that ties me down most — our magazine, the work I love best . . . I am saddest of all because of our four great Clubs which thousands of you help me with so generously. These Clubs helped the Blind Children, the Spastic Children and have helped my little Children's Home here in Beaconsfield. My animal-loving readers have helped numberless sick and injured animals, through my Busy Bees Club, for many years. Thousands of pounds have been raised for all these fine causes, and every week your well-earned, generous gifts have been coming in. It has been a great delight to me to know I have about 500,000 children working week in and week out to help me. Hundreds of parents and teachers have helped too . . .

Poem written during Government discussion on the
Abolition of Capital Punishment (1950)

To Hang — or not to Hang — that
is the Question!

Two Points of View

What — you'd have them *hung* — not give them a chance!
Poor fellows, they're mentally ill!
They need kindly treatment — reforming, you know —
And first-rate psychiatrist's skill!
I'm told they're unhappy, and warped in their minds,
We've *no* right to let a man swing
Simply because he has strangled a child
And raped her — yes, poor little thing,
I grant you it's shocking — but *I* think it's wrong
To hang that poor man till he's dead —
Reform him! He'll make a good citizen yet —
This *hanging* — it makes me see red!

Then *I* said, 'Well, *mothers* can see red at times —
The red of a little girl's blood,
And loud in our ears we can hear the weak cries
Of a child with her cheek in the mud.
She sobs for her father, and maybe to God,
But only the nightwind sighs
As a monster rapes and strangles and gloats,
Then carries away his prize
To dump in a ditch, or under a hedge —
And see him when morning's here
As he reads of the crime and tut-tuts to his wife,
'*Another* sex-murder, my dear!'

No — don't interrupt me — and DON'T say again
That Death is too hard for this man;
Was Death then so easy for that little girl,

Whose few years were so short a span?
You've pity to spare for the raper, who knows
That in lust he would murder again,
But you've none for the child, and little for those
Who mourn her in horror and pain.

And you ask me WHY I would hang this man!
Though you know it's our only hope
To stop any fiend who would rape and kill —
He's a coward — and he *fears* the rope!
You're not quite sure if I'm right — or not?
You'll think about it — alone?
Well, if you're doubtful, *I'm* certain of this —
`You haven't a child of your own!"

ENID BLYTON

Children's Reading Taste

(*The Library Association Record*, September 1949)

We thank MR. S. C. DEDMAN *for permission to print below a letter received by him from* MISS ENID BLYTON *regarding his paper on "Children's Reading Taste" given at the Eastbourne Conference.*

"It is nice to know that there is at least one librarian who knows what there is in the children's books on his shelves, and who can pick out the essentials in a good book for boys and girls. You librarians do a fine work with children and you hold a very responsible job — it should actually be almost in the nature of a vocation, I think.

"You are quite right when you say that children's books should be morally sound. This is the most important thing in any book for children. One should also be a born storyteller — then style and language come beautifully and naturally, making the book easy and delightful to read. Many authors have this style, from Homer onwards — it is a sign of the good storyteller. For children it is doubly important — however fine a story one has thought of, it is no use unless one has a natural "story-telling style", which carries the children along without being obtrusive.

"It always amazes me when people deride books for being what they call "escapist". Any intelligent person must surely know, if he thinks about it, that a large part of our finest literature is escapist — take *Treasure Island* for instance. Escapist literature should only be scorned when it is badly written or conceived, not because it is "escapist". This has become the kind of cliché used by the less intelligent reviewers, critics or librarians.

"All adventure stories are 'escapist' — mine among them. I cannot think why some people use this adjective in a derogative sense — such stories fulfil a very real need — and one of the finest, Eric Williams' *The Wooden Horse* is better than any fiction.

"But only about thirty of my books are 'escapist'. I write Nature books, 'home stories' of family life, religious books, readers of all kinds for schools — I think few of the general public know that my educational and religious books number almost as many as my story-books — and are also best-sellers. In the educational world I wear the label of 'Educational writer'. In the religious world I am solidly backed by ministers of all creeds, and labelled 'writer on religious subjects'. In the librarian and bookshop world I am labelled 'story-teller for children'. I consider all the three equally important, and it is because of my religious convictions, my educational training (I am a trained Froebel Kindergarten Teacher) and my gift for story-telling that I think my books are successful. They give children a feeling of security as well as pleasure — they know that they will never find anything wrong, hideous, horrible, murderous or vulgar in my books, although there is plenty of excitement, mystery and fun — and the children are always real live characters, exactly like the readers. After all, I have children of my own, and hear them talk and quarrel and plan — if I didn't know how to present them, I would be a very poor mother!

"I'm not out only to tell stories, much as I love this — I am out to inculcate decent thinking, loyalty, honesty, kindliness, and all the things that children *should* be taught. I was speaking to Mr. Basil Henriques the other day (the Juvenile Delinquents' Magistrate) and we both agreed that if only we could raise up just *one* generation of first-rate children, we needn't worry about the future! But oh, the difficulties of getting even one generation."

The Summer Storm (Play)

The Characters

Sally Hanly: Daughter of Robert Hanly, well-known writer of light comedies. Not yet 21. Small, slight, very pretty. Has had two years at the University and is hoping to take her degree the next year. Is very popular, a merry, affectionate girl, whose life has gone easily, so that no demands have been made on her character. It is therefore surprising to her family when she shows such a strong reaction to events and goes with great determination to follow her own way with a sense of duty; compassion — and unhappiness.

Jane Hanly: Also a daughter of the Hanlys, the same age as Sally. Plain, plump always the second-string when Sally is with her. She is at the University too, but does not attract the opposite sex as does Sally. A loyal and good-natured girl, always struggling against the jealousy she feels for Sally, but not admitting to it. Only when she falls in love does she blossom out into a kind of beauty.

Robert Hanly: Their father, a celebrated writer of comedies, a simple pleasant man, rather weak, devoted to his family, whom he considers that he knows inside-out. A goodlooking, likeable fellow, unobtrusively managed by his wife, oddly youthful in his ways owing to a streak of immaturity in his character.

Mary Hanly: A quiet, sweet-faced woman, loving her family deeply, faults and all. Calm and pleasant on the surface, but capable of strong reactions, which can be sensed despite her apparently calm and cheerful dealings with her household. She has a real sense of humour.

Andrew Hanly: The son. About nineteen and down from his first year at Balliol. A typical undergrad, restless, amusing, talkative, omniscient — but quite a wise and responsible young fellow when trouble breaks. Loves his family, and regards them with humour.

Mervyn Villiers: A well-known actor of about 35 or so, who has played the chief parts in Robert Hanly's plays for many years. He has a great opinion of himself, is rather mannered, a little meretricious, like the parts he is used to playing — and hopes to marry the pretty little Sally.

John Preston: A young law student, about 27, genuinely attracted by Jane, and superficially by Sally. He is tall and rather awkward, with none of Mervyn's assured walk and movements, or sophisticated manner. He has an ordinary, very pleasant face, and good manners, is rather shy, not used to girls, but good at his law work. Meets everything, good or bad, unshaken, and in spite of his awkwardness, has a real attraction ... the attraction of a big, well-mannered, rather clumsy but devoted dog.

Peter Johnson: Over 50, but old for his age, due to his time in prison. Silver-haired and handsome, slow in his movements, and a little strange in his speech and ways — haunted by the happenings of twenty years ago, lonely and friendless, yet capable of a difficult and unselfish decision when suddenly faced with a living memory of the woman he once loved.

Malcolm McDougal: Male servant to Peter Johnson — a typical Scot of about 55.

Mrs. McDougal: His wife — a typical kindly outspoken Scotswoman, buxom and pleasant-faced, grey-haired and competent.

Correspondence with Peter McKellar

Professor Peter McKellar, now Professor of Psychology at Otago University, New Zealand, first wrote to Enid Blyton in early February 1953, requesting information on the writer's imagery processes for a psychological study he was then pursuing at Aberdeen University. Enid Blyton wrote nine letters to the psychologist during the five years following and material from these was subsequently referred to by Peter McKellar in his book *Imagination and Thinking* (London: Cohen and West; New York: Basic Books 1957). The book is referred to from time to time in these extracts from the correspondence.

Enid Blyton to Peter McKellar, February 15th, 1953

Thank you for your interesting letter. Of course I'll help you if I can.

I don't really understand myself how my imagination works. It is a thing completely beyond my control, as I imagine it is with most imaginative writers. Where I am lucky is that I have such easy *access* to my imagination — i.e. I do not have to 'wait for inspiration' as so many do. I have merely to 'open the sluice gates' and out it all pours with no effort or labour of my own. This is why I can write so much and so quickly — it's all I can do to keep up with it, even typing at top speed on my typewriter.

In my case the imagery began as a young child. In bed I used to shut my eyes and 'let my mind go free'. And into it would come what I used to call my 'night stories' — which were, in effect, all kinds of imaginings in story form — sometimes I was the 'I' in the story, sometimes I wasn't. I thought all children had the same 'night stories' and was amazed when one day I found they hadn't.

Because of this imagining I wanted to write — to put down what I had seen and felt and heard in my imagination. I had a gift for words, so it was easy. (That has been in my family for some time.)

I am a very well-balanced person, quick in the uptake, not in the least temperamental. I never wanted to write for anyone but children (which was odd, in a child, I think).

Now I will tell you as clear and simply as I can, how I write my stories, and use my imagination.

First of all, you must realise that when I begin a completely new book with new characters, I have no idea at all what the characters will be, where the story will happen, or what adventures or events will occur. All I know is that the book is to be say, an 'Adventure' tale, or a 'Mystery' or a 'fairy-tale' and so on, or that it must be a certain length — say 40,000 words.

I shut my eyes for a few minutes, with my portable typewriter on my knee — I make my mind a blank and wait — and then, as clearly as I would see real children, my characters stand before me in my mind's eye. I see them in detail — hair, eyes, feet, clothes, expression — and I always know their Christian names but never their surname. (I get these out of a telephone directory afterwards!) More than that, I know their characters — good, bad, mean, generous, brave, loyal, hot-tempered and so on. I don't know how I know that — it's as instinctive as sizing up a person in real life, at which I am quite good. As I look at them, the characters take on movement and life — they talk and laugh (I hear them) and perhaps I see that one of them has a dog, or a parrot, and I think — 'Ah — that's good. That will liven up the story.' Then behind the characters appears the setting, in colour, of course, of an old house — a ruined castle — an island — a row of houses.

That's enough for me. My hands go down on my typewriter keys and I begin. The first sentence comes straight into my mind, I don't have to think of it — I don't have to think of anything.

The story is enacted in my mind's eye almost as if I had a private cinema screen there. The characters come on and off, talk, laugh, sing — have their adventures — quarrel — and so on. I watch and hear everything, writing it down with my typewriter — reporting the dialogue (which is always completely natural) the expressions on the faces, the feelings of delight, fear and so on. I don't know what anyone is going to say or do. I don't know what is going to happen. I am in the happy position of being able to write a story and read it for the first time, at one and the same moment. The odd thing is that if a character comes in singing a song or reciting a poem, I hear it and take it down immediately, rhyme and all — though if I were actually writing a poem about something myself, I would, like most poets, have to think hard about metre and correct rhyming. But this imaginative creative work is something quite different from *thinking* work —

with me, at any rate. If I am writing 'real' poetry, as distinct from ordinary verse, I have to work hard over it — and welcome the sudden gift of a complete line or two, or the happy word — *these* come from the 'under-mind' or whatever you call it — the hard thinking comes from my upper conscious mind. I use my 'under-mind' a tremendous lot. I send things down to it and let them simmer there, forgotten. The answer comes up complete when I want it. I believe mathematicians do this.

Another odd thing is that my 'under-mind' seems to be able to receive such directions as 'the story must be 40,000 words long'. Because, sure enough, no matter what length I have to write to (it varies tremendously) the book ends almost to the word — the right length. This seems to me peculiar. Another odd thing is that sometimes something crops up in the story which I am sure is wrong, or somehow out of place. Not a bit of it! It rights itself, falls into place — and now I dare not alter a thing I think is wrong. I have never yet found my 'under-mind' to make a mistake, though I make plenty myself in ordinary life. It's much cleverer than I am! I once tried to write a book in the usual way — sitting down, writing out a plot — inventing a list of characters — making a list of chapters and so on. I couldn't write a page, not a single page: it was labour — it was dull — it was, in a word, completely uninspired! When children write to me (and hundreds write every week) they say so often 'I love your books because they are so real — I feel I am having the adventure too.' If I invented the adventures they wouldn't feel like that: I am indeed lucky. When I am writing a book, in touch with my under-mind, I am very happy, excited, full of vitality. I could go on till the book is finished but my arms get tired of being held over the typewriter. When I go to bed, to sleep, I see the characters again in my dreams, but the adventures they have then are fantastic, not credible and balanced as they are when I am awake. They get mixed up with my dreams, I suppose. When I have finished a book, the characters fade away at once — as if my under-mind had said — 'There — that's done — I'm empty and waiting for my next call.'

I don't pretend to understand all this. To write book after book without knowing what is going to be said or done sounds silly — and yet it happens. Sometimes a character makes a joke, a really funny one, that makes me laugh as I type it on my paper — and I think, 'Well, I couldn't have thought of that myself in a hundred years'! And then I think, 'Well, who *did* think of it then?'

. . . it is only when I write imaginative stuff that I write in the ways I have described. I think that such prolific writers as Dickens were probably the same — and Homer's intensely real flashes of thought in his poems seem to me the same. They are so exactly *right* when they really are the products of one's under-mind, super-mind, other-mind, whatever you like to call it: one learns to recognise it in other writings — Shakespeare is full of it — superb! Christopher Fry has it. All these writers are different — but I am sure they are the same in one way — they draw from their under-mind easily and surely . . .

I lead an ordinary life, with husband and girls, and I don't think any stranger meeting me would know I was a writer or anything else. I don't feel any different from other people except that I sometimes think my mind works more quickly, which sounds very conceited . . .

It might also interest you to know that my books are translated into dozens of different languages — Malay French Fijian, Japanese, Indian, Finnish, Icelandic, Greek, all kinds — and yet, although my characters are typically British children, with the British ideals of fair play, loyalty, generosity and so on, all these nations love my books, and clamour for them. The one that clamours most, oddly enough, is Germany. Even the adults read them there — I'd love to be told why and how this should be — perhaps you can enlighten me! . . .

I should perhaps say that I recognise many things that are thrown up from my under-mind, transmuted and changed — a castle seen long ago — a dog — a small child — woods long forgotten, in a new setting . . .

Peter McKellar to Enid Blyton, February 23rd, 1953

. . . You have given a most lucid and invaluable account of your imagery, and I am specially interested in the fact that it all began with hypnagogic imagery — the 'night stories' to which you refer. One of the interesting things about human imaging, it strikes me, is the very small part of human imaginings that has been recorded, an infinitely small part of what has been experienced by people. It is most interesting to discover a writer who has made a systematic account to record such a large part of her imaging in the way you have. Very little seems to be known about 'night stories', though vivid imaging has been itself pretty fully studied. The pioneer work of E. R. Jaensch: *Eidetic Imagery* (Kegan Paul, 1930), you will probably know. I note with interest your feeling as a child that everybody must have such imagery, and such night stories. The usual incidence of eidetic imagery, in ordinary waking life, with adults is in the vicinity of about 7 per cent. (It is very much greater with children.) My own study of the largely-uninvestigated night stories or hypnagogic images indicates that they occur with about 40 per cent of adults, though as I haven't got very far with the investigation these figures would be very approximate.

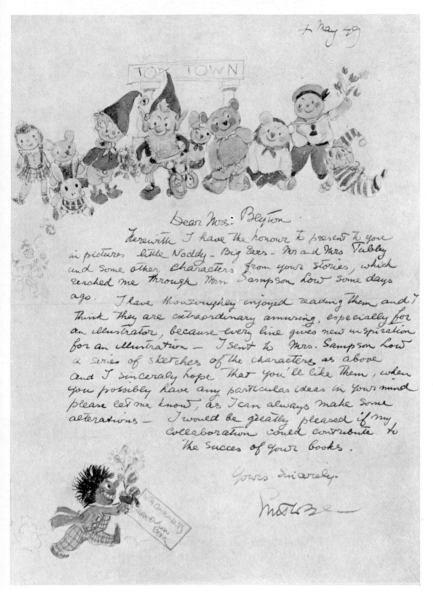

+ May 49

Dear Mrs. Beyton.

Herewith I have the honour to present to you
in pictures little Noddy - Big Ears - Mr and Mrs Tubby
and some other Characters from your stories, which
reached me through Mrs Sampson Low some days
ago. I have thouroughly enjoyed reading them and I
think they are extraordinary amusing, especially for
an illustrator, because every line gives new inspiration
for an illustration - I sent to Mrs. Sampson Low
a series of sketches of the characters, as above
and I sincerely hope that you'll like them, when
you possibly have any particular ideas in your mind
please let me know, as I can always make some
alterations - I would be greatly pleased if my
collaboration could contribute to
the succes of your books.

Yours sincerely.

Reproduction of Van Beek's letter with first detailed sketches of Toyland characters

With the first Noddy fro
Enid Blyton's pantomi
Noddy in Toyland

Party for the 100,000th me
ber of the Enid Blyt
Magazine Club, 1957

They refer, of course, only to the having of them and not to any very marked development of the faculty concerned. They are usually of a brief, and fleeting kind. Some of those I have accounts of are amusing, some a little terrifying, some visual, others auditory, but I have a few cases of similarly vivid imagery before sleep, for touch, temperature and even smell experiences. Your detailed account of your own, your development of this usually neglected tendency, and your putting it all to such a useful purpose, is of extreme interest to this study ...

You did kindly offer to answer any additional questions. There are just one or two that arise. The first relates to your postscript about your recognising some, but I take it not all, of the things imaged as things previously seen and heard. If there is anything you feel you would like to add to this it would be of great interest. I find with the hypnagogic images that some people are totally unable to recognise the imagery as involving anything they remember ever having previously seen. Others, however, find the before sleep imagery closely related usually to the experiences of the previous day. The difference between the two may prove to be important. Again, you mention that your 'private cinema screen' began with the before sleeping imagery. I take it, however, that the major part of your writing is done with similar imagery in the ordinary waking state. Do, however, the 'night stories' themselves still go on (as opposed to the actual dreams to which you refer), and do you find that these night stories also yield story material? Anything you could add about the relation between the before sleep and the ordinary day-time imagery would be of great interest. My only other question is the obvious one of whether you have tried out other methods of recording the stories than typing. If you have, as you probably will have, did you find it less satisfactory? (in short, is the total situation, complete with the movements of typing, the best for recording these stories?) ...

Enid Blyton to Peter McKellar, February 26th, 1953

Thank you for your very interesting letter. I'm very glad mine was of use to you. To tell you the truth I'd be very pleased if I could find an explanation of the goings-on of my sub-conscious!! It startles me sometimes.

Before I forget — I've told the publisher of the Little Noddy books (my most popular series for the youngest age-group) to send your small daughter the first three of these books (there are 6 or 7) because I think she may like them. If you read them yourself to her you will see how her imagination gets hold of Little Noddy, and makes him come alive to her! One of the great reasons for reading imaginative books to very young children is to stir their imaginations and their thinking — to set their minds ticking — and it's interesting to see how even a 2½ year old will sometimes take enormous strides forward as soon as he is read to — but the books or stories must, of course, be absolutely suited to his understanding.

I think hundreds upon hundreds of writers have just the same power of imagination as I have — but I have noticed that only a *very* small percentage have the easy access to it that I have. Some 'wait for inspiration', some labour and wrestle with their imagination (and the labour shows in their work!), the lucky few have their imagination at their command, and then the whole thing is effortless — a sheer delight. That is where I am so lucky — the gates are so easy to open and also, I think, the fact that I am so close to my imagination prevents my being badly-balanced, temperamental or moody as so many creative people are.

My night 'images' were always more than merely 'images' — they were a coherent line of events in the form of a narrative. My simile of a 'private cinema screen' is the best I can think of. But it's a 3-dimensional screen, complete with sound, smell and taste — and feeling! This is why I can describe things so realistically in my stories, 'as if I had been there'. I *have* been there — but only in my imagination! This is probably why all the artists that work for me find my stories easy to illustrate — they visualise the picture at once from the words.

I did not know that I was 'training' my under-mind (or subconscious) in its ability to create and imagine, but I was, of course, and have been all these years. I knew how to get in touch with it, I knew how to be at one with it. I knew how to pull out the imaginings or put them into words — and now, with so much practice, a whole book is formed in a few days, characters alive and complete, incidents, jokes, everything — and my conscious mind has nothing whatever to do with it except record what it sees — by means of my typewriter. Sometimes I find it very strange. For instance, I have been asked to write a book, which will deal with a scout or scouts, with kindness to animals and with a definite religious thread going through it. No more instructions than that.

Now the ordinary writer would begin to think consciously about the book, plans would take shape in his mind, he would arrange a scheme and so on — and then write the book according to what he had consciously planned.

All I have done is to say firmly to myself — there must be a scout or scouts — animals — and ethics — and I leave it at that and don't think another word about it. But those conscious directions penetrate down into the imagination, and when, on Monday, I sit down to begin the book, it will already be complete in my imagination — characters (a scout or scouts will be there) setting, animals, everything. No thought or planning will have gone to the book — it will well up spontaneously and rhythmically, suited for the particular age of child, and will be the right length. This is sometimes rather weird, as you can imagine.

Your question about recognising things that are thrown up from my imagination is an interesting one. There are, for instance, many islands in my stories, many old castles, many caves — all things that have attracted me in my travels. These things come up time and again in my stories, changed, sometimes *almost* unrecognisable — and then I see a detail that makes me say — yes — that's one of the Cheddar Caves, surely! Characters also remind me of people I have met — I think my imagination contains all the things I have ever seen or heard, things my conscious mind has long forgotten — and they have all been jumbled about till a light penetrates into the mass, and a happening here or an object there is taken out, transmuted, or formed into something that takes a natural and rightful place in the story — or I *may* recognise it — or I may not — I don't think that I use anything I have not seen or experienced — I don't think I could. I don't think one can take out of one's mind more than one puts in. In the same way I do not think, for instance, that a man can write a funny book if he has no sense of humour — however powerful his imagination — because his mind does not deal with humour! Our books are facets of ourselves.

My before-sleep imagery (when falling off to sleep) is nothing whatever to do with so-called 'night stories' — completely different — just a jumble, fleeting, and of no account. The 'night stories' I had were always coherent — and went on evolving like a proper story till I fell asleep. I don't have the same kind of 'night stories' or imaginings now that I had as a child — I have command over that, whatever it is, and use it when I want to, and banish it otherwise. I do no 'day-dreaming'. I *work* with my subconscious, it doesn't run away with me! It used to, of course, now I would not let it — it is in harness, and works all the better for it — and makes for a well-balanced personality. (I don't believe I have answered your questions properly — you must ask again if not.) It's so difficult to explain something unusual and so elusive.

You want to know about typing — I always type, for quickness, but I can of course *write* a story by hand just as well. But typing keeps up with my imagination better. The story evolves so very quickly when I write a book. I could probably dictate just as well, but I'd have to bother with a machine and records then and that would 'break the spell'!

You can quote what you like from anything I have said or written if it's of any help — but it would be nice if you could let me see a proof to make sure everything is absolutely accurate!

I was interested in your brief reports of student's hypnagogic imagery. Have you read *Timeless Moment*? There is a great deal of interesting and thoughtful material there about all these things. Few people, I imagine, experience the 'Timeless Moment' (mystics do, of course, but that's rather different). I have only experienced one and have never forgotten it and never will. I wonder if you ever have? The man who wrote *Timeless Moment* experienced one, and described it extremely well. I'm not a mystic, I'm a very ordinary, cheerful sort of person, but I must say that things of this kind intrigue me very much.

You will be very sorry you ever wrote to me! I do wish you could throw some light on these strange things. I struggle to explain myself to myself — but when you are at one and the same time, creator and interpreter, using your unconscious and your conscious intermingled for hours, it is sometimes very muddling! Which is really which? . . .

Enid Blyton to Peter McKellar, January 28th, 1955

. . . I have recently tried a new medium of writing — that is, writing a play . . . [see page 161] . . . I thought you might like to know how an imagination, apparently harnessed only to the writing of books, can adapt itself, and pour itself out in quite a different medium. It took me nearly three weeks to write the play, but I could write another in a week now that I know how to harness my imagination to the new medium. I have just finished a book for Macmillans — the 8th in a popular series that has been translated into many languages. I began it on Monday, and finished it this afternoon (Friday). It is 60,000 words long and flowed like its title (*River of Adventure*). All the same I know quite well that if I had had to miss even a day in the writing of it I might have had to give it up. Once the river is dammed anywhere, it won't flow again in that particular direction — which is why I *must* write a book at 'full flow'. I wish you could explain to me why I have these limitations and their opposites! It puzzles me very much at times! . . .

Peter McKellar to Enid Blyton, April 25th, 1957

. . . At what I hope you will not regard as at long last — it is a very great pleasure to send you this copy of my book.

It is only a small return for the most valuable and interesting introspections with which you have provided me, and which are now recorded in print in the form you approved. I hope you will like it. What pleases me is the way in which your creative processes, though atypical in many ways, nevertheless fit the general theory of original and creative thinking — which has for me been a great mystery.

I hope you will find the book, as a whole, of some interest. It takes a pretty broad sweep from thinking as represented by the students' examination answer: the dream; the work of art; oddities like number forms, colour associations and hypnagogic imagery; grossly abnormal thinking; to the kinds of thinking we call theorising in science.

My impression is there is a lot of room for research in this field; too much that has so far been done has dealt merely with the history of the psychology of thinking; too little has attempted to make a new contribution, however tiny . . .

. . . A start on the psychology of literary creativeness seems to me to be being made when we attempt to record, as accurately as human introspection permits, how individual creative thinkers *have* thought. Later I hope somebody will be able to generalise this knowledge into principles which apply to creative thinking as a whole . . .

Enid Blyton to Peter McKellar, May 13th, 1957

I have just finished reading your remarkably interesting book, and I really must write to congratulate you most warmly . . . You cover a very wide field, as you should, of course, but the reader never gets lost or bored — and your masterly little recapitulations at the end of each chapter are most satisfying — tying all loose ends up neatly for any untidy-minded reader. I do that for children very often!

I must say that I agree with all your ideas, as far as my own particular knowledge goes. I am no 'mystic', as you know, and therefore think that supernatural manifestations can always be reduced to common-sense explanations. You cover so many interesting phases of mind, all of which aroused my curiosity, making me stop and consider, and delve into my own experiences. You used many happy phrases, apt for the readers understanding — like the 'magic lantern' idea for hypnagogic imagery. I hadn't thought of that simile before, but it is, of course exactly right. I've been experimenting with this kind of imagery so different from my own way of imagining which really consists of a kind of opening of 'sluice gates' and allowing a flow of cinematograph pictures and sounds to flood into my conscious mind, from the 'under-mind'. *Quite* different from the magic lantern slides of hypnagogic pictures. I find that the gargoylish and grotesque type do not come along as frequently as the more ordinary type — such as clouds, waves, fountains, the moving, interchanging things — or still pictures in colour (or uncoloured) beautifully etched in every detail, such as a brilliant golden gorse-bush against a clear blue sky, each thorn put in meticulously — or a child's head in perfect silhouette that I can 'stare' at for a long time before it dissolves. Never the kind of fast-moving cinematic picture, complete with sound-track that my conscious mind pulls up from my under-mind when writing. All the same, I think that my hypnagogic imagery (which I find easy to induce now I've tried to) is only composed of things in my visual memory, nothing really new — even the gargoylish faces are more like the kind of thing one seeks to find in cloud shapes — just a shape *like* something, which one's eye completes on its own and we say 'there's a horse's head in that cloud' and so on. I have sometimes heard noises in the hypnagogic imagery, but have always assumed (probably quite wrongly) that they were *outside* noises — a sudden snore from my husband, sounding like a commanding voice — the sudden rattle of my window, which may sound like some kind of spoken or shouted sentence. They have always seemed to me to be too *real* to be imagined — they must come from *outside* me, not inside my mind.

I feel I would also like to comment on your '*presque vu*' reports. For some reason I had not heard the experiences called by that name, but it is really a very good definition. I have only once had this experience, in my teens, under 'laughing gas'. I have had gas many times, but only once did I ever experience '*presque vu*' — and then it was in one respect different from the things you report in that instead of '*almost seeing*', I *did* see and grasp everything, or so I thought! — and then lost it. This is what happened. I have never forgotten it and its extraordinary clarity has always remained with me. I found myself (apparently bodiless but still firmly myself) being drawn through space at a speed so great that I thought I must be going at the pace of light itself. I seemed to go through vibrating *waves* of light, and thought that I must be passing many suns and many universes. (I love astronomy, hence my suppositions, I suppose!) Finally, after a long, incredibly long journey in an incredibly short time I arrived somewhere. This Somewhere was, as far as I could make out, in my dazed and amazed state, a place of wonderful light (not daylight or sunlight) — and I saw, or knew, that there were Beings there — no shape, nothing tangible — but I knew they were great and holy and ineffable. Then I knew I was going to hear the secret of Everything — and Everything was explained to me, simply and with the utmost lucidity. I was overjoyed — filled with wonder and delight. I knew the reasons behind existence, time, space, evil, goodness, pain — and I rejoiced, and marvelled that no one had guessed such things before. Then I knew I must go back to my

214

body, wherever it was, through all the long eras of time and vastness of space, and as I left in sorrow, my spirit cried out, or seemed to cry out 'Let me tell everyone this wonderful thing I know, this secret that explains everything and will bring such rejoicing and happiness!' And as I went back down aeons of time, I was told I must not divulge the secret and I cried out why — and as I went, I was told why, and I said 'At least let *me* always remember', but no, I was not even to be allowed to remember even one small detail myself, and I cried out again — 'But why may I not remember?' And then, just at the very moment when I returned to my body in the dentist's chair, I was told why I must not even hug the knowledge to myself, and it was such a logical and wonderful reason that I accepted it joyfully, in the fullest understanding, and found myself opening my eyes, and smiling happily in the chair, completely overcome with what I thought had been a true and overwhelming revelation. That is the only *presque vu* experience I have had, and as you will agree, it was more than *presque vu* — it was '*complitement vu*' — and yet ended by being completely lost. I can still get back the feeling at the end of it of acquiescing joyfully in my forgoing of the secret, and yet hugging to myself the certainty that 'all's well with the world', despite everything!*

This experience has nothing to do with religion, it wasn't a 'vision', only something amazingly produced by the gas — but I kept hold of my identity all the time, and did not lose the reporter sense of the practised writer, who instinctively retains all that is essential to her true 'news-story'. I have told only two or three people of this experience, as I did not think it sounded believable . . .

Your mescaline experiences must have been rather terrifying. They would be to me. I dread the feeling of losing my identity, of not being able to control my own mind! . . .

* Enid related this experience to her daughter Gillian, but substituted the garden seat at Green Hedges for the 'dentist's chair' and placed the time of this experience as the middle 1950s.

The Blyton Line

A psychologist's view by Michael Woods

(An extract from 'Blyton Revisited', a special edition of *LINES*, Autumn 1969)

Imagine an author with an output of over two hundred books, loved by millions, not only in this country but in most of the English speaking world and the continent of Europe. Suppose, too, that this author not only ran a twice-monthly magazine and contributed to many famous journals, but also wrote many songs, plays and poems. Surely nobody could but admire and respect such phenomenal success — such variety and such creativity? Yes of course, but not if it belongs to a children's author called Enid Blyton.

Enid Blyton was probably one of the most successful writers of children's books this country has known. A visit to any public library will make this clear; usually every one of Enid Blyton's books the library possesses is out on loan! But what of the writer herself? What information will we find about her? Surely such a large stone in the pond of children's books must have created some ripples in the adult section. But not Enid Blyton. She has remained virtually ignored, even by those adults who are most concerned with children and children's books. Even comics have fared better, and have been taken seriously as phenomena of our times by sociologists and others. It is virtually impossible to find any information about Enid Blyton, apart from a few lines in *Who's Who 1969*, which forgot to include her age and the fact that she died in November 1968.

If one draws a dividing line at puberty, the reactions on either side to the name Enid Blyton will be vastly different. One might almost use it as a test to determine whether a young person is mature enough to be admitted into a cinema to see an 'X' film. Amongst her vast public of children, just a whisper of her name conjures up feelings of excitement and anticipation; amongst adults reactions range from derision to nausea. What is it about Enid Blyton's works that causes such strong feelings? Such admiration on the one side, and anger on the other? Can it be jealousy on the part of the adults at her fantastic success through doing something that appears so obvious and simple? Perhaps it is, but my feelings are that the answer lies deeper than that. Adults may crave background details as necessary for realism and atmosphere in a story, but to a child, however, they are just an irritation that gets in the way of the main action. It is action they want, and with Enid Blyton it is action they get.

The same is true for characterisation. Invariably the main characters are groups of four or five children, usually siblings and their cousins, ranging in age from about seven to fourteen, roughly the age boundaries of Blyton readers. Groups this size are usually safe because of their numbers. They are not so large as to be unwieldy. One may suppose they reflect, perhaps, the nuclear family, and offer far less opportunities for tension within the group than, say, units of three — the eternal triangle. It seems a deliberate policy on Enid Blyton's part to define the characters in her books only in the haziest terms. It is very difficult to tell children apart, especially in a series like the 'Secret Seven'. Those children who do stand out are complete oddities; George, the girl who tries to be a boy in the 'Five' series, and Philip, the boy who talks to animals in the 'Adventure' series. Elaborate characterisation may be necessary in an adult novel, but in children's fiction it is probably a waste of time at best. Children's imaginations readily supply characters to suit their own needs, and Enid Blyton's policy of being vague about her characters enables the young reader to identify more easily with them.

Another inescapable point about Enid Blyton's writing is its strong upper-middle-class bias. Vague mention is made of 'Cook', the children are shown in one drawing arriving in a chauffeur-driven car, and other minions are always at hand to arrange things for them, without any hint of worldly remuneration. The children adopt a superior attitude, not only to the crooks, but also to the cooks of the world, and Enid Blyton tosses this off casually as though it is the only right and natural order of things.

Apart from its convenience in so many ways, for instance, being on hobnobbing terms with police inspectors and being able to conjure up impossible things like horse-drawn caravans and helicopters, this superior setting carries much weight with the young readers, in rather the same way that having army officers drawn from the upper echelons of society is supposed to inspire confidence in the troops. It does so by subtly adding to the fantasy element of the story, and with a few deft strokes places it well and truly beyond the experience of the majority of her readers.

Enid Blyton encourages the judgement of others by superficialities. Everybody is most clearly labelled 'good' or 'bad', 'us' or 'them' in the author's own old-fashioned stereotype. Crooks always have rough voices, and are humourless and incredibly stupid. The children are always polite and nice to each other, they are always laughing — especially at others less fortunate than themselves. In the *Mountain of Adventure* which is set in Wales, the local people seem to say nothing else but 'Look you, whateffer' and nearly choke themselves on food. In *The Six Bad Boys* which is a rare and unsuccessful attempt at social realism, Enid's own obvious middle-class prejudices are even more in evidence:

Bob, a middle-class boy from a broken home, meets up with a delinquent gang of working-class boys. 'None of the boys was very clever,' she writes. 'Patrick [introduced as 'a wild Irish boy'] had a streak of cunning that the gang found useful'.. When Bob met the gang their leader Fred . . . rose to the occasion. He had sized up Bob at once — a boy a bit above them in station . . . (and later) 'All four boys admired Bob and liked him, and because he was better dressed than they were and came from a better home they were proud to have him share their cellar.'

Another primary attraction is the inevitable inclusion of a strong animal interest. Of course the animals are usually dogs, and, in fact, one of the 'Famous Five' in the series of that name is actually 'Timmy', George's dog. Like all Blyton animals he always appears to know exactly what is going on and 'woofs' in the appropriate places. Even more fantastic is 'Kiki', a parrot in the 'Adventure' series, who comments on and takes part in everything that happens. This imputation of human attributes to animals appeals to children, because it is something that they secretly believe to be true anyway. For adults though, this is one of the most infuriating aspects of Enid Blyton's writing, not merely because it is patronising, but because it seems a deliberate attempt on the author's part to cash in on children's gullibility, and perpetuate a lie.

We have now established some of the ingredients of the successful 'Blyton' formula: superior social status, the absence of anything that smacks of the work-a-day world, the high fantasy level and the strong animal interest. These factors have played a large part in establishing Enid Blyton's success but they would hardly be enough without a very good and usually well-written story. There are naturally enough a few rough corners and hurriedly patched up endings, the suspense though is admirably controlled and is exciting often at times even at an adult level.

Some critics observed, not without justification considering Enid Blyton's phenomenal output and variety of styles, that the books were written by a syndicate following a formula much as we have described above. This may be true, but it does not really help with an explanation. Each Blyton book carries the inimitable 'Blyton' stamp just as it bears her babyish signature with those coy dots beneath. For me Enid Blyton is a real person. No syndicate would allow itself to exhibit such foibles. The secret of success lies not in calculated exploitation by a cynical adult or adults of a vast number of gullible children. I do not honestly believe she was clever enough for that. She was, I am sure, really a child at heart, a person who never developed emotionally beyond the basic infantile level.

'Mother, Mother!', the typical Enid Blyton adventure story is rarely without this familiar evocation in its first few lines, and of course there is dear old Mummy (never 'Mum' you may observe) ready at hand to offer succour and attention in abundance. Often the request is for food and Mother chides goodnaturedly but abundantly, 'Darling, you have only just had your breakfast.' Mother is suitably faceless and universal. The food is more reminiscent of an orgy in an Edwardian emporium than a modern child's idea of a good 'blow-out'. Enid Blyton writes of tongues, ham, pies, lemonade and ginger-beer. This is not just food it is archetypal feasting, the author's longing for the palmy days of her own childhood.

It is in these opening lines that the author catches the child's imagination to prepare it for the adventure ahead. Once a firm home base is established, once the young reader sees that the writer has her priorities right, he can follow her through the most improbable hair-raising deeds. It parallels the young child's need to cling to its mother in a strange environment, emerging only gradually to explore its new surroundings and fleeing back to its mother at the first sign of danger. But Enid Blyton never goes too far, the children are wrapped in a cocoon of middle-class niceness which demands respect from even the beastliest villain. There is never any real threat to the children, no upsetting fears or panicky terrors; it is all so nicely under control.

Another interesting feature of these opening chapters is that Enid Blyton often has the father killed off or maimed in some way before the book opens; those who survive the massacre are inevitably amiable, pipe-smoking buffoons, as harmless as toothless tigers. An exception is George's father, 'Uncle Quentin', who is a rather irritable scientist, but he is never very much in evidence. When it is necessary to introduce a man, he is typically a walking compendium of everything within, but in all other ways a complete goon.

Bill Cunningham of the 'Adventure' series is a good example. He is actually a policeman, not your ordinary 'copper' of course, but something referred to mysteriously as 'high-up'. In another series, 'The Secret Seven', the children's mentor is also a policeman; this time an Inspector. Such characters help the plot along by enabling the author to cut corners and get crooks arrested and jailed in a paragraph. The policeman of course also symbolises super-authority and one word of praise for the children is enough: ('Well done you kids, we have had half the police force in the country looking for this little lot.') Care is taken however to keep this potentially threatening authority figure well into the background for most of the time and he is usually shown as tolerant and thoroughly non-threatening: one of Enid Blyton's most obvious failings is that she cannot handle men.

(By the way, here is a puzzle for the cynically minded. What exactly is Bill Cunningham's relationship to the widowed Mrs. Mannering? Does he arrange adventures to suit himself to get those children away while he has Mrs. Mannering all to himself? Those children normally so shrewdly observant seem to be peculiarly blind to what must be going on while they are away.)

For most adults who write children's books, once the communication barrier has been largely overcome, the main problem is to write what children want to read and yet remain intellectually honest to themselves in presenting the world as it really is. For Enid Blyton it seems unlikely that any such dilemma raised its head: she was a child, she thought as a child, and she wrote as a child; of course the craft of an extremely competent adult writer is there, but the basic feeling is essentially pre-adolescent. Piaget has shown us that children tend to make moral judgement purely in terms of good and bad and that it is only with the advent of adolescence that the individual is able to accept different levels of goodness and to judge the actions of others according to the circumstances. Enid Blyton has no moral dilemmas and her books satisfy children because they present things clearly in black and white with no confusing intermediate shades of grey. For the adult of course this is what makes life interesting; for the child ambiguity is untenable. The reason Enid Blyton was able to write so much (most of her books appeared in the ten-year period, 1945-1955) was because she did not have to make any effort to think herself back into childhood or wrestle with her conscience about the falsity of what she wrote.

Gossip about the famous naturally feeds on public doubts as to the validity of the eminent personages' adopted pose. Clerics become debauchers; politicians, embezzlers and generals, cowards. Inevitably Enid Blyton was labelled by rumour as a child-hater. If true, such a fact should come as no surprise to us, for as a child herself all other children can be nothing but rivals to her. Perhaps this is why she so constantly put her bold adventurers in dark tunnels and on lonely islands, while canny adults like Bill Cunningham, Mrs. Mannering and Uncle Quentin remained behind, enjoying holidays as they ought to be enjoyed, without children or animals to bother them!

Books by Enid Blyton
1922—1968

Each book is entered under the first publication date. Many were reissued several times and sometimes changed publisher. This list does *not* include reprints, new editions and omnibus editions.

Series such as the Holiday books are entered under the first only — details being given there of the number in the series.

Some books are sometimes called *Enid Blyton's book of*... and sometimes just *Book of*... In this list the title most frequently found has been given, e.g. *Gay Street book* not *Enid Blyton's Gay Street book*, *Enid Blyton's nature lover's book* not *Nature lover's book*.

Translations have not been included, but UNESCO Index Translatorium 1970 listed the most translated authors for 1967 as follows: Lenin 222, Simenon 143, Enid Blyton 128.

Articles and stories in periodicals have not been included.

SOURCES OF REFERENCE

The English catalogue of books, 1923–1952
British books in print, 1965
Reference catalogue of current literature. Books in print at December 31st, 1960
Cumulative book index, 1928–1971
National Union catalog (Library of Congress), pre-1956
National Union catalog (Library of Congress), 1956–1967
British Museum catalogue
British Museum catalogue Supplements, 1956–1970

1922
  Child Whispers   J. Saville

1923

Real Fairies: poems — J. Saville
Responsive Singing Games — J. Saville

1924

The Enid Blyton Book of Fairies — Newnes
Songs of Gladness: words by Enid Blyton,
music by Alec Rowley — J. Saville
The Zoo Book — Newnes

1925

The Enid Blyton Book of Bunnies — Newnes
Reading Practice, Nos. 1–5, 8, 9, 11
(1925–6. Nos. 6, 7, 10 not published) — Nelson
Silver and Gold, illus. Lewis Baumer — Nelson

1926

The Bird Book, illus. by Ronald Green — Newnes
The Book of Brownies, illus. by Ernest Aris — Newnes
Tales Half Told — Nelson
The Teachers' Treasury, 3 vols. Edited
by Enid Blyton — Newnes
Sunny Stories for Little Folks. Edited by
Enid Blyton. Followed by Enid Blyton's
Sunny Stories 1937–52 — Newnes

1927

The Animal Book — Newnes
A Book of Little Plays — Nelson
The Play's the Thing! Musical plays for
children with music by Alec Rowley.
Reprinted by Newnes in 1940 in 2
volumes as Plays for Older Children and
Plays for Younger Children — Home Library Book Co.

1928

Aesop's Fables: retold — Nelson
Let's Pretend, illus. by I. Bennington
Angrave — Nelson
Modern Teaching. Practical suggestions for
junior and senior schools. General editor
Enid Blyton. 6 vols. Also Modern
teaching in the Infant School, 4 vols,
1932 — Newnes

Old English Stories: retold	Nelson
Pinkity's Pranks and other Nature Fairy *Stories: retold*	Nelson
Tales of Brer Rabbit: retold	Nelson

1929

Nature Lessons	Evans
Tarrydiddle Town	Nelson

1930

The Knights of the Round Table. John O'London's Children's Library	Newnes
Tales from the Arabian Nights. John O'London's Children's Library	Newnes
Tales of Ancient Greece. John O'London's Children's Library	Newnes
Tales of Robin Hood. John O'London's Children's Library	Newnes
Pictorial Knowledge. 10 vols. Enid Blyton was assistant editor and contributed verse section	Newnes

1933

Cheerio! A book for boys and girls	Birn Bros.
Five Minute Tales: sixty short stories for children	Methuen
Let's Read	Birn Bros.
My First Reading Book	Birn Bros.
Read To Us	Birn Bros.

1934

The Adventures of Odysseus. Stories from World History retold	Evans
The Enid Blyton Poetry Book	Methuen
The Old Thatch Series, 8 vols., 1934-5	W. & A. K. Johnston
The Red Pixie Book	Newnes
Round the Year with Enid Blyton. 4 parts: Spring, Summer, Autumn, Winter	Evans
The Story of the Siege of Troy. Stories from World History retold	Evans
Tales of the Ancient Greeks and Persians. Stories from World History retold	Evans

223

Tales of the Romans. Stories from World
History retold   Evans
Ten Minute Tales   Methuen
Treasure Trove Readers. Junior series
  compiled by Enid Blyton   Wheaton

1935
The Children's Garden   Newnes
The Green Goblin Book   Newnes
Hedgerow Tales   Methuen
Nature Observation Pictures. 32 pictures in
  4 folders from *The Birds of the British
  Isles* by T. A. Coward, selected with
  footnotes by Enid Blyton   Warne
Six Enid Blyton Plays   Methuen

1936
Birds of the Wayside and Woodland. Edited
  and with introductory chapters by
  Enid Blyton. By Thomas A. Coward   Warne
The Famous Jimmy, illus. by Benjamin
  Rabier   Muller
Fifteen Minute Tales   Methuen
The Yellow Fairy Book   Newnes

1937
Adventures of the Wishing Chair, illus. by
  Hilda McGavin   Newnes

1938
The Adventures of Binkle and Flip, illus. by
  Kathleen Nixon   Newnes
Billy-Bob Tales, illus. by May Smith   Methuen
*Heyo, Brer Rabbit! Tales of Brer Rabbit
  and his Friends*   Newnes
Mr. Galliano's Circus   Newnes
The Old Thatch, second series, 8 vols.,
  1938–9   W. & A. K. Johnston
The Secret Island   Blackwell

1939
*The Blyton-Sharman Musical Plays for
  Juniors.* 6 parts. Words by Enid Blyton   Wheaton
Boys' and Girls' Circus Book   News Chronicle

Malcolm Saville, Mr. Clark Ramsey, publicity manager of Newnes, Enid
Blyton and Richmal Crompton at a performance of *Noddy in Toyland* (Stoll
Theatre, 1957)

Enid considering book illustrations at Green Hedges

Jersey's tribute to Enid Blyton—Battle of Flowers commemoration stamp, 1970, showing float with Noddy characters (*reproduced by permission of the States of Jersey Postal Committee*)

Daily Sketch, May 28th, 1957

"These are his Enid Blytons . . ."

Cameo Plays Book 4. Edited by George
H. Holroyd. Book 4 only by Enid
Blyton   Arnold
The Enchanted Wood   Newnes
How the Flowers Grow, and Other Musical
Plays   Wheaton
Hurrah for the Circus!, illus. by E. H.
Davie   Newnes
Naughty Amelia Jane   Newnes
School Plays: six plays for schools   Blackwell
The Wishing Bean and other plays   Blackwell

1940
Birds of our Gardens, illus. by Roland
Green and Ernest Aris   Newnes
Boys' and Girls' Story Book   Newnes
Children of Cherry Tree Farm, illus. by
Harry Rountree   Country Life
Children of Kidillin. First published under
pseudonym of Mary Pollock   Newnes
The Little Tree House, being the Adven-
tures of Josie, Click and Bun, illus. by
Dorothy M. Wheeler. Reprinted in
1951 as Josie, Click and Bun and the
Little Tree House   Newnes
Mr. Meddle's Mischief, illus. by Joyce
Mercer and Rosalind M. Turvey   Newnes
Naughtiest Girl in the School   Newnes
The News Chronicle Boys' and Girls' Book   News Chronicle
The Secret of Spiggy Holes   Blackwell
Tales of Betsy-May, illus. by J. Gale
Thomas   Methuen
Three Boys and a Circus. First published
under pseudonym of Mary Pollock   Newnes
The Treasure Hunters, illus. by E. Wilson
and Joyce Davies   Newnes
Twenty Minute Tales   Methuen

1941
The Adventures of Mr. Pink-Whistle   Newnes
The Adventurous Four   Newnes
The Babar Story Book. Told by Enid
Blyton. The first half reprinted in
1942 as Tales of Babar   Methuen

225

A Calendar for Children	Newnes
Enid Blyton's Book of the Year	Evans
Five O'clock Tales	Methuen
The Further Adventures of Josie, Click and	
Bun, illus. by Dorothy M. Wheeler	Newnes
The Secret Mountain	Blackwell
The Twins at St. Clare's	Methuen

1942

The Children of Willow Farm, illus. by	
Harry Rountree	Country Life
Circus Days Again	Newnes
Enid Blyton Happy Story Book	Hodder & Stoughton
Enid Blyton Readers. Books 1–3	Macmillan
Enid Blyton's Little Books. First of series	Evans
Five on a Treasure Island	Hodder & Stoughton
The further adventures of Brer Rabbit	Newnes
Hello, Mr. Twiddle, illus. by Hilda	
McGavin	Newnes
I'll Tell You a Story, illus. by Eileen A.	
Soper	Macmillan
I'll Tell You Another Story	Macmillan
John Jolly at Christmas Time	Evans
Land of Far-Beyond	Methuen
Mary Mouse and the Doll's House	Brockhampton
More Adventures on Willow Farm	Country Life
Naughtiest Girl Again	Newnes
The O'Sullivan Twins	Methuen
Shadow the Sheep Dog	Newnes
Six O'Clock Tales, illus. by Dorothy M.	
Wheeler	Methuen

1943

The Adventures of Scamp. Published under	
the pseudonym of Mary Pollock	Newnes
Bimbo and Topsy, illus. by Lucy Gee	Newnes
The Children's Life of Christ	Methuen
Dame Slap and her School, illus. by	
Dorothy M. Wheeler	Newnes
Five Go Adventuring Again	Hodder & Stoughton
John Jolly by the Sea	Evans
John Jolly on the Farm	Evans
The Magic Faraway Tree, illus. by	
Dorothy M. Wheeler	Newnes

Merry Story Book, illus. by Eileen A.
   Soper   Hodder & Stoughton
More Adventures of Mary Mouse   Brockhampton
The Mystery of the Burnt Cottage, illus. by
   J. Abbey   Methuen
Polly Piglet, illus. by Eileen A. Soper   Brockhampton
The Secret of Killimooin   Blackwell
Seven O'Clock Tales   Methuen
Smuggler Ben. Published under pseudo-
   nym of Mary Pollock   Laurie
Summer Term at St. Clare's   Methuen
The Toys Come to Life, illus. by Eileen
   A. Soper   Brockhampton

1944

At Appletree Farm   Brockhampton
Billy and Betty at the Seaside   Valentine and Sons
A Book of Naughty Children   Methuen
The Boy Next Door, illus. by A. E.
   Bestall   Newnes
The Christmas Book, illus. by Treyer
   Evans   Macmillan
Claudine at St. Clare's   Methuen
Come to the Circus, illus. by Eileen A. Soper   Brockhampton
The Dog that went to Fairyland   Brockhampton
Eight O'Clock Tales, illus. by Dorothy
   M. Wheeler   Methuen
Enid Blyton Readers. Books 4–6   Macmillan
Enid Blyton's Nature Lover's Book   Evans Bros.
Five Run Away Together, illus. by Eileen
   A. Soper   Hodder & Stoughton
The Island of Adventure, illus. by Stuart
   Tresilian   Macmillan
Jolly Little Jumbo   Brockhampton
Jolly Story Book, illus. by Eileen A. Soper   Hodder & Stoughton
Little Mary Mouse Again   Brockhampton
The Mystery of the Disappearing Cat,
   illus. by J. Abbey   Methuen
Rainy Day Stories, illus. by Nora S.
   Unwin   Evans
The Second Form at St. Clare's, illus. by
   W. Lindsay Cable   Methuen
Tales from the Bible, illus. by Eileen A.   Methuen
   Soper

Tales of Toyland, illus. by Hilda McGavin   Newnes
The Three Golliwogs   Newnes

1945

The Blue Story Book, illus. by Eileen A.
Soper   Methuen
The Brown Family, illus. by E. *and* R.
Buhler   News Chronicle
The Caravan Family, illus. by William
Fyffe   Lutterworth
The Conjuring Wizard and other stories,
illus. by Eileen A. Soper   Macmillan
Enid Blyton Nature Readers. Nos. 1–20   Macmillan
The Family at Red Roofs, illus. by W.
Spence   Lutterworth
Fifth Formers at St. Clare's, illus. by W.
Lindsay Cable   Methuen
The First Christmas, photographs by
Paul Henning   Methuen
Five go to Smugglers' Top   Hodder & Stoughton
Hallo, Little Mary Mouse, illus. by Olive
F. Openshaw   Brockhampton
Hollow Tree House, illus. by Elizabeth
Wall   Lutterworth
John Jolly at the Circus   Evans
Mystery of the Secret Room   Methuen
Naughtiest Girl is a Monitor   Newnes
Round the Clock Stories, illus. by Nora
S. Unwin   National Magazine Co.
The Runaway Kitten, illus. by Eileen A.
Soper   Brockhampton
Sunny Story Book   Hodder & Stoughton
Teddy Bear's Party, illus. by Eileen A.
Soper   Brockhampton
The Twins go to Nursery-Rhyme Land,
illus. by Eileen A. Soper   Brockhampton

1946

Amelia Jane Again   Newnes
The Bad Little Monkey, illus. by Eileen A.
Soper   Brockhampton
The Castle of Adventure, illus. by Stuart
Tresilian   Macmillan

The Children at Happy House, illus. by
Kathleen Gell — Blackwell
Chimney Corner Stories, illus. by Pat
Harrison — National Magazine Co.
The Enid Blyton Holiday Book. First of a
series. Followed by second to twelfth
Holiday Books — Sampson Low
Enid Blyton Nature Readers. Nos. 21–30 — Macmillan
First Term at Malory Towers — Methuen
Five go off in a Caravan, illus. by Eileen
A. Soper — Hodder & Stoughton
The Folk of the Faraway Tree, illus. by
Dorothy M. Wheeler — Newnes
Gay Story Book, illus. by Eileen A. Soper — Hodder & Stoughton
Josie, Click and Bun Again, illus. by
Dorothy M. Wheeler — Newnes
Little White Duck and other stories, illus.
by Eileen A. Soper — Macmillan
Mary Mouse and her Family, illus. by
Olive F. Openshaw — Brockhampton
Mystery of the Spiteful Letters, illus. by
J. Abbey — Methuen
The Put-em-rights, illus. by Elizabeth Wall — Lutterworth
The Red Story Book — Methuen
The Surprising Caravan, illus. by Eileen
A. Soper — Brockhampton
Tales of Green Hedges, illus. by Gwen
White — National Magazine Co.
The Train that Lost its Way, illus. by
Eileen A. Soper — Brockhampton

1947

The Adventurous Four Again — Newnes
At Seaside Cottage, illus. by Eileen A.
Soper — Brockhampton
Before I go to Sleep: a book of Bible stories
and prayers for children at night — Latimer House
Enid Blyton's Treasury — Evans for Boots
Five on Kirrin Island Again — Hodder & Stoughton
The Green Story Book, illus. by Eileen A.
Soper — Methuen
The Happy House Children Again, illus.
by Kathleen Gell — Blackwell

Here Comes Mary Mouse Again	Brockhampton
The House at the Corner, illus. by Elsie Walker	Lutterworth
Jinky Nature Books. 4 parts	Arnold
Little Green Duck and other stories	Brockhampton
Lucky Story Book, illus. by Eileen A. Soper	Hodder & Stoughton
Mischief at St. Rollo's. Published under the pseudonym of Mary Pollock	Laurie
More about Josie, Click and Bun, illus. by Dorothy M. Wheeler	Newnes
The Mystery of the Missing Necklace	Methuen
Rambles with Uncle Nat, illus. by Nora S. Unwin	National Magazine Co.
The Saucy Jane Family, illus. by Ruth Gervis	Lutterworth
A Second Book of Naughty Children, illus. by Kathleen Gell	Methuen
The Second Form at Malory Towers	Methuen
The Secret of Cliff Castle. Published under the pseudonym of Mary Pollock	Laurie
The Smith Family. Books 1–3	Arnold
The Valley of Adventure, illus. by Stuart Tresilian	Macmillan
The Very Clever Rabbit	Brockhampton

1948

The Adventures of Pip	Sampson Low
The Boy with the Loaves and Fishes, illus. by Elsie Walker	Lutterworth
Brer Rabbit and his Friends	Coker
Brer Rabbit Book. First of a series followed by second to eighth *Brer Rabbit Books*	Latimer House
Come to the Circus, illus. by Joyce M. Johnson. This is a different book from the one of the same title published in 1944 by Brockhampton	Newnes
Enid Blyton Readers. Book 7	Macmillan
Enid Blyton's Bedtime Series. 2 parts	Brockhampton
Five go off to Camp	Hodder & Stoughton
How do you do, Mary Mouse	Brockhampton
Just time for a Story, illus. by Grace Lodge	Macmillan
Jolly Tales	Johnston

Let's Garden, illus. by William McLaren	Latimer House
Let's have a Story, illus. by George Bowe	Pitkin
The Little Girl at Capernaum, illus. by Elsie Walker	Lutterworth
Mister Icy-Cold	Blackwell
More Adventures of Pip	Sampson Low
The Mystery of the Hidden House, illus. by J. Abbey	Methuen
Nature Tales	Johnston
Now for a Story, illus. by Frank Varty	Harold Hill
The Red-spotted Handkerchief and other stories, illus. by Kathleen Gell	Brockhampton
The Sea Adventure, illus. by Stuart Tresilian	Macmillan
The Secret of the Old Mill, illus. by Eileen A. Soper	Brockhampton
Six Cousins at Mistletoe Farm, illus. by Peter Beigel	Evans
Tales after Tea	Laurie
Tales of the Twins, illus. by Eileen A. Soper	Brockhampton
They Ran Away Together, illus. by Jeanne Farrar	Brockhampton
Third Year at Malory Towers, illus. by Stanley Lloyd	Methuen
We want a Story, illus. by George Bowe	Pitkin

1949

The Bluebell Story Book	Gifford
Bumpy and his Bus, illus. by Dorothy M. Wheeler	Newnes
A Cat in Fairyland	Pitkin
Chuff the Chimney Sweep	Pitkin
The Circus Book	Latimer House
The Dear Old Snow Man	Brockhampton
Don't be Silly, Mr. Twiddle	Newnes
The Enchanted Sea	Pitkin
Enid Blyton Bible Pictures, Old Testament, illus. by John Turner	Macmillan
The Enid Blyton Bible Stories, Old Testament. 14 titles	Macmillan
Enid Blyton's Daffodil Story Book	Gifford
Enid Blyton's Good Morning Book, illus. by Don and Ann Goring	National Magazine Co.

Five get into Trouble, illus. by Eileen A. Soper	Hodder & Stoughton
Humpty Dumpty and Belinda	Collins
Jinky's Joke and other stories, illus. by Kathleen Gell	Brockhampton
Little Noddy goes to Toyland, illus. by Harmsen Van Beek	Sampson Low
Mr. Tumpy and his Caravan	Sidgwick and Jackson
The Mountain of Adventure	Macmillan
My Enid Blyton Bedside Book. First of a series. Followed by Enid Blyton's second to twelfth *Bedside Books*	Barker
The Mystery of the Pantomime Cat	Methuen
Oh, What a Lovely Time	Brockhampton
A reference Book to Enid Blyton Nature Plates	Macmillan
Reference Book to Old Testament Bible Plates	Macmillan
Robin Hood Book	Latimer House
The Rockingdown Mystery, illus. by Gilbert Dunlop	Collins
The Secret Seven, illus. by George Brook	Brockhampton
Stories and Notes to Enid Blyton Nature Plates. A teacher's edition of Readers	Macmillan
A Story Party at Green Hedges, illus. by Grace Lodge	Hodder & Stoughton
The Strange Umbrella	Pitkin
Tales after Supper	Laurie
Those Dreadful Children, illus. by Grace Lodge	Lutterworth
Tiny Tales	Littlebury
The Upper Fourth at Malory Towers	Methuen

1950

The Astonishing Ladder and Other Stories, illus. by Eileen A. Soper	Macmillan
A Book of Magic	Coker
A Complete List of Books by Enid Blyton. Foreword by Enid Blyton	John Menzies
Enid Blyton's Little Book No. 1. First of a series. Followed by *Nos. 2–6*	Brockhampton
The Enid Blyton Pennant Series. 30 parts	Macmillan
Enid Blyton Readers. Books 10–12	Macmillan

Five Fall into Adventure, illus. by Eileen A. Soper	Hodder & Stoughton
Hurrah for Little Noddy	Sampson Low
In the Fifth at Malory Towers, illus. by Stanley Lloyd	Methuen
The Magic Knitting Needles and other stories	Macmillan
Mister Meddle's Muddles, illus. by Rosalind M. Turvey and Joyce Mercer	Newnes
Mr. Pinkwhistle Interferes	Newnes
The Mystery of the Invisible Thief	Methuen
The Pole Star Family, illus. by Ruth Gervis	Lutterworth
The Poppy Story Book	Gifford
Rilloby Fair Mystery, illus. by Gilbert Dunlop	Collins
Round the Year with Enid Blyton	Evans
Round the Year Stories	Coker
Rubbalong Tales, illus. by Norman Meredith	Macmillan
The Seaside Family, illus. by Ruth Gervis	Lutterworth
Secret Seven Adventure, illus. by George Brook	Brockhampton
The Ship of Adventure, illus. by Stuart Tresilian	Macmillan
Six Cousins Again, illus. by Maurice Tulloch	Evans
Tales about Toys	Brockhampton
The Three Naughty Children and other stories, illus. by Eileen A. Soper	Macmillan
Tricky the Goblin and other stories, illus. by Eileen A. Soper	Macmillan
We do Love Mary Mouse	Brockhampton
Welcome Mary Mouse, illus. by Olive F. Openshaw	Brockhampton
What an Adventure	Brockhampton
The Wishing Chair Again	Newnes
Yellow Story Book, illus. by Kathleen Gell	Methuen

1951

Benny and the Princess and other stories	Pitkin
The Big Noddy Book, illus. by Harmsen Van Beek. First of a series. Followed	

by the second to eighth *Big Noddy Books*	Sampson Low
The Buttercup Farm Family, illus. by Ruth Gervis	Lutterworth
Buttercup Story Book	Gifford
Down at the Farm	Sampson Low
Father Christmas and Belinda	Collins
Feefo, Tuppeny and Jinks. This is an abridged edition of the *Green Goblin Book* published by Newnes in 1935	Staples Press
Five on a Hike Together, illus. by Eileen A. Soper	Hodder & Stoughton
The Flying Goat and other stories	Pitkin
Gay Street Book, illus. by Grace Lodge	Latimer House
Hello Twins	Brockhampton
Here Comes Noddy Again	Sampson Low
Hurrah for Mary Mouse	Brockhampton
Last Term at Malory Towers, illus. by Stanley Lloyd	Methuen
Let's Go to the Circus	Odhams
The Little Spinning Mouse and other stories	Pitkin
The Magic Snow-bird and other stories	Pitkin
The Mystery of the Vanished Prince, illus. by Treyer Evans	Methuen
Noddy and Big Ears have a Picnic	Sampson Low
Noddy and his Car	Sampson Low
Noddy has a Shock	Sampson Low
Noddy has more Adventures	Sampson Low
Noddy goes to the Seaside	Sampson Low
Noddy off to Rocking Horse Land	Sampson Low
Noddy Painting Book	Sampson Low
Noddy's House of Books	Sampson Low
A Picnic Party with Enid Blyton, illus. by Grace Lodge	Hodder & Stoughton
Pippy and the Gnome and other stories	Pitkin
A Prize for Mary Mouse	Brockhampton
The Proud Golliwog	Brockhampton
The Queen Elizabeth Family, illus. by Ruth Gervis	Lutterworth
The Runaway Teddy Bear and other stories	Pitkin
The Six Bad Boys, illus. by Mary Gernat	Lutterworth
A Tale of Little Noddy	Sampson Low

'*Too-wise*' *the Wonderful Wizard and other stories*   Pitkin

Up the Faraway Tree, illus. by Dorothy M. Wheeler   Newnes

Well Done, Secret Seven, illus. by George Brook   Brockhampton

1952

Bright Story Book, illus. by Eileen A. Soper   Brockhampton

The Children's Jolly Book. With W. E. Johns and others   Odhams

The Circus of Adventure, illus. by Stuart Tresilian   Macmillan

Bible Pictures, New Testament   Macmillan

Come Along Twins   Brockhampton

Enid Blyton Tiny Strip Books. First of a series   Sampson Low

Enid Blyton's Animal Lover's Book   Evans

Enid Blyton's Colour Strip Book   Sampson Low

Enid Blyton's Omnibus, illus. by Jessie Land   Newnes

Five have a Wonderful Time, illus. by Eileen A. Soper   Hodder & Stoughton

The Mad Teapot   Brockhampton

Mandy, Mops and Cubby Again   Sampson Low

Mandy, Mops and Cubby Find a House   Sampson Low

Mary Mouse and her Bicycle, illus. by Olive F. Openshaw   Brockhampton

Mr. Tumpy plays a Trick on Saucepan   Sampson Low

My First Enid Blyton Book. First of a series. Followed by the second and third *Enid Blyton Books*   Latimer House

My First Nature Book, illus. by Eileen A. Soper. First of a series. Followed by the second and third *Nature Books*   Macmillan

The Mystery of the Strange Bundle, illus. by Treyer Evans   Methuen

Noddy and Big Ears   Sampson Low

Noddy and the Witch's Wand   Sampson Low

Noddy Colour Strip Book, illus. by Harmsen Van Der Beek   Sampson Low

Noddy goes to School   Sampson Low

Noddy's Ark of Book   Sampson Low

Noddy's Car gets a Squeak	Sampson Low
Noddy's Penny Wheel Car	Sampson Low
The Queer Adventure, illus. by Norman Meredith	Staples Press
Reference Book to New Testament Bible Plates	Macmillan
The Rubadub Mystery, illus. by Gilbert Dunlop	Collins
Secret Seven on the Trail, illus. by George Brook	Brockhampton
Snowdrop Story Book	Gifford
The Story of my Life	Pitkin
The Two Sillies and other stories retold by Enid Blyton	J. Coker
The Very Big Secret, illus. by Ruth Gervis	Lutterworth
Welcome Josie, Click and Bun, illus. by Dorothy M. Wheeler	Newnes
Well Done, Noddy	Sampson Low

1953

The Children's Book of Prayers. Chosen by Enid Blyton	Muller
Clicky the Clockwork Clown	Brockhampton
The Enid Blyton Bible Stories. New Testament. 14 books	Macmillan
Enid Blyton's Christmas Story, illus. by Fritz Wegner	Hamish Hamilton
Five Go Down to the Sea, illus. by Eileen A. Soper	Hodder & Stoughton
Go Ahead Secret Seven, illus. by Bruno Kay	Brockhampton
Gobo and Mr. Fierce	Sampson Low
Here Come the Twins	Brockhampton
Little Gift Books. Translated by Enid Blyton, illus. by Pierre Probst. First of a series	Hackett
Mandy makes Cubby a Hat	Sampson Low
Mary Mouse and the Noah's Ark, illus. by Olive F. Openshaw	Brockhampton
Mr. Tumpy in the Land of Wishes	Sampson Low
My Enid Blyton Story Book, illus. by Willy Schermelé	Juvenile Productions

The Mystery of Holly Lane, illus. by Treyer Evans	Methuen
The New Big Noddy Book	Sampson Low
New Noddy Colour Strip Book	Sampson Low
Noddy and the Cuckoo's Nest	Sampson Low
Noddy at the Seaside	Sampson Low
Noddy Cut-Out Model Book	Sampson Low
Noddy gets Captured	Sampson Low
Noddy is Very Silly	Sampson Low
Noddy's Garage of Books	Sampson Low
Playways Annual. By Enid Blyton and others	Lutterworth
The Secret of Moon Castle	Blackwell
Snowball the Pony, illus. by Iris Gillespie	Lutterworth
The Story of Our Queen, illus. by F. Stocks May	Muller
Visitors in the Night	Brockhampton
Well really Mr. Twiddle!, illus. by Hilda McGavin	Newnes

1954

The Adventure of the Secret Necklace, illus. by Isabel Veevers	Lutterworth
The Castle Without a Door and other stories	Pitkin
The Children at Green Meadows, illus. by Grace Lodge	Lutterworth
Enid Blyton's Friendly Story Book, illus. by Eileen A. Soper	Brockhampton
Enid Blyton Magazine Annual. First of four	Evans
Enid Blyton's Marigold Story Book	J. Gifford
Enid Blyton's Noddy Pop-up Book	Sampson Low
Enid Blyton's Noddy Giant Painting Book	Sampson Low
Five go to Mystery Moor	Hodder & Stoughton
Good Work, Secret Seven, illus. by Bruno Kay	Brockhampton
The Greatest Book in the World, illus. by Mabel Peacock	British & Foreign Bible Society
How Funny You Are, Noddy!	Sampson Low
Little Strip Picture Books. A series	Sampson Low
The Little Toy Farm and other stories	Pitkin
Mary Mouse to the Rescue	Brockhampton
Merry Mister Meddle!, illus. by Rosalind M. Turvey and Joyce Mercer	Newnes

More about Amelia Jane, illus. by Sylvia I.
Venus   Newnes
The Mystery of Tally-Ho Cottage   Methuen
Noddy and the Magic Rubber   Sampson Low
Noddy's Castle of Books   Sampson Low

1955

Away goes Sooty, illus. by Pierre Probst   Collins
Benjy and the Others, illus. by Kathleen
Gell   Latimer House
Bible Stories from the Old Testament, illus.
by Grace Lodge   Muller
Bible Stories from the New Testament, illus.
by Grace Lodge   Muller
Bimbo and Blackie Go Camping, illus. by
Pierre Probst   Collins
Bobs, illus. by Pierre Probst   Collins
Christmas with Scamp and Bimbo   Collins
Enid Blyton's Favourite Book of Fables.
From the Tales of La Fontaine   Collins
Enid Blyton's Little Bedtime Books. 8 books   Sampson Low
Neddy the Little Donkey, illus. by Romain
Simon   Collins
Enid Blyton's Sooty, illus. by Pierre Probst   Collins
Enid Blyton's What Shall I Be?, illus. by
Pierre Probst   Collins
Finding the Tickets: Play   Evans
Five have Plenty of Fun   Hodder & Stoughton
Foxglove Story Book   J. Gifford
Gobbo in the Land of Dreams   Sampson Low
Golliwog Grumbled   Brockhampton
Holiday House, illus. by Grace Lodge   Evans
Laughing Kitten. Photographs by Paul
Kaye   Harvill
*Mandy, Mops and Cubby and the White-
wash*   Sampson Low
Mary Mouse in Nursery Rhyme Land   Brockhampton
Mischief Again. Photographs by Paul
Kaye   Collins
Mr. Pinkwhistle's Party   Newnes
Mr. Sly-One and Cats: Play   Evans
Mr. Tumpy in the Land of Boys and Girls   Sampson Low
More Chimney Corner Stories, illus. by
Pat Harrison   Macdonald

Mother's Meeting: Play	Evans
Noddy in Toyland	Sampson Low
Noddy meets Father Christmas	Sampson Low
Playing at Home. With S. Schweitzer	Methuen
Ring o' Bells Mystery	Collins
River of Adventure, illus. by Stuart Tresilian	Macmillan
Run-abouts Holiday, illus. by Lilian Chivers	Lutterworth
Secret Seven Win Through, illus. by Bruno Kay	Brockhampton
The Troublesome Three, illus. by Leo	Sampson Low
Who Will Hold the Giant?: Play	Evans
You Funny Little Noddy!	Sampson Low

1956

Be Brave, Little Noddy!	Sampson Low
Bom the Little Toy Drummer	Brockhampton
The Clever Little Donkey, illus. by Romain Simon	Collins
Colin the Cow-boy, illus. by R. Caille	Collins
A Day with Mary Mouse, illus. by Frederick White	Brockhampton
A Day with Noddy	Sampson Low
Enid Blyton's Animal Tales	Collins
Enid Blyton's Book of her famous play Noddy in Toyland	Sampson Low
Enid Blyton's Noddy Playday Painting Book	Sampson Low
Five on a Secret Trail, illus. by Eileen A. Soper	Hodder & Stoughton
Four in a Family, illus. by Tom Kerr	Lutterworth
Let's have a Party. Photographs by Paul Kaye	Harvill
Mystery of the Missing Man, illus. by Lilian Buchanan	Methuen
Noddy and his Friends. A pop-up picture book	Sampson Low
Noddy and Tessie Bear	Sampson Low
Noddy Nursery Rhymes	Sampson Low
The Noddy Toy Station Books. Nos. 1–5	Sampson Low
Rat-a-tat Mystery	Collins
Scamp at School, illus. by Pierre Probst	Collins
Story Book of Jesus, illus. by Elsie Walker	Macmillan

Three Cheers Secret Seven, illus. by
    Burgess Sharrocks   Brockhampton

1957

Bom and His Magic Drumstick   Brockhampton
Children's Own Wonder Book. Containing
    contributions by Enid Blyton and
    others   Odhams
Do Look Out, Noddy!   Sampson Low
Enid Blyton's Bom Painting Book   Dean
Five go to Billycock Hill, illus. by Eileen
    A. Soper   Hodder & Stoughton
Mary Mouse and the Garden Party, illus. by
    Frederick White   Brockhampton
Mystery of the Strange Messages, illus. by
    Lilian Buchanan   Methuen
New Testament Picture Books 1–2   Macmillan
Noddy and Bumpy Dog   Sampson Low
Noddy's New Big Book   Sampson Low
Secret Seven Mystery, illus. by Burgess
    Sharrocks   Brockhampton

1958

Birthday Kitten, illus. by Grace Lodge   Lutterworth
Bom goes Adventuring, illus. by R. Paul-
    Höye   Brockhampton
Clicky gets into Trouble, illus. by Molly
    Brett   Brockhampton
Five get into a Fix, illus. by Eileen A.
    Soper   Hodder & Stoughton
Mary Mouse goes to the Fair, illus. by
    Frederick White   Brockhampton
Mr. Pink-Whistle's Big Book   Evans
My Big-Ears Picture Book   Sampson Low
My Noddy Picture Book   Sampson Low
Noddy has an Adventure   Sampson Low
The Noddy Shop Book. Nos. 1–5   Sampson Low
Noddy's Own Nursery Rhymes   Sampson Low
Puzzle for the Secret Seven, illus. by
    Burgess Sharrocks   Brockhampton
Rumble and Chuff, illus. by David Walsh   Juvenile Productions
The School Companion. A practical guide
    to work and play, together with a

special section for the very young and
a quick reference encyclopedia for the
older child. By Enid Blyton and others   New Educational Press
You're a Good Friend, Noddy!   Sampson Low

1959

A.B.C. with Noddy   Sampson Low
Bom and the Clown   Brockhampton
Bom and the Rainbow   Brockhampton
Dog Stories. This is *Three Boys and a*
Circus first published by Newnes 1940,
and *Adventures of Scamp,* first pub-
lished by Newnes 1943   Collins
Hullo Bom and Wuffy Dog, illus. by R.
Paul-Höye   Brockhampton
Mary Mouse has a Wonderful Idea, illus.
by Frederick White   Brockhampton
Noddy and Bunkey   Sampson Low
Noddy goes to Sea   Sampson Low
Noddy's Car Picture Book   Sampson Low
Ragamuffin Mystery   Collins
Secret Seven Fireworks, illus. by Burgess
Sharrocks   Brockhampton

1960

Adventure of the Strange Ruby   Brockhampton
Adventure Stories   Collins
Bom goes to Magic Town   Brockhampton
Cheer Up, Little Noddy!   Sampson Low
Clicky and Tiptoe, illus. by Molly Brett   Brockhampton
Five on Finniston Farm, illus. by Eileen
A. Soper   Hodder & Stoughton
Good old Secret Seven, illus. by Burgess
Sharrocks   Brockhampton
Happy Day Stories, illus. by Marcia Lane
Foster   Evans
Here Comes Bom, illus. by R. Paul-Höye   Brockhampton
Mary Mouse goes to Sea, illus. by
Frederick White   Brockhampton
Mystery Stories   Collins
Noddy Goes to the Fair   Sampson Low
Noddy's One, Two, Three Book   Sampson Low
Noddy's Tall Blue Book. Also Green,

Orange, Pink, Red and Yellow Books.
Six books in all   Sampson Low
Old Testament Picture Books   Macmillan
Tales at Bedtime, illus. by Hilda McGavin   Collins
Will the Fiddle, illus. by Grace Lodge   Instructive Arts

1961
The Big Enid Blyton Book   Hamlyn
Bom at the Seaside, illus. by R. Paul-Höye   Brockhampton
Bom goes to the Circus, illus. by R. Paul-
Höye   Brockhampton
Five go to Demon's Rocks, illus. by Eileen
A. Soper   Hodder & Stoughton
Happy Holiday, Clicky, illus. by Molly
Brett   Brockhampton
Mary Mouse Goes Out for the Day, illus.
by Frederick White   Brockhampton
Mr. Plod and Little Noddy   Sampson Low
Mystery of Banshee Towers, illus. by
Lilian Buchanan   Methuen
The Mystery That Never Was, illus. by
Gilbert Dunlop   Collins
Noddy's Toyland Train Picture Book   Sampson Low
Shock for the Secret Seven, illus. by
Burgess Sharrocks   Brockhampton

1962
A Day at School with Noddy   Sampson Low
Five have a Mystery to Solve, illus. by
Eileen A. Soper   Hodder & Stoughton
The Four Cousins, illus. by Joan Thomp-
son   Lutterworth
Fun with Mary Mouse, illus. by R. Paul-
Höye   Brockhampton
Look out Secret Seven, illus. by Burgess
Sharrocks   Brockhampton
Noddy and the Tootles   Sampson Low
Stories for Monday   Oliphants
Stories for Tuesday   Oliphants

1963
The Boy who Wanted a Dog, illus. by
Sally Michel   Lutterworth
Brer Rabbit Again   Dean

Five are Together Again, illus. by Eileen
  A. Soper   Hodder & Stoughton
Fun for the Secret Seven, illus. by Burgess
  Sharrocks   Brockhampton
Tales of Brave Adventure retold   Dean

1964

Enid Blyton's Sunshine Picture Story Book.
  First of a series   World Distributors
Happy Hours Story Book   Dean
Mary Mouse and the Little Donkey, illus.
  by R. Paul-Höye   Brockhampton
Noddy and the Aeroplane   Sampson Low
Story Book for Fives to Sevens   Parrish
Storytime Book   Dean
Tell-a-story Books   World Distributors
Trouble for the Twins   Brockhampton

1965

The Boy Who Came Back, illus. by Elsie
  Walker   Lutterworth
Easy Reader. First of a series   Collins
Enid Blyton's Brer Rabbit's a Rascal Dean
Enid Blyton's Sunshine Book   Dean
Enid Blyton's Treasure Box   Sampson Low
Learn to Count with Noddy   Sampson Low
Learn to Go Shopping with Noddy Sampson Low
Learn to Read About Animals with Noddy Sampson Low
Learn to Tell the Time with Noddy Sampson Low
The Man who Stopped to Help, illus. by
  Elsie Walker   Lutterworth
Noddy and His Friends. A nursery picture
  book   Sampson Low
Noddy Treasure Box   Sampson Low
Tales of Long Ago. Retold by Enid Blyton Johnstone

1966

Enid Blyton's Bedtime Annual. First of a
  series   Manchester
Enid Blyton's Playbook. First of a series Collins
The Fairy Folk Story Book   Collins
Fireside Tales   Collins
Gift Book   Purnell
The Happy House Children   Collins

John and Mary series, illus. by Fromont. Brockhampton
   9 books, 1966–8
Pixie Tales Collins
Pixieland Story Book Collins
Stories for Bedtime Dean
Stories for You Dean

1967
  Holiday Annual Stories Low Marston
  Holiday Magic Stories Low Marston
  Holiday Pixie Stories Low Marston
  Holiday Toy Stories Low Marston
  Noddy and his Passengers Sampson Low
  Noddy and the Magic Boots. (With *Noddy's*
    Funny Kite.) Cover bears the title
    Noddy's Funny Kite Sampson Low
  Noddy and the Noah's Ark Adventure
    Picture Book Sampson Low
  Noddy in Toyland Picture Book Low Marston
  Noddy Toyland ABC Picture Book Sampson Low
  Noddy's Aeroplane Picture Book Sampson Low
  The Playtime Story Book. Nos. 1–4 World Distributors

1968
  Adventures on Willow Farm Collins
  Brownie Tales Collins
  The Playtime Book. Nos. 9–12 World Distributors
  Once Upon a Time Collins

Enid Blyton also contributed stories and poems to a number of anthologies.

INDEX

INDEX